NEW BRITISH FICTION

Series editors:
Philip Tew
Rod Mengham

Published
Bradley Buchanan: **Hanif Kureishi**
Kaye Mitchell: **A.L.Kennedy**
Robert Morace: **Irvine Welsh**
Stephen Morton: **Salman Rushdie**

Forthcoming
Sonya Andermahr: **Jeanette Winterson**
Frederick M. Holmes: **Julian Barnes**
Rod Mengham: **Jonathan Coe**
Mark Rawlinson: **Pat Barker**
Philip Tew: **Zadie Smith**
Lynn Wells: **Ian McEwan**
Wendy Wheeler: **A.S. Byatt**

New British Fiction Series
Series Standing Order

ISBN 1–4039–4274–9 hardback
ISBN 1–4039–4275–7 paperback
(*outside North America only*)

You can receive future titles in this series as they are published by placing a standing order. Please contact your bookseller or, in the case of difficulty, write to us at the address below with your name and address, the title of the series and the ISBN quoted above.

Customer Services Department, Palgrave Ltd
Houndmills, Basingstoke, Hampshire RG21 6XS, England

NEW BRITISH FICTION

Salman Rushdie

Fictions of Postcolonial Modernity

Stephen Morton

First published 2008 by
PALGRAVE MACMILLAN
Houndmills, Basingstoke, Hampshire RG21 6XS and
175 Fifth Avenue, New York, N.Y. 10010
Companies and representatives throughout the world.

PALGRAVE MACMILLAN is the global academic imprint of the Palgrave Macmillan division of St. Martin's Press, LLC and of Palgrave Macmillan Ltd. Macmillan® is a registered trademark in the United States, United Kingdom and other countries. Palgrave is a registered trademark in the European Union and other countries.

ISBN-13: 978–1–4039–9700–5 hardback
ISBN-10: 1–4039–9700–4 hardback
ISBN-13: 978–1–4039–9701–2 paperback
ISBN-10: 1–4039–9701–2 paperback

This book is printed on paper suitable for recycling and made from fully managed and sustained forest sources. Logging, pulping and manufacturing processes are expected to conform to the environmental regulations of the country of orgin.

A catalogue record for this book is available from the British Library.

A catalog record for this book is available from the Library of Congress.

10 9 8 7 6 5 4 3 2 1
17 16 15 14 13 12 11 10 09 08

Printed and bound in China

CONTENTS

GENERAL EDITORS' PREFACE

This series highlights with its very title two crucial elements in the nature of contemporary British fiction, especially as a field for academic research and study. The first term indicates the originality and freshness of such writing expressed in a huge formal diversity. The second evokes the cultural identity of the authors included, who, nevertheless, represent through their diversity a challenge to any hegemonic or narrow view of Britishness. As regards the fiction, many of the writers featured in this series continue to draw from and adapt long traditions of cultural and aesthetic practice. Such aesthetic continuities contrast starkly with the conditions of knowledge at the end of the twentieth century and the beginning of the twenty-first century, a period that has been characterised by an apprehension of radical presentness, a sense of unprecedented forms of experience and an obsession with new modes of self-awareness. This stage of the survival of the novel may perhaps be best remembered as a millennial and post-millennial moment, a time of fluctuating reading practices and of historical events whose impact is largely still unresolved. The new fiction of these times reflects a rapidly changing cultural and ideological reality, as well as a renewal of the commitment of both writers and readers to both the relevance and utility of narrative forms of knowledge.

Each volume in this series will serve as an introductory guide to an individual author chosen from a list of those whose work has proved to be of general interest to reviewers, academics, students and the general reading public. Each volume will offer information concerning the life, work, and literary and cultural contexts appropriate to the chosen subject of each book; individual volumes will share the same overall structure with a largely common organisation of materials. The result is intended to be suitable for both academic and general readers: putting accessibility at a premium, without compromising an ambitious series of readings of today's most vitally interesting British novelists, interpreting their work, assessing their influences and exploring their relationship to the times in which they live.

Philip Tew and Rod Mengham

ACKNOWLEDGEMENTS

Thanks to the staff and students in English at the University of Southampton (past and present) for sharing thoughts and ideas that have helped to shape this book. I am particularly grateful to Stephen Bygrave, Bryan Cheyette, David Glover, Lucy Hartley, Aamer Hussein, James Jordan, Stephanie Jones, Gail Macdonald, Nicky Marsh, Peter Middleton and Sujala Singh. I have also benefited from conversations with Elleke Boehmer, Robert Eaglestone, John McLeod, James Procter, Mubbashir Rizvi, Mark Shackleton and Neelam Srivastava. Thanks also to the anonymous reader of this book in manuscript form for their perceptive comments, to Rod Mengham and Phil Tew, to Kate Wallis and Kitty Van Boxel at Palgrave Macmillan, and to Vidhya Jayaprakash at Newgen Imaging Systems for their patience and hard work. I am also very grateful to Janet Dickinson for compiling the index with insight and efficiency. I am also grateful to the staff at the University of Southampton libraries and the staff at the science reading room in the British Library for their tireless help in tracking down books and relevant material for this study. Finally, thanks to Susan Kelly for her love, patience and support.

I would also like to thank the School of Humanities and the English Discipline at the University of Southampton for granting me a semester's research leave to complete this book in 2007, and for the award of a University Annual Grant in 2005 to conduct preliminary research into Rushdie's fiction and criticism.

PART I

Introduction

TIMELINE

1947   Ahmed Salman Rushdie born in Bombay.
India declares political independence.

1947–1948   Hundreds of thousands die in widespread communal bloodshed after partition.

1948   Mahatma Gandhi assassinated by Hindu extremist.
Muhammed Ali Jinnah, the first governor general
of Pakistan, dies.
War between India and Pakistan over disputed
territory of Kashmir.

1951   Jinnah's successor Liaquat Ali Khan is assassinated.

1951–1952   Congress Party of India wins first general elections
under leadership of Jawaharlal Nehru

1956   Constitution proclaims Pakistan an Islamic republic

1958   Martial law declared in Pakistan and General
Ayyub Khan takes over

1960   Harold Macmillan 'Winds of Change' speech, Cape
Town, South Africa
John F. Kennedy elected as US President

1961   Adolf Eichmann on trial in Israel for role in Holocaust
Bay of Pigs: attempted invasion of Cuba
Berlin Wall constructed
Yuri Gagarin first person in Space
Silicon chip patented
Rushdie sent to Rugby School, Warwickshire, England

1962   Cuban Missile Crisis
Marilyn Monroe dies
Independence for Uganda; followed this decade by Kenya
(1963), Northern Rhodesia (1964), Southern Rhodesia
(1965), Barbados (1966)
India loses border war with China

1963   John F. Kennedy assassinated in Dallas
Martin Luther King Jr delivers 'I Have a Dream' speech

1964   Nelson Mandela sentenced to life imprisonment
Commercial pirate radio challenges BBC monopoly
Death of Prime Minister Jawaharlal Nehru

1965   US sends troops to Vietnam
Second War between India and Pakistan over Kashmir
Rushdie studies history at King's College, Cambridge.

1966   Nehru's daughter Indira Gandhi becomes prime minister
of India
Star Trek series debut on NBC television
Jean Rhys, *The Wide Sargasso Sea*

1967   Six-Day War in the Middle East
World's first heart transplant
Abortion Act legalises termination of pregnancy in UK
Sergeant Pepper's Lonely Hearts Club Band album released by
The Beatles

1968   Anti-Vietnam War protestors attempt to storm American
Embassy in Grosvenor Square
Martin Luther King Jr assassinated

Robert F. Kennedy assassinated
Student protests and riots in France

1969 Civil rights march in Northern Ireland attacked by Protestants
Apollo 11 lands on the Moon with Neil Armstrong's famous first steps
Rock concert at Woodstock
Yasser Arafat becomes leader of PLO
Booker Prize first awarded; winner P. H. Newby, *Something to Answer for*

1970 Popular Front for the Liberation of Palestine (PFLP) hijacks five planes
Students activists and bystanders shot in anti-Vietnam War protest at Kent State University, Ohio, four killed, nine wounded

1971 Internment without trial of terrorist suspects in Northern Ireland begins
India and Pakistan in conflict after Bangladesh declares independence

1972 Bloody Sunday in Derry, 14 protestors killed outright or fatally wounded by British troops
Aldershot barracks bomb initiates IRA campaign with seven dead
Massacre of Israeli athletes at Munich Olympics
Watergate scandal
Samuel Beckett, *Not I*

1973 US troops leave Vietnam
Zulfiqar Ali Bhutto becomes prime minister of Pakistan.
Arab–Israeli 15-day Yom Kippur War

1974 IRA bombings in Guildford (five dead) and Birmingham (21 dead)
India explodes first nuclear device in underground test

1975   Microsoft founded
Zadie Smith born in North London
Salman Rushdie, *Grimus*
Indira Gandhi declares state of emergency in India after being found guilty of electoral malpractice; over the next two years nearly 1,000 political opponents imprisoned and programme of compulsory birth control introduced.

1977   *Star Wars* released
UK unemployment tops 1,600,000
Nintendo begins to sell computer games
Indira Gandhi's Congress Party loses general elections
Riots erupt over allegations of vote-fixing by Zulfiqar Ali Bhutto's Pakistan People's Party (PPP). General Zia ul-Haq stages military coup

1978   Soviet troops occupy Afghanistan
General Zia becomes president of Pakistan
First test-tube baby born in Oldham, England

1979   Iranian Revolution establishes Islamic theocracy
Zulfiqar Ali Bhutto hanged
Margaret Thatcher becomes British PM after Conservative election victory
USSR invades Afghanistan
Lord Mountbatten assassinated by the IRA

1980   Iran–Iraq War starts
Iranian Embassy siege in London
CND rally at Greenham Common airbase, England
US pledges military assistance to Pakistan following Soviet intervention in Afghanistan
Indira Gandhi returns to power
IRA hunger strike at Belfast Maze Prison over political status for prisoners

1981   Widespread urban riots in UK including in Brixton, Holloway, Toxteth, Handsworth, Moss Side
AIDS identified

First IBM personal computer
Salman Rushdie, *Midnight's Children*, which wins Booker Prize for Fiction

1982 Falklands War with Argentina, costing the UK over £1.6 billion

1983 Klaus Barbie, Nazi war criminal, arrested in Bolivia
Beirut: US Embassy and barracks bombing, killing hundreds of members of multinational peacekeeping force, mostly US marines
US troops invade Grenada
Microsoft Word first released
Salman Rushdie, *Shame*, which wins Prix du Meilleur Livre Etranger (France)

1984 HIV identified as cause of AIDS
Troops storm Golden Temple to counter Sikh militants pressing for self-rule
Indira Gandhi assassinated by Sikh bodyguards, following which her son, Rajiv, takes over.
IRA bomb at Conservative Party Conference in Brighton kills four
Gas leak at Union Carbide pesticides plant in Bhopal, India. Thousands are killed immediately, many more subsequently die or are left disabled
British Telecom privatisation shares sale
Martin Amis, *Money: A Suicide Note*
Julian Barnes, *Flaubert's Parrot*
Graham Swift, *Waterland*

1985 Famine in Ethiopia and Live Aid concert
Damage to ozone layer discovered
Mikhail Gorbachev becomes Soviet Premier and introduces *glasnost* (openness with the West) and *perestroika* (economic restructuring)
My Beautiful Laundrette film released (dir. Stephen Frears, screenplay Hanif Kureishi)
Jeanette Winterson, *Oranges Are Not the Only Fruit*

1986   Abolition of Greater London Council and other metropol-
itan county councils in England
Rushdie travels to Nicaragua
Challenger shuttle explodes
Chernobyl nuclear accident
US bombs Libya
Peter Ackroyd, *Hawksmoor*

1987   Remembrance Sunday: eleven killed by Provisional IRA
bomb in Enniskillen
Salman Rushdie, *The Jaguar Smile*
Jeanette Winterson, *The Passion*
Ian McEwan, *The Child in Time*, which wins Whitbread
Novel Award

1988   US shoots down Iranian passenger flight
General Zia, the US ambassador and top Pakistan army
officials die in mysterious air crash
Pan Am flight 103 bombed over Lockerbie, 270 people killed
Soviet troop withdrawals from Afghanistan begin
Benazir Bhutto's PPP wins general election in Pakistan
Salman Rushdie, *The Satanic Verses*

1989   Death sentence issued against Rushdie by Iranian leader-
ship (Khomeini)
Fall of Berlin Wall
Exxon Valdez oil disaster
Student protestors massacred in Tiananmen Square,
Bejing
Kazuo Ishiguro, *The Remains of the Day*, which wins Booker
Prize for Fiction
Jeanette Winterson, *Sexing the Cherry*

1990   Fall of Thatcher; John Major becomes Conservative PM
Nelson Mandela freed from jail
Benazir Bhutto dismissed as prime minister of Pakistan
on charges of incompetence and corruption
Hanif Kureishi, *The Buddha of Suburbia*, which wins
Whitbread First Novel Prize

A. S. Byatt, *Possession*
Salman Rushdie, *Haroun and the Sea of Stories*

1991   Soviet Union collapses
First Iraq War with 12-day Operation Desert Storm
Apartheid ended in South Africa
Prime Minister Nawaz Sharif begins economic liberali-
sation programme, Islamic Shariah law formally incorpo-
rated into Pakistan's legal code
Hypertext Markup Language (HTML) helps create the
World Wide Web
Hanif Kureishi: screenplays for *Sammy and Rosie Get Laid*
and *London Kills Me*
Pat Barker, *Regeneration*
Salman Rushdie, *Imaginary Homelands*

1992   'Black Wednesday' stock market crisis when UK forced to
exit European Exchange Rate Mechanism
Destruction of Babri Mosque in Ayodhya, India, trigger-
ing widespread communal riots
Salman Rushdie *The Wizard of Oz*

1993   With Downing Street Declaration, PM John Major and
Taoiseach Albert Reynolds commit Britain and Ireland to
joint Northern Ireland resolution
Pakistan's President Khan and Prime Minister Sharif both
resign under pressure from military. General election
brings Benazir Bhutto back to power
Midnight's Children wins the Booker of Bookers
Irvine Welsh, *Trainspotting*

1994   Tony Blair elected leader of Labour Party following death
of John Smith
Channel Tunnel opens
Nelson Mandela elected President of South Africa
Provisional IRA and loyalist paramilitary cease-fire
Homosexual age of consent for men in the UK lowered to 18
Jonathan Coe, *What a Carve Up!*
Salman Rushdie, *East, West*

1995   Oklahoma City bombing
Srebrenica massacre during Bosnian War
Hanif Kureishi, *The Black Album*
Salman Rushdie, *The Moor's Last Sigh*

1996   Indian Congress Party suffers worse ever defeat as Hindu
nationalist BJP emerges as the largest single party
Breaching cease-fire, Provisional IRA bombs London's
Canary Wharf and Central Manchester
Graham Swift, *Last Orders*, which wins Booker Prize
Film of Irvine Welsh's *Trainspotting* (dir. Danny Boyle), star-
ring Ewan McGregor and Robert Carlyle

1997   Tony Blair becomes Labour PM after landslide victory
Nawaz Sharif returns as prime minister of Pakistan after
his Muslim League party wins elections
Princess Diana dies in Paris car crash
Hong Kong returned to China by UK
Jonathan Coe, *The House of Sleep*, which wins Prix Médicis
Etranger (France)
Ian McEwan, *Enduring Love*
Rushdie co-edits *The Vintage Book of Indian Writing
1947–1997* with Elizabeth West

1998   Good Friday Agreement on Northern Ireland and
Northern Ireland Assembly established
India and Pakistan carry out nuclear tests
Twenty-eight people killed by splinter group Real IRA
bombing in Omagh
Julian Barnes, *England, England*

1999   Euro currency adopted
Macpherson Inquiry into Stephen Lawrence murder
accuses London's Metropolitan Police of institutional
racism
Brief war between India and Pakistan in Kashmir
NATO bombs Serbia over Kosovo crisis
Anti-globalisation protest and riots in Seattle
Salman Rushdie, *The Ground Beneath her Feet*

2000 Anti-globalisation protest and riots in Genoa
Hauliers and farmers blockade oil refineries in fuel price
protest in the UK
Kazuo Ishiguro, *When We Were Orphans*
Will Self, *How the Dead Live*
Zadie Smith, *White Teeth*

2001 9/11 Al-Qaeda attacks on World Trade Center and
Pentagon
Bombing and invasion of Afghanistan
Riots in Oldham, Leeds, Bradford, and Burnley, Northern
England
Labour Party under Blair re-elected to government
Ian McEwan, *Atonement*
Salman Rushdie, *Fury*

2002 Communal Riots in Gujarat, following the deaths of 59
Hindu pilgrims in a train fire
Bali terrorist bomb kills 202 people and injures a further
209

2003 Invasion of Iraq and fall of Saddam Hussein
Death of UK government scientist Dr David Kelly, and
Hutton Inquiry
Worldwide threat of Severe Acute Respiratory Syndrome
(SARS)
The Royal Shakespeare Company premiers the play adap-
tation of Midnight's Children

2004 BBC Director General Greg Dyke steps down over Kelly
affair
Bombings in Madrid kill 190 people and injure over 1,700
Congress Party wins Indian General elections
Expansion of NATO to include seven ex-Warsaw Pact
countries
European Union expands to 25 countries as eight ex-
communist states join
Jonathan Coe, Like a Fiery Elephant: The Story of
B. S. Johnson

Andrea Levy, Small Island, which wins Orange Prize for Fiction

Alan Hollinghurst, The Line of Beauty, which wins Booker Prize for Fiction

2005 7/7 London suicide bombings on transport system kill 52 and injure over 700 commuters in morning rush hour

Hurricane Katrina kills at least 1,836 people and floods devastate New Orleans

After four failed bombings are detected, Brazilian Jean Charles de Menezes is shot and killed by Metropolitan Police officers at Stockwell Underground Station

Ian McEwan, Saturday

Zadie Smith, On Beauty, which wins 2006 Orange Prize for Fiction

Salman Rushdie, Shalimar the Clown

2006 Jeanette Winterson awarded the OBE

Airline terror plot thwarted, causes major UK airline delays

Israel–Hezbollah war in Lebanon

Five prostitutes killed in Ipswich in a six-week period

Saddam Hussein executed by hanging in controversial circumstances

2007 Rushdie accepts a knighthood from the British monarchy

1

INTRODUCTION:
SALMAN RUSHDIE
AND FICTIONS OF
POSTCOLONIAL
MODERNITY

The sound of 'Mountbatten's ticktock' in Salman Rushdie's second novel *Midnight's Children* is not only a narrative device for building suspense and focusing attention on an event such as the count-down to a bomb detonation; for the sound of the ticking clock also evokes the technological instrument of modernity used to meas-ure the chronological transition from the period of British colo-nial rule in India to India's political independence in 1947. By highlighting this temporal transition, and its subsequent anti-climax, Salman Rushdie not only draws attention to the fault lines in India's political independence in his fiction but also suggests that India's postcolonial modernity is itself a fictional composite of different political and cultural discourses borrowed from the South Asia's rich and complex cultural history as well as the European enlightenment.

Salman Rushdie is perhaps best known for his magical realist style of writing and for his irreverent treatment of historical, polit-ical and religious themes in novels such as *Midnight's Children*, *Shame*, *The Satanic Verses*, *Haroun and the Sea of Stories* and *The Moor's Last Sigh*. Indeed Rushdie's winning of the prestigious Booker prize in 1981 and the 1993 Booker of Bookers' prize for the best novel in the past 25 years, for his novel *Midnight's Children*, have established a prominent place for Rushdie's fiction in the canon of contemporary world literature. Rushdie's name has also garnered much notoriety since the Ayatollah Khomeini of Iran called on Muslims around the world to kill Rushdie for what Khomeini and some sections of the international Muslim community saw as Rushdie's blasphemous representation of the *Qur'ān* and the Prophet Muhammad in his novel *The Satanic Verses* (1988).

My argument in this book is that it is crucial to read Rushdie's writing in relation to both critical and popular understandings of nationalism, secularism and political violence in postcolonial South Asia, as well as the historical experience of South Asian migrants to Britain in order to understand the complex and multiple socio-political worlds that Salman Rushdie's fiction represents. Since Rushdie's fiction has always been concerned with the limitations of language and narrative to describe events in the world, it is not possible to separate entirely Rushdie's fictional writing from the critical reception of his work. The literary critic Edward Said has argued that 'texts are worldly, to some degree they are events, and, even when they appear to deny it, they are nevertheless part of the social world, human life, and of course the historical moments in which they are located and interpreted' (Said 1991: 4). In light of Said's claim about the worldliness of texts and their reception, this study seeks to assess the ways in which Rushdie's fiction re-imagines the worlds of South Asian history, politics and culture after colonialism, as well as crossing the cultural and geographical worlds of South Asia, Britain and the United States. More specifically, the study investigates the ways in which Rushdie's novels are bound up with wider debates about the legacies of colonial modernity in India, Pakistan and Britain, the meaning of secularism in India's political discourses, the emergency period in India, the experience of migration and displacement from India to Pakistan and South Asia to Britain, the rise of communal violence in both India and Pakistan, the conflict over Kashmir, the politicisation of Islam in Pakistan and Iran and the contemporary discourses of terrorism and anti-Americanism.

This is not to suggest, however, that Rushdie's novels are a transparent reflection of social and political reality. Rather, by focusing on Rushdie's use of formal literary devices, such as unreliable narration, analepsis, digression, irony, hyperbole, repetition, the grotesque, satire, allegory, collage and intertextuality, the study will consider how Rushdie's fiction and essays raise

questions about the historical, social and political worlds it presents and, in so doing, encourage readers to imagine an alternative
political future.

Critics have often described the literary fiction of Salman
Rushdie as postmodern, precisely because it questions realist
modes of knowledge and representation. Rushdie's use of literary
devices such as the ticking clock, for instance, highlight the ways
in which historical events – such as India's independence – are
constructed in and through narrative discourse. The literary critic
Linda Hutcheon (1988) has described Rushdie's *Midnight's Children*
and *Shame* as examples of postmodern historiographic metafic-
tion because of the ways in which these novels employ literary
self-consciousness to draw attention to the process of writing
through which historical events, such as the Amritsar massacre or
the forced displacement of India's Muslim population after partition, are constructed and made intelligible as facts. And critics
such as Rudolf Bader (1984) and Patricia Merivale (1994) have
noted formal similarities between Rushdie's *Midnight's Children*
and Günter Grass's postmodern historical novel about the rise of
National Socialism and the holocaust in twentieth-century
Germany, *The Tin Drum* (1959). Such readings are certainly borne
out by Rushdie's own comments on how *The Tin Drum* influenced
his own fictional writing by opening 'doors in the head' and telling
him to 'Go for broke. Always try and do too much. Dispense with
safety nets' (Rushdie 1992: 277). Yet to read Rushdie as an avatar of
postmodernism is to ignore the ways in which Rushdie's literary
style is precisely a response to the historical condition of South
Asia's postcolonial modernity from the diasporic standpoint of a
British Indian Muslim.

RUSHDIE AND SOUTH ASIAN MODERNITY

If Rushdie's fiction seems to imply an undertone of scepticism
about the political achievements of South Asia's modernisation in
the aftermath of India's independence and partition, this is partly
a consequence of the colonial history of South Asian modernity.
For the South Asian historian Partha Chatterjee, 'because of the
way in which [South Asian] modernity has been intertwined with
the history of colonialism, we have never quite been able to believe
that there exists a universal domain of free discourse, unfettered

by differences of race or nationality' (Chatterjee 1997: 275). While political theorists such as Hans Kohn argue that the nation state became the dominant political form of modernity in Western Europe because it was coeval with the rise of democracy and industrialisation, Chatterjee stresses that the nation state 'has been the cause of the most destructive wars ever seen; it has justified the brutality of Nazism and Fascism; it has become the ideology of racial hatred in the colonies and has given birth to some of the most irrational revivalist movements as well as to the most oppressive political regimes in the contemporary world' (Chatterjee 1986: 2). For this reason, Chatterjee calls into question the universal claims of Western modernity on the grounds that the values of Western modernity perpetuate the colonial domination of non-European countries. In a similar vein, Navnita Chadha Behera argues that the British colonial administration introduced new forms of statecraft in India, including economic relationships based on individual property rights and forms of social regulation based on overarching categories, such as religion and language. In so doing '[c]olonial modernity sought to unify the diversity of the [Indian] social world' (Behera 2000: 39).

The image of Mountbatten's ticking clock in Rushdie's *Midnight's Children* is apposite for understanding the temporal dynamics of postcolonial modernity because it suggests that the teleological transition from colonialism to independence is shaped and determined by British colonial rule. In this respect, Mountbatten's ticktock does not merely foreshadow India's political independence but also portends the partition of India along ethnic lines and the communal violence and mass population transfer that ensued. For the smooth transition of India from colonial state to postcolonial nation state which Mountbatten's ticktock prefigures, and which Salman Rushdie satirises in *Midnight's Children*, is called into question by the British colonial administration's involvement in the engineering of India's partition and the 'humanly catastrophic population transfers and expulsions [that] have gone hand in hand with the policy of partition' (Cleary 2002: 21). Indeed, historians have suggested that Sir Cyril Radcliffe and Lord Mountbatten's involvement in the partition of Bengal and Punjab aided and abetted the communal violence and statelessness for many South Asians that followed India's independence (Bennett-Jones 2002: 58–61; Khan 2007).

If India's partition was largely a response to the political demands of its Muslim population and the cynical efforts by Britain's outgoing colonial administration to exploit communal antagonisms between India's Muslim and Hindu populations, Prime Minister Nehru's secular vision of India's democracy, his plans for India's economic development and his principle of Third World non-alignment in matters of foreign policy during the Cold War seemed to offer an alternative model for India's political modernity in the aftermath of colonialism. Rushdie's references to the political legacy of Nehru's vision of India's political modernity in novels such as *Midnight's Children* and *The Moor's Last Sigh* may at times satirise Nehru's vision of India's postcolonial modernity, and so appear to encourage readers to regard decolonisation in South Asia as a political failure. Rushdie's parody of Nehruvian ideas such as non-alignment with the United States or the Soviet Union, a secular socialism that celebrates India's diversity, and industrialisation certainly highlights the fault lines in India's social and political foundations. Yet, as this book will suggest, Rushdie does so in order to imagine the conditions of possibility for a radical democratic transformation in South Asian society, rather than simply announcing the failure of India's national independence.

The work of Salman Rushdie has been the focus of much critical attention during the past two decades, with several studies appearing on his work. Many of these studies offer commentaries on Rushdie's fiction (Cundy 1996; Goonetilleke 1998; Grant 1999; Kortenaar 2004). Only one study has attempted to place Rushdie's fictional corpus in a broad historical context by comparing Rushdie's fiction to Third World writers such as Marquez, Achebe and Ngugi (Brennan 1989). Despite a growing interest in partition, secularism and communalism in South Asian studies (Bharucha 1998; Asad 2003), there have been no sustained book-length studies of how Rushdie's writing contributes to an understanding of decolonisation, secularism and political violence in South Asia. Two major bodies of work make this task particularly urgent. On the one hand, historical studies of communalism in South Asia have shown how the legacy of Nehru's rhetoric of secularism masked the dominant position of Hindus within Indian society (Mufti 1998; Pandey 2006). On the other hand, studies of the violence associated with India's partition and emergency period have revealed the political context which made it possible for different communities to torture, rape and kill individuals identified as dangerous (Butalia 1998; Menon and Bhasin 1998; Tarlo 2003). By situating Rushdie's fiction in the context of debates about secularism and political violence in postcolonial South Asia, this study demonstrates the important contribution Rushdie's writing makes to understanding the relationship between imperialism, political violence and religion in the twenty-first century.

This book examines the representation of decolonisation, secularism and political violence in Rushdie's literary and critical work from *Midnight's Children* to *Shalimar the Clown*. It traces the parallels between the official representation of national independence, partition, secularism, political violence and Rushdie's fictional representation of these events in South Asian history. It begins with a consideration of how Rushdie's novel *Midnight's Children* (1981) contests Nehru's rhetoric of national liberation from a historical perspective after India's emergency period, and ends with an analysis of the Kashmir crisis, US foreign policy in South Asia at the end of the twentieth century, and Rushdie's representation of Kashmir and the US-led war on terrorism in *Shalimar the Clown* (2005). Where previous treatments of Rushdie's fiction have tended to focus on either Rushdie's literary and cultural influences (Cundy 1996; Jussawalla 1999; Sanga 2001) or the way in which his fictional construction of South Asian history is part of a postmodern literary technique (Hassumani 2002; Kortenaar, 2004), this study seeks to move the discussion forward by paying particular attention to the political events and popular discourses that inflect Rushdie's writing. It will (a) focus on the ways in which Rushdie's fiction and essays question and complicate the meaning of secularism and national independence after the partition of India, the emergency period (1975–1977) and the rise of communal violence; and (b) examine how Rushdie's fiction negotiates the political challenges and opportunities that religious fundamentalism and political violence posed to the ruling authorities in India and Pakistan from 1947 to the present.

MIGRATION AND THE WORLDLINESS OF RUSHDIE'S WRITING

While many of Rushdie's novels are partly located in South Asia, his fiction is also marked by the experience of migration, and the different economic and political conditions that enable, prevent or (in some cases) force people to migrate. In his essay 'Imaginary Homelands', for example, Rushdie reflects on a photograph taken in 1946 of what was to become his childhood home in Bombay. For Rushdie, the photograph not only evokes the loss of his childhood, but also a feeling of loss for the place left behind. Against this feeling of loss, Rushdie argues that he sought to reclaim this lost sense of place and homeland in fiction. Yet, in doing so, Rushdie recognises that his 'physical alienation from India' along with that of other diasporic Indian writers 'almost inevitably means that we will not be capable of reclaiming the thing that was lost; that we will, in short, create fictions, not actual cities or villages, but invisible ones, imaginary homelands, Indias of the mind' (Rushdie 1992: 2).

This idea of an imaginary homeland or an India of the mind is crucial for grasping the migrant sensibility underpinning much of Rushdie's writing. Indeed, novels such as *Midnight's Children* and *The Satanic Verses* are in various ways marked by the experience of migration. In *Midnight's Children*, the first-person narrator Saleem Sinai reflects on the loss of his family home in Bombay and his subsequent move to Karachi following the partition of India, and in *The Satanic Verses* the protagonist Saladin Chamcha, following his arrival in Britain, metamorphoses into a demonic half-man, half-goat figure and is brutally assaulted by policemen, who suspect him of being an illegal immigrant.

Rushdie has also compared the experience of writing from the standpoint of a migrant to the practice of translation. Invoking the etymological root of the word 'translation' from the Latin word *translatus* meaning 'bearing across', Rushdie argues that 'Having been borne across the world [British Indian writers] are translated men' (Rushdie 1992: 17). While 'It is normally supposed that something always gets lost in translation', Rushdie clings 'obstinately, to the notion that something can also be gained' (Rushdie 1992: 17). In saying this, however, Rushdie is not suggesting that the culture that is being translated in fiction can be recovered in its totality; rather, Rushdie's fiction is constituted of partial and fragmentary memories of his homeland. As Rushdie explains, 'The shards of memory acquired greater status, greater resonance, because they were *remains*; fragmentation made trivial things seem like symbols, and the mundane acquired numinous qualities' (Rushdie 1992: 12).

Following the proscription of Rushdie's novel *The Satanic Verses* in India; the burning of the novel in Bradford, England; the subsequent pronouncement of a death sentence on Rushdie by the Ayatollah Khomeini of Iran in 1989; and Rushdie's retreat into hiding and protection by the British secret service, Rushdie's personal freedom, especially his freedom to travel and to make public appearances, was severely restricted. Despite the security restrictions imposed on Rushdie after the death sentence issued by the Ayatollah Khomeini, a sense of worldliness continues to inflect Rushdie's writing after the 'Rushdie affair'. *The Moor's Last Sigh* for instance is structured around a cosmopolitan vision of India's diverse cultural and economic history. Yet, this sense of worldliness in Rushdie's writing after the death sentence issued by Khomeini is also marked by the threat of proscription, death or incarceration by a repressive authority figure such as the cultmaster Khattam-Shud in *Haroun and the Sea of Stories*; the artist Vasco Miranda in *The Moor's Last Sigh*, who orders Moraes Zogoiby to recount his family story or face death; or the repressive political leader Babur in *Fury* who imprisons the protagonist Malik Solanka in Lilliput-Blefuscu.

The migrant vantage point that underpins much of Rushdie's fictional and non-fictional writing is not above criticism. In an essay on Salman Rushdie's *Shame*, the Indian Marxist critic Aijaz Ahmad raises a question about Rushdie's status in the counter-canon of 'Third World Literature' and argues that Rushdie inscribes the 'Third World' in the 'plottings and thematics' of his first three novels, in particular:

> the colonial determination of our modernity, the conditions and corruptions of post-coloniality, the depiction of the Zia and Bhutto periods in Pakistan as emblematic of Third World *caudillos* and dictators in general, myths of nationhood and independence, the myths and gods of India, Third World migrants in metropolitan cities, the world of Islam and so on. (Ahmad 1992: 126)

Furthermore, Ahmad contends that many critics have conjectured that Rushdie's 'forms of narrativization ... belong, in essence, to a generally non-Western, specifically Indian form of non-mimetic narration, derived, finally, from the *Ramayana* and the *Mahabharata* and exemplifying, in the words of Raja Rao, the characteristically Indian penchant for obsessive digressions and the telling of an interminable tale' (Ahmad: 126). For Ahmad, however, this critical reading of Rushdie obscures his debt to the conventions of European modernism and postmodernism as well as his 'ideological moorings in the High Culture of the modern metropolitan bourgeoisie' (Ahmad: 127). To correct this mistaken reading of Rushdie, Ahmad argues that Rushdie's fiction uses the metaphor of migrancy as a metaphor for the 'ontological condition of all human beings' as well as the 'social condition of the "Third World" migrant' (Ahmad: 127). The effect of this conflation of postcolonial narratives of migration with postmodernist theories of subjectivity is, according to Ahmad's Marxist critique of Rushdie, the packaging of Third World culture for Western consumption. As Ahmad puts it,

> This idea of the availability of *all* cultures of the world for consumption by an individual consciousness was, of course, a much older European idea, growing in tandem with the history of colonialism as such, but the perfection and extended use of it in the very fabrication of modernism ... signalled a real shift, from the age of old colonialism *per se* to the age of modern imperialism proper, which was reflected also in the daily lives of metropolitan consumers in a new kind of shopping: the supermarket. (Ahmad: 128)

In Ahmad's view, the presentation of different commodities from India, Manchester, France and Persia without reference to their history and context was equivalent to the new critical idea that 'each literary text constituted a self-enclosed and sufficient unit for analysis' (128). Furthermore, with the advent of postmodernism, Ahmad argues that the 'idea of belonging is itself seen now as bad faith, a mere "*myth* of origins" and the "experience of loss" is celebrated' (128).

This celebration of not belonging or rather belonging in too many places at once prompts Ahmad to raise questions about the structural relationship between metropolitan intellectuals who mine 'the resource and raw material of "Third World Literature" for archival accumulation and generic classification in the *metropolitan* university' on the one hand, and the contemporary 'age of late capitalism in which the most powerful capitalist firms, originating in particular imperialist countries but commanding global investments and networks of transport and communication, proclaim themselves to be *multi*nationals and *trans*nationals' (130) on the other. According to the logic of Ahmad's analogy, the activity of reading postcolonial literary texts corresponds to the activity of multinational corporations plundering the resources of the global South for profit, and the 'excess of belonging', which Ahmad imputes to the migrant sensibility of Rushdie's writing, is equivalent to the multinational corporation's disavowal of its '*origins* in the United States or the Federal German Republic' (130).

Apart from the rather obvious fact that this compressed analogy reveals a broader economic reductionism in Ahmad's argument that describes the literary production and reception of Rushdie's texts in terms of the laws of surplus value and commodity fetishism, Ahmad proceeds to make some thought-provoking observations about Rushdie's migrant sensibility. In the conclusion to the essay, for example, Ahmad invokes Raymond Williams' distinction between exile and vagrancy in an essay on George Orwell to clarify the political stance of Rushdie as a migrant writer before and after the death sentence issued by the Ayatollah Khomeini. For Williams, there is an important distinction that needs to be made between the condition of exile in which 'there is usually a principle' and the condition of vagrancy or self-exile, in which 'there is always only relaxation' (Williams cited in Ahmad 157). For Ahmad, 'after Khomeini's sentencing of him, Rushdie's "vagrancy" has turned paradoxically and tragically, into a full-scale exile' (157).

Graham Huggan in *The Postcolonial Exotic* has attempted to distance himself from the Marxist critique of postcolonial writers and intellectuals posited by Aijaz Ahmad by formulating a more nuanced account of the postcolonial aesthetic in an era of globalisation. In Huggan's argument, the literary representation of the postcolonial world is a form of exoticism, or a particular mode of aesthetic representation of the postcolonial world that domesticates the foreign: a mode which Huggan names the postcolonial exotic. In contrast to nineteenth-century and early twentieth-century forms of exoticism that 'conceal imperial authority through exotic spectacle' (Huggan 2001: 15), Huggan argues that 'Late twentieth-century exoticisms are the products, less of the expansion of the nation state than of a worldwide *market*'. In other words, 'exoticism has shifted ... from being a more or less privileged mode of aesthetic perception to an increasingly global mode of mass-market consumption' (Huggan: 15).

For Huggan, contra Ahmad, the aesthetic form of postcolonial texts is not determined by global market forces; rather, what Huggan calls 'the postcolonial exotic' is 'a site of discursive conflict between a local assemblage of more or less related oppositional practices and a global apparatus of assimilative institutional/commercial codes' (28). Against the charge made by Ahmad and others that postcolonial writers such as Salman Rushdie are the 'lackeys' of global capitalism and that readers of postcolonial fiction participate in the global commodification of the postcolonial world, Huggan contends that such charges 'underestimate [the] power [of postcolonial writers] to exercise agency over their own work', as well as the agency and diverse cultural composition of the readers of postcolonial texts 'who by no means form a homogeneous or readily identifiable consumer group' (Huggan: 30). What is more, Huggan suggests that writers such as Salman Rushdie, Arundahti Roy and Chinua Achebe employ, in very different ways, a strategy of writing, which he calls 'strategic exoticism', or 'the means by which postcolonial writers/thinkers, working from within exoticist codes of representation, either manage to subvert these codes … or succeed in redeploying them for the purposes of uncovering differential relations of power' (Huggan: 32). In a reading of Rushdie's *Midnight's Children*, Huggan argues that the novel draws attention 'to itself as an object of Western consumption' by demonstrating its awareness of the way in which India's history is already mediated by Orientalist representations of India in Anglo-Indian fiction (Huggan 2001: 72–73).

Rushdie's self-consciousness is not merely literary, however, but is also concerned to expose injustice, corruption and oppression within the social and political structures of postcolonial South Asia, against the historical backdrop of a global political transition from a progressive Third World nationalist vision based on the Bandung spirit of non-alignment to the rise of religious fundamentalisms in South Asia and the Middle East at the end of the Cold War. Such a concern is not simply motivated by a desire to expose the limitations of decolonisation, but rather to highlight the necessity for the social and political redemption of a secular, democratic and tricontinental nationalism to counter the forces of *both* neoliberal globalisation and religious fundamentalisms.

Against the conflation of Rushdie's fiction with his privileged, metropolitan location in Britain or the United States, and the charge that Rushdie's fiction participates (either critically or uncritically) in the postmodern exoticisation of South Asia for a Western audience, this study argues that the worldliness of Rushdie's fiction and essays offer important insights into the meaning of secularism in India's political discourses, the emergency period in India, the experience of migration and displacement from India to Pakistan and South Asia to Britain, the rise of communal violence in both India and Pakistan, the conflict over Kashmir, the rise of Islamic fundamentalism in Pakistan and Iran, and the contemporary discourses of terrorism and anti-Americanism in the aftermath of the terrorist attacks of September 11 2001.

Chapter 3 examines how Rushdie interrogates the emancipatory rhetoric of India's secular democracy in his novel *Midnight's Children* through a critical parody of Nehru's speeches and Indira Gandhi's declaration of a state of emergency. The chapter then proceeds to compare the representation of political violence in *Midnight's Children* and his third novel *Shame*. If *Midnight's Children* gives voice to the people through the destruction of Saleem Sinai's body, the acts of violence carried out by Sufiya Zenobia in *Shame* articulate the violence of state repression in Pakistan. Yet in both novels Rushdie suggests that it is the political formation and partition of South Asia after decolonisation that gives rise to such political violence.

Chapter 4 considers how Rushdie represents the relationship between migration and religion in *The Satanic Verses*. With reference to debates in Islamic historical scholarship, the reception of *The Satanic Verses* and Dipesh Chakrabarty's idea of provincialising Europe, the chapter argues that Rushdie uses Islamic history to make sense of postcolonial migration from South Asia to Britain, even as he questions the truth claims of religious ideas such as revelation. The chapter then proceeds to consider how Rushdie develops these concerns in *Haroun and the Sea of Stories* and in his short story 'The Prophet's Hair'.

Chapter 5 begins by examining how the crisis of India's secular constitution from the Emergency period (1975–1977) to the riots that followed the destruction of the Babri mosque in December 1992 is reflected in the narrative structure and rhetoric of Rushdie's novel *The Moor's Last Sigh*. Focusing on the significance of Rushdie's use of a protagonist of mixed-race ancestry, the chapter proceeds to consider how *The Moor's Last Sigh* calls into question Nehru's claims to promote cultural and religious toleration in India by tracing the rise of the Hindu right. If *The Moor's Last Sigh* traces the breakdown in Nehru's modernising vision of a secular Indian nation state, *The Ground Beneath Her Feet* questions the political, economic and cultural dominance of Europe and North America that is often associated with modernity and globalisation. Chapter 5 assesses how Rushdie's South Asian rock 'n' roll novel challenges the cultural dominance of American and European modernity.

Chapter 7 considers how Rushdie's novels *Fury* and *Shalimar the Clown* register the increasing importance of American economic and political influence in India, Pakistan and Kashmir. After a critical analysis of Rushdie's geopolitical imagination in *Fury* and his essays on the US-led wars in Afghanistan and Iraq, the chapter proceeds to focus in particular on Rushdie's representation of the crisis in Kashmir in *Shalimar the Clown* and the phenomena of anti-Americanism in the first decade of the twenty-first century.

The conclusion assesses the legacy of Rushdie's fiction and criticism and its importance for understanding Islamophobia and discourses of terrorism in the twenty-first century through the framework of Rushdie's responses to the attacks on America of September 11 2001, and with reference to the controversy surrounding *The Satanic Verses*. Against Samuel Huntingdon (1996), I argue that Rushdie's fiction offers an important challenge to the geopolitical opposition between the religious and the secular in contemporary political discourse, even though his recent journalistic writings seem to endorse the Bush administration's wars in Afghanistan and Iraq in the first decade of the twenty-first century. The final section is an appendix, which provides an overview of Rushdie's critical reception, as well as mapping the trajectory of Rushdie's geopolitical imagination in his essays and other critical writings.

2

A BIOGRAPHICAL READING

Rushdie's life is not anterior to the body of his fictional writing, but inextricably bound up with it. Yet his background as a secular Indian Muslim who moved to Britain and subsequently to the United States is often read as a transparent reflection of his fictional writing. While Rushdie's cosmopolitan background may certainly help to situate his fiction in a cultural and political context, it can also lead to crude *ad hominem* readings (as in the case of *The Satanic Verses* affair), which dismiss Rushdie's fiction on the basis of his biographical background rather than critically engaging with the literary texts themselves (see Kuortti 1997a) For this reason, I would argue that the life of Salman Rushdie, or the events which become associated with the proper name of Salman Rushdie, are written in and through the fictional texts themselves.

THE LIFE OF RUSHDIE'S WRITING

Ahmed Salman Rushdie was born in Bombay (now Mumbai) on 19 June 1947, almost two months before India gained independence from Britain. Rushdie's family were affluent Indian Muslims: his father was a barrister and a Cambridge graduate with a taste for owning books and telling stories to his children, and his maternal grandfather, Ataullah Butt, had been a medical doctor with progressive views on gender codes, such as not forcing his daughters to adhere to the rules of *purdah* within the household by wearing a headscarf (Idris 2006: 315). Such a liberal, secular and affluent family background is partly reflected in Rushdie's characterisation of Saleem Sinai's grandfather Ahmed in *Midnight's Children*, who loses his religious faith after banging his nose against the ground while attempting to pray in his Kashmir home at the start of the novel, and is subsequently lambasted by his wife for refusing to respect the rules of *purdah*. Although the Rushdie family was influenced by European culture and education, and adopted a liberal secular outlook, they were nonetheless identified as Indian Muslims in the aftermath of India's independence and partition, and according to Ian Hamilton, 'Anis Rushdie's business came under threat from both the Hindu mobs and the new post-Independence courts' (Hamilton 1995/1996: 92).

After attending the Cathedral and John Connon Church of England mission school in Bombay during the 1950s, Rushdie was sent to the prestigious Rugby School in England for his secondary education in 1961, at which he was awarded a Queen's Medal for History, and scholarships to study at Balliol College, Oxford, and King's College, Cambridge. During this time, his father moved his family from their home in Bombay to a flat in Kensington, South West London, in 1962 and then to Karachi, Pakistan, two years later. Under pressure from his father, Rushdie enrolled to read for a degree in History at King's in October 1965 and studied there until the summer of 1968 (Hamliton 1995/6: 96). If social and cultural life in Pakistan during this period was increasingly influenced by the Islamic revivalism of Maulana Mawdudi and the Islamic Party, England in the 1960s was defined by a counter-culture that not only advocated a liberal life style based on sex, drugs and rock 'n' roll, but also publicly opposed the US war in Vietnam. It was this diasporic cultural formation – as a secular Indian Muslim opposed to the strict codes of Islamic law and as a Cambridge student swept up by the liberal values and anti-imperialism of Britain's counter-culture – that partly informed Rushdie's historical interest in Islam for a special subject on 'Mohammed and the rise of Islam' in his History Tripos at Cambridge.

The literary critic Timothy Brennan has suggested that Rushdie's provocative representation of the Satanic Verses episode in his eponymous novel was a sign of the 'soixante-huitard' sensibility of a 'uniquely situated cosmopolitan' (2006: 74) and an education in the cultural traditions of the British Empire, especially the English novel, rather than a sustained engagement with the cultural traditions and forms of South Asia. As well as *The Satanic Verses*, Rushdie's novel *The Ground Beneath Her Feet* is inflected by the 1960s British zeitgeist in its references to Pirate radio, rock 'n' roll, and LSD. Yet to say that Rushdie's intertextual engagement with the *Qur'ān*, *The Conference of Birds* or Hindu epics such as the *Ramayana* or the *Mahabharata* is 'meta-fictional' – as Brennan does – is to overlook the precise political and cultural significance of Rushdie's literary collage in novels such as *The Satanic Verses*. For in juxtaposing the Thatcher government's privatisation of the public sector and its war against Britain's new Caribbean and South Asian citizen-migrants with a fictionalised account of events in the life of the Prophet Muhammad from seventh-century Arabia and a story of a group of pilgrims led by a woman prophet in twentieth-century South Asia, Rushdie not only highlights the way in which the birth of Islam is a worldly event which takes place inside history but also calls into question the cultural and political dominance of the West – as symbolised by Thatcher's Britain – in the current phase of neoliberal globalisation. Such a concern is further developed in Rushdie's novel *The Ground Beneath Her Feet* (1999), which challenges the global cultural dominance of American popular culture by suggesting that rock 'n' roll was invented in Mumbai.

Despite Rushdie's promising academic performance at school in the 1950s, he graduated from Cambridge with a lower second-class degree. This apparent dip in Rushdie's academic performance might be accounted for by his active interest in the theatre during his time at Cambridge, for according to Ian Hamilton, Rushdie had played in 'student productions of Ionesco, Brecht, Ben Jonson and others' (Hamilton 1995/1996: 97). Rushdie's interest in acting continued when he returned to Karachi in 1968, where his family were living, and took a job with Pakistan's television service. He convinced Karachi TV to let him produce and act in Edward Albee's 'The Zoo Story', but the censors banned the production because of the use of the word 'pork' in the play (Hamilton: 97). Rushdie's experience of trying to find work in Pakistan during the late 1960s finds a parallel in his third novel *Shame* (1983), which offers a dark image of state repression, corruption and religious authoritarianism in Pakistan under the rule of its two successive but fictional political leaders, Iskander Harappa and Raza Hyder.

Rushdie returned to London in 1969 to live with his sister at a rented house in Fulham. Following several attempts to act in productions at the Oval House in Kennington, South London, Rushdie proceeded to work as a copywriter for different advertising companies and to work on his first novel 'The Book of the Pir', which he completed in 1971, but abandoned after several rejections from publishers. This book featured 'a Muslim guru in some unnamed

Eastern land, who gets taken up by a military junta and installed as the figurehead President of its corrupt regime' (Hamilton: 100). Following this setback Rushdie continued to work as a copywriter for the major advertising company, and worked on his next novel. During this period Rushdie met Clarissa Luard, later his first wife, who came from an upper middle-class background (Idris 2006: 316). After the publication of his first novel *Grimus* (1975), a work that combines the generic conventions of science fiction, folklore and the quest narrative to tell the story of Flapping Eagle, an American Indian, who tries to rescue his sister Bird Dog, who is a captive of the European magician, Grimus, Rushdie travelled to India and Pakistan with Clarissa Luard, and subsequently started work on his next novel about India, 'Madame Rama' (Idris: 316).

Grimus is often regarded as an 'early failed novel', perhaps because, as Timothy Brennan has claimed, the novel 'lacks a *habitus*' (Brennan 1989: 70). But if the failure of *Grimus* is due in part to its hybridisation of different cultural codes from Dante's *Inferno* and Joyce's *Ulysses* to American Indian myth, Attar's *The Conference of Birds*, and Hindu epic without a final synthesis to frame the novel as a determinate allegory of a particular national culture, such a refusal of synthesis may in fact be the point. As Roger Y. Clark has argued in *Stranger Gods: Salman Rushdie's Other Worlds*, 'Instead of parodying and downgrading the quests of Dante and Attar [in *Grimus*], Rushdie conflates them with a never-ending cycle of death and rebirth, of eschatology and cosmogony' (Clark 2001: 59). Put another way, the status of *Grimus* as a failed novel in Rushdie criticism may reveal as much about the secular value systems upon which Western literature and culture are based, as it does about the intelligibility of the novel's handling of transcendental themes such as the infinite and the afterlife.

The manuscript for Rushdie's next novel, 'Madame Rama' was rejected by publishers; however, Rushdie went on to develop it by switching the third-person narrator to the first person. This unpublished manuscript is significant because it became the first draft of *Midnight's Children*, which Rushdie completed in 1979, just two years after the end of the emergency period India had ended. Following his marriage to Clarissa Luard in 1976, Rushdie fathered his first child, Zafar, in 1979. Rushdie's use of a first-person narrator in *Midnight's Children* may invite comparisons between his own life and that of his protagonist, Saleem Sinai. Like Rushdie, Saleem was born around the time of India's independence in 1947 into a secular

Indian Muslim family. However, such comparisons are complicated by Saleem's confession that he is an unreliable narrator, and
by fantastic events in the novel such as Saleem's ability to hear the
voices of the Indian population through a magic radio concealed in
his nose, and by his suggestion that he caused significant historical
events in India's history, such as the language riots. By presenting
Saleem's body as an allegory of the national body politic, Rushdie
ultimately constructs Saleem as an everyman whose body is oblit-
erated by the forces of history to which he is handcuffed.

Just as the biography of Saleem Sinai in *Midnight's Children* can
be read as an allegory of India, so the life of Sufiya Zenobia, the
main character in Rushdie's third novel *Shame* (1983), can be interpreted as a symbol of Pakistan. Sufiya's tendency to blush and her
murderous alter ego are a thinly veiled criticism of the state
repression inflicted on the people by her father. Yet, for the Indian
literary critic Aijaz Ahmad, Rushdie's representation of Pakistan
in *Shame* is one-dimensional because it focuses on the corruption
and criminality of the ruling political elite and excludes the

> dailiness of lives lived under oppression, and the human bonding – of
> resistance, of decency, of innumerable heroisms of both ordinary and
> extraordinary kinds – which makes it possible for large numbers of
> people to look each other in the eye, without guilt, with affection and
> solidarity and humour, and makes life, even under oppression,
> endurable and frequently joyous. (Ahmad 1992: 139)

The left-wing position that Rushdie adopted in his opposition
to the war in Vietnam in the 1960s and 1970s found further expression in Rushdie's visit to Nicaragua in 1986 as a guest of the
Sandinista government, which was documented in his 1987 travelogue, *The Jaguar Smile*. Rushdie's representation of Daniel Ortega
and the Sandinistas is generally sympathetic, drawing links
between India's struggle against Britain and the Sandinistas' struggle against the counter-revolutionary army *la Contra*, which was
backed by the Reagan administration and the CIA. In one passage,
for instance, Rushdie compares the mythologisation of Sandino
with that of Gandhi (21). In 1988, Rushdie married the American
author Marianne Wiggins, after divorcing his first wife Clarissa
Luard in 1987 and having a two-year affair with the writer Robyn
Davidson, whom he had met during a visit to Australia with the
writer Bruce Chatwin.

If the end of the Cold War and the global expansion of western capitalist markets was paralleled by a political shift in many Third World countries away from a socialist ideology based on the principle of non-alignment with either the West or the Soviet Union to religious, ethnic or anti-Western nationalist movements (Brennan 2006: 68), the publication and reception of Rushdie's novel *The Satanic Verses* (1988) seems to anticipate some of these global political developments. For Rushdie's fictional representation of Mahound (a derogatory term used by some European writers to demonise and discredit the Prophet), his parodic depiction of the Prophet's wives as sex workers, and the inadvertent suggestion that the *Qur'ān* itself was ghost written by Satan became the object of an intense debate between representatives of an anti-Western, religious nationalism, such as the Ayatollah Khomeini of Iran, who defended the sacred status of the Qur'ān and the Prophet, and called on Muslims to kill Rushdie on the one hand, and representatives of a Western, neo-imperialist, secular ideology, such as the British MP Chris Patton, who defended Rushdie's right to free speech on the other.

As I explain in Chapter 4, the controversy that *The Satanic Verses* provoked was partly based on the way in which the novel collapsed the secular, cultural conventions of European imaginative literature and the cultural conventions of Urdu and Arabic literary forms, as well as the fantastic conventions of Bombay cinema into a hybrid literary form, which refuse a straightforward realist interpretation of the novel. The constant refrain of Rushdie's narrator in *The Satanic Verses* – 'it was and it was not so' (35) – may undermine attempts by careful readers to find a stable correspondence between words and things, such as fictional characters and events in the 'Jahilia' chapters of the novel and those described in historical sources such as the medieval Islamic historian al-Tabari's account of the life of the Prophet. In this respect, *The Satanic Verses* can be seen to develop Rushdie's philosophical challenge to historical realism that is also evident in *Midnight's Children* and *Shame*. Yet this indeterminate connection between the fictional worlds of *The Satanic Verses* and the historical worlds of seventh-century Arabia and late-twentieth-century Britain and South Asia does not rule out the possibility that parts of the novel can be read as a thinly veiled, if ambivalent, attack on Islam and the Prophet. Indeed if, as Roger Y. Clark has argued, the insidious, satanic narrator of *The Satanic Verses* is rather like Iago in Shakespeare's play

Othello in his subtle and devilish manipulation of Gibreel Farishta (Clark 2001: 128–181), this narrator also seems to play a manipulative and dangerous game with its readers.

One possible clue to understanding what is at stake in Rushdie's fictional representation of Islamic history lies in his representation of an Imam residing in Kensington, who is against history. If Rushdie's Imam is interpreted as a fictional version of the Ayatollah Khomeini during his period of exile in Paris just before the Iranian revolution in 1979, it is possible to read Rushdie's characterisation of the Ayatollah as a coded criticism of Islamic fundamentalism as a political ideology and as the authoritative interpretation of Islam. Such a criticism of the Kensington Imam's anti-historicism suggests that Rushdie's fictional reworking of Islamic history is not simply an attack on Islam *per se*, but an attempt to explore the birth of Islam as an event that happened within history. In an essay titled 'In Good Faith', Rushdie argued that Gibreel Farishta's visionary dreams of himself as an Islamic angel who communicates the message of Allah to Mohammad were intended to encourage discussion and debate about the meaning of divine revelation, and the historical context in which the *Qur'ān* was written. Yet, Rushdie's profane representation of the Prophet's wives as sex workers, and the novel's perhaps unwitting suggestion that a Satanic figure dictated the entire *Qur'ān* prompted the novel's proscription in India, South Africa, Pakistan, Saudi Arabia, Egypt, Somalia, Bangladesh, Sudan, Malaysia, Indonesia and Qatar; the burning of the novel in Bradford, West Yorkshire; street agitations in India and Pakistan; the murder of the Japanese translator and the wounding of the Norwegian and Italian translators; and the religious leader of Iran, Ayatollah Khomeini, publicly calling upon Muslims to kill Rushdie.

The 'Rushdie affair', as it has since become known, is often invoked to exemplify the clash of civilisations between the Islamic world and the West. For the British state's defence and protection of Rushdie and his right to free speech is often taken as a sign of the British government's disregard for the religious beliefs of Britain's Muslim population. If the British conservative government of the late 1980s defended Rushdie and *The Satanic Verses* in order to re-assert a certain post-imperial idea of Britain's secular culture against the rise of Islamic nationalism, however, Rushdie's novel contains an explicit criticism of Margaret Thatcher's Conservative government, and its treatment of black Britons.

Following the Ayatollah's call for Rushdie's murder in 1989, Rushdie was offered protection by the Special Branch of the British police, and subsequently went into hiding with his second wife Marianne Wiggins. Rushdie's next novel *Haroun and the Sea of Stories* was published in 1990 and combined the form of a fantasy story about a storyteller who loses his voice with an allegory of censorship. After Rushdie's marriage with Marianne Wiggins ended in 1993, Rushdie went on to publish a collection of short stories titled *East, West* in 1994. During this time, Rushdie also made several public appearances at readings, granted interviews, and became an honorary professor at the Massachusetts Institute of Technology in 1993. The appearance of Rushdie's sixth novel *The Moor's Last Sigh* in 1995 continued the critique of religious fundamentalism established in *Shame* and *The Satanic Verses* by offering a satirical representation of the right-wing Hindu political leader of Bombay, Bal Thackeray, and the Hindu fundamentalist group, the Shiv Sena. Yet, in doing so, Rushdie also raised questions about the political legacy of Jawaharlal Nehru's secular socialism in the aftermath of the communal riots that followed the destruction of the Babri Mosque at Ayodhya in 1992.

Rushdie met the editor Elizabeth West in 1994; they married in 1997 and had a son the same year. West and Rushdie collaborated on the *Vintage Book of Indian Writing 1947–1997* (1997), and wrote a controversial introduction in which they stated that Indian literature written in English was not only stronger than literatures written in Indian languages but also represented the 'most valuable contribution India has yet made to the world of books' (Rushdie 1997: x). Following pressure from the European Union and Britain, the Iranian government lifted the execution order pronounced by Ayatollah Khomeini, and withdrew the reward money for Rushdie's assassination in 1998.

In 1999 Rushdie published *The Ground Beneath Her Feet*, a novel set in a parallel reality, which re-writes the myth of Orpheus and Eurydice to trace the rise of an Indian rock 'n' roll group called VTO, the romantic relationship that develops between the bands' two musicians, Ormus Cama and Vina Apsara, and their success in the United States. Rushdie's move from London to New York at the end of the twentieth-century was partly an attempt to escape what he perceived as the 'backbiting' literary culture of London and British politics (Idris 2006: 325), the other reason was to live with Padma Lakshmi, an Indian model and cookbook author (Rushdie later divorced Elizabeth West and married Padma Lakshmi). According to Farhad Idris, Rushdie's New York lifestyle and his public criticism of British cultural and political institutions prompted two British Asian Members of Parliament to raise questions about Rushdie's gratitude for the protection afforded him by the British government and the cost of this protection to the state (Idris 2006: 325). Nevertheless, Rushdie's acceptance of a knighthood from the British monarchy in 2007 would seem to confirm his rejection of the more radical, anti-establishment position reflected in his earlier essays and fiction.

Rushdie's eighth novel *Fury* (published in August 2001) brings together the worlds of late capitalist New York at the end of the twentieth century and a series of coups in the fictional Indian Ocean state of Lilliput-Blefuscu. The novel's preoccupation with the figure of the literary celebrity in the global marketplace prompted some critics to argue that the novel was a thinly veiled and rather solipsistic autobiography, which represents New York through the one-dimensional lens of the American media. Yet Rushdie's exploration of anti-Americanism, the plight of the postcolonial immigrant in late twentieth-century America, and the political efficacy of Third World nationalism in the aftermath of the Cold War seem to prefigure the Bush administration's war on terror, and the rhetoric of a clash of civilisations, which followed the attacks on America of September 11 2001.

Rushdie's post-9/11 editorials in *The Washington Post* and *The New York Times* on the attacks on America of September 11 2001, the US-led invasions of Afghanistan and Iraq, and the London bombings of July 7 2005, have tended to adopt what Rushdie describes as a liberal position of support for the Bush administration's wars in Afghanistan and Iraq, and criticism of Islamic fundamentalism, as I argue in Chapter 7. Yet, Rushdie's ninth novel *Shalimar the Clown* (2005) complicates this position by re-imagining the conflict between India and Pakistan over Kashmir from India's independence to the present, and highlighting the shortcomings of US foreign policy in South Asia. What Rushdie's representation of US foreign policy from a South Asian perspective in *Shalimar the Clown* highlights is a broader tendency in his writing to rethink the geographical axes and cultural histories of modernity from the standpoint of a postcolonial writer. And it is with this tendency that this book is concerned.

PART II
Major Works

3

MIDNIGHT'S CHILDREN AND *SHAME*

Rushdie's second novel *Midnight's Children* (1981) and his third novel *Shame* (1983) address the radical social and political changes brought about by India's independence, partition and the formation of Pakistan. The genocide and abduction of thousands of refugees on both sides of the India–Pakistan border that followed partition; the war between India and Pakistan over Kashmir; and the authoritarian political leadership of Indira Gandhi and Zulfiqar Ali Bhutto are just a few examples of the violence and repression associated with the formation of the divided postcolonial state. By employing self-reflective rhetorical and narrative devices, Rushdie interrogates the promises of political leaders such as Jawaharlal Nehru, Indira Gandhi, General Zia and Iskander Harappa, as well as the official narratives of national independence in order to address the division between the political elite and the people.

This is not to say that Rushdie's fiction adopts a socialist position that simply exposes the claims of the political elite as false in favour of the true voice and historical experience of the people. For in *Midnight's Children* and *Shame* Rushdie also satirises the ideologies of communism and socialism that are often associated with the people. Yet by focusing on the material effects of national independence in India and Pakistan, Rushdie exposes the violence associated with postcolonial modernity as a counterpoint to what he calls the 'optimism disease' of national liberation.

'IN THE END IT ALL BLOWS UP IN YOUR FACE': TERROR, FREEDOM AND POSTCOLONIAL MODERNITY IN *MIDNIGHT'S CHILDREN*

Salman Rushdie's second novel *Midnight's Children* (1981) has been variously read as an allegory of India's national independence (ten Kortenaar 1995); a postmodern novel, which, through its exoticist representation of India in the English language, commodifies Indian society and culture for Western consumption (Huggan 2001); and an exemplary postcolonial text that juxtaposes stories and cultural practices from different religious and cultural perspectives (Clark 2001). Such interpretations have certainly helped to elucidate the political limitations, as well as the rhetorical complexity and thematic concerns of *Midnight's Children*. Yet, as the first part of this chapter argues, what *Midnight's Children* crucially foregrounds is the dialectical relationship between terror and freedom that characterised postcolonial modernity after the event of national liberation.

The Limits of Nehruvian Secularism in *Midnight's Children*

In contrast to the violent, anti-colonial insurgency movements in Algeria and Ireland, the history of India's national independence is often associated with the non-violent, non-cooperation movement led by Mohandas K. Gandhi (see Young 2001). This is not to suggest that violent, anti-colonial insurgents did not operate in India. Indeed, as the South Asian historian Peter Heehs has argued, there were many active groups of violent, anti-colonial insurgents in early-twentieth-century India (Heehs 2004). However, these extremist groups were not successful in mobilising popular support for the nationalist cause in colonial India. Instead, the transition from colonialism to national independence in India is often regarded as the result of a popular and non-violent struggle for national independence, which was led by an elite political class.

Apart from the cinematic rendering of the Amritsar massacre, in which the British military leader, General Dyer, ordered troops to fire on a group of protesters in the Punjab town of Amritsar, Rushdie's representation of India's national independence in *Midnight's Children* is not overtly concerned with terrorism in colonial India as such. Yet, as this chapter suggests, it is in Rushdie's monstrous figuration of the body of the first-person narrator, Saleem Sinai, as a metaphor for the nation that the terror of postcolonial modernity is registered. For *Midnight's Children* is primarily concerned with the democratic promises of Nehru's nationalist rhetoric of modernisation and the failure of that rhetoric to deliver social transformation and secularisation after the event of national liberation. As Neil ten Kortenaar explains, 'The Nehruvian state is best described as a "project", with all the connotations that word has acquired in the twentieth century of progress, hubris, large-scale mobilization, and mass participation' (ten Kortenaar 2004: 138). Yet this secular project failed to mobilise the various different social, linguistic and religious groups that constitute the nation. By literalising the metaphors of Nehru's nationalist rhetoric, Rushdie proceeds to expose the terror of postcolonial freedom, epitomised in India's partition and communal violence, as well as the Indo-Pakistan war and the state of emergency declared by Indira Gandhi in 1975. In so doing, Rushdie foregrounds how the freedom which the event of India's national independence seemed to promise was also founded on the exclusion of socially subordinate, 'subaltern' groups and communities who were deemed to be minorities on the grounds of race, class, language or religion.

This founding exclusion of subaltern groups from the elite narrative of India's national independence can be seen as a form of political violence, which parallels discussions of violence or terror in contemporary social and political theory. In a discussion of Hegel's 'Absolute Freedom and Terror' in *The Phenomenology of Spirit*, for example, the social theorist Judith Butler has argued that Hegel's discussion of the Reign of Terror in France after the revolution of 1789 exemplifies the failure of abstract universal principles such as freedom to recognise the particularity of the individual. As Butler puts it, 'The universal can be the universal only to the extent that it remains untainted by what is particular, concrete and individual. Thus it requires the constant and meaningless vanishing of the individual, which is dramatically displayed by the Reign of Terror' (Butler, Laclau and Zizek 2000: 23). In Butler's analysis, abstract universal principles such as freedom are predicated on the liquidation of the particular or the individual, which in concrete terms is equivalent to an act of terror.

The liquidation of the particular and the individual by the universal is similarly evident in Rushdie's *Midnight's Children*, especially in Saleem's claim to represent the entire population through a corporeal radio transmitter that is produced by an obstruction in his nasal passage. As this chapter will suggest, Saleem's hyperbolic claim to embody the nation and the subsequent destruction of his body mirrors the false universality of national liberation, and its claim to represent the entire population.

Midnight's Children is ostensibly an autobiography, which traces the birth and maturation of the first-person narrator Saleem Sinai. Yet, as Neil ten Kortenaar has argued, Saleem's narrative is simultaneously a narrative of India's national independence, and it is for this reason that the story of Saleem Sinai in *Midnight's Children* has been described as a national allegory (Kortenaar 2004: 29–47). Saleem's receipt of a letter from the Indian Prime Minister Jawaharlal Nehru on the eve of India's independence on 15 August 1947, the date on which Saleem is born, prompts Saleem to regard himself as an important historical figure who is responsible for the nation's destiny:

> Newspapers celebrated me; politicians ratified my position. Jawaharlal Nehru wrote: "Dear Baby Saleem, My belated congratulations on the happy incident of your moment of birth! You are the newest bearer of that ancient face of India which is also eternally young. We shall be watching over your life with the closest attention; it will be, in a sense, the mirror of our own. (Rushdie 1981: 122)

It is partly Nehru's letter to Saleem and the publicity he receives from national newspapers such as the *Times of India* that prompts Saleem to imagine himself as a figure of national importance. Indeed, Nehru's letter provides Saleem with a license to employ frequent hyperbolic descriptions of how events in his own family life influence and even cause events of national significance, such as the Amritsar massacre, the riots over language, India's independence and subsequent partition and the Indo-Pakistan war of 1965.

Saleem's hyperbolic self-fashioning as a national hero may at first seem to be a consequence of his elite, cosmopolitan family background. For Saleem traces his origins back to his grandfather Aadam Aziz, a medical doctor who is born in Kashmir and subsequently undertakes medical training in Germany where he becomes associated with European anarchists, before returning to India. Aziz's association with European anarchists could be seen to parallel the association of Indian nationalists such as Aurobindo Ghose and Bal Gangadhar Tilak with anarchists and revolutionary thinkers in Russia, Germany and Ireland during the early twentieth century (see Heehs 2004). Yet, as Neil ten Kortenaar has suggested, Aadam Aziz's discovery of secular humanism and the loss of his religious faith during his visit to Europe bears a striking resemblance to the influence of Western thinking on Jawaharlal Nehru's secular vision of India's postcolonial modernity:

> Aziz learns to identify with a political state of his own, fully modern in the sense of secular and democratic, but in which he can see his own image and not that of his European friends ... His Indianness does not precede his internationalism but arises in response to it'. (ten Kortenaar 29)

In ten Kortenaar's reading, Aziz, like Rushdie, is a nationalist successor to Nehru, who claims a cosmopolitan perspective that is outside the homogenisation associated with communalism (13).

Yet this elite, cosmopolitan narrative is undermined by the revelation that Saleem's progenitors are false and that his genealogy is invented. At the end of book one, Saleem discovers that he is the bastard offspring of William Methwold, a British colonial landowner, and Vanita, one of Methwold's domestic servants. This discovery clearly undermines the elite genealogy that Saleem invents for himself as the son of wealthy landowners, but it also complicates the analogy between Saleem's birth and the birth of Nehru's nationalist project. For not only is Saleem an Anglo-Indian – 'An Anglo', as Padma puts it (118) – but he is also the product of an illegitimate relationship between a British colonial landowner and a subaltern.

Subaltern Histories and Anglo-Indian Hybridity in *Midnight's Children*

For Loretta Mijares, the hybridity of Anglo-Indians often forces them into a position of economic and social marginalisation in

India (Mijares 2003: 128). Yet for Rushdie, as Mijares proceeds to argue, Saleem's hybrid identity as an Anglo-Indian is a metaphor for the multiple and overdetermined genealogy of India rather than a concern with the marginality of the Anglo-Indian *per se* (132–133). Moreover, the 'ambiguity surrounding Saleem's birth does not centre on whether he is to grow up Indian or English, but rather whether he will be rich or poor' (134). As a consequence, Mijares concludes, Rushdie is not really concerned with the plight of the Anglo-Indian in decolonised space.

By focusing on Rushdie's treatment of the Anglo-Indian, however, Mijares overlooks the subaltern element of Saleem's genealogy, as well as Saleem's relationship to the socially and economically subordinate or subaltern characters in *Midnight's Children*, such as Tai, Mary Pereira, Joseph D' Costa, Padma, Parvati, Picture Singh and Shiva. For some of Rushdie's critics, the subaltern is marginalised and at times even demonised in *Midnight's Children*. Deepika Bahri argues, for instance, that *Midnight's Children* does not contribute significantly to the representation of the subaltern; indeed, she proceeds to suggest that Rushdie figures the subaltern as a terrifying mob that threatens the coherence of the nation state (Bahri 2003: 164–169). In a similar vein, Neil ten Kortenaar argues that the history that is deconstructed in *Midnight's Children* is not 'history in the sense of a past recoverable by radical historians seeking the traces and empty spaces left in the archives by classes other than the middle classes and by groups other than intellectuals. That is the project of the Subaltern Studies historians; it is not Rushdie's'. Instead, Kortenaar argues that '*Midnight's Children* is a meditation on the writing of history and, in particular, of that official history that constitutes the nation' (ten Kortenaar 1995: 42). As both Kortenaar and Bahri suggest, Rushdie's project in *Midnight's Children* is one of deconstructing official bourgeois nationalist history, rather than attempting to articulate the traces of subaltern histories that remain to be written.

To be sure, the first section of Saleem's autobiographical narrative seems to privilege the experiences of the middle-class Sinai family, of which Saleem claims to be a part. Yet this is not to suggest that Rushdie forecloses Marxist and feminist readings of Saleem's national narrative. Indeed, the revelation of Saleem's true genealogy and his subsequent socio-economic downfall clearly registers his class position. The difficulty with *Midnight's Children* is that it incorporates antagonistic social and political narratives without really addressing the power relations between these narratives. As a consequence, certain narratives seem to be marginalised, or at least subordinated to the march of Saleem's self-conscious historical narration. Like the Muslim characters, Mian Abdullah and Nadir Khan, who supported a secular state in India well before independence and partition, these subaltern narratives and histories are often swept under the carpet. Yet the traces of these subaltern histories are, nevertheless, inscribed in Saleem's narrative, and it is these traces that threaten the authority and coherence of the bourgeois nation state.

Midnight's Children and the Third World Alternative between Capitalism and Communism

One important example of a subaltern history that is partially swept under the carpet is that of the working class in *Midnight's Children*. Saleem's account of his grandfather recalls how he used to carry around a copy of Lenin's *What is to be Done?* a text in which Lenin tried to formulate a revolutionary theory for mobilising and organising the international workers' struggle. This detail is not entirely unrelated to the history of anti-colonial nationalist struggles in *Midnight's Children*. As Robert Young points out in *Postcolonialism: An Historical Introduction*, postcolonial thought has always been engaged in the translation and revision of Marxist (and Leninist) thought in a way that is conscious of the local conditions of the rural peasantry and the industrial proletariat in colonial and postcolonial societies (Young 2001). In the case of India, Young cites the debate between the leader of the Indian communist party M. N. Roy and Lenin in the 1920s and 1930s over the nationalist question. Roy opposed nationalism as a viable form of social transformation in India because he believed that the nationalist struggle in India was essentially bourgeois and would do nothing to change the rigid class structure in Indian society. However, Lenin believed that anti-colonial nationalism was an important strategy in India because it would overthrow the rule of British imperial capitalism, even if it temporarily gave political and economic power to upper middle-class political elites.

Such debates do not really feature at the forefront of *Midnight's Children*, however. Indeed, as previously mentioned, Kortenaar argues that Saleem's grandfather Aadam Aziz seems to be more like Nehru in his political optimism and modernising outlook. Furthermore, after Nehru's declaration of India's independence, Saleem's official (but not biological) father, Ahmed Sinai, starts to turn white along with many other businessmen (Rushdie 1981: 179). This magical metamorphosis could be read as a sign that India's political independence from the British has not led to a corresponding social revolution in its class and patriarchal structures. For in his father's symbolic whiteness, Saleem recognises the limitations of national independence, and the way that the 'businessmen of India' had become 'masters of their own destinies' at the expense of the rest of the country (179). The skin pigmentation disorder which afflicts India's business-men could perhaps be seen as a racialised symptom of neo-colo-nialism, or the complicity of India's elite professional class in the global economic exploitation of India's relatively cheap labour power and natural resources. Rather than simply endorsing Ahmed Sinai's capitalist ventures in neo-colonialism, however, Saleem is subsequently drawn to the communist politics of Picture Singh and Parvati. Indeed, it is significant that Saleem proceeds to contrast his father's business, as a capitalist comprador, with his own social downfall and incipient class-consciousness later in the novel:

I, who had been raised in India's other true faith, which we may term Businessism … began zealously to turn red and then redder, as surely and completely as my father had once turned white, so that now my mission of saving-the-country could be seen in a new light; more rev-olutionary methodologies suggested themselves. (1981: 397)

The contradictions between India's political independence and its economic dependency are also foregrounded in a passage where Saleem juxtaposes the government's announcement to the world 'that it could accept no more development loans unless the lenders were willing to wait indefinitely for repayment' with the following parenthetical comment:

But let me not overstate the case: although the production of finished steel reached only 2.4 million tons by the [Five Year] plan's end in 1961, and although, during those five years, the number of landless and unemployed masses actually increased, so that it was greater than it had ever been under the British Raj, there were also substantial gains. The production of iron ore was almost doubled; power capacity did double; coal production leaped from thirty-eight million to fifty-four million tons. Five billion yards of cotton textiles were produced each year. Also large numbers of bicycles, machine tools, diesel engines, power pumps and ceiling fans. But I can't help ending on a downbeat: illiteracy survived unscathed; the population continued to mushroom. (Rushdie 1981: 206)

What Saleem implies but does not explicitly state in this parenthetical comment about India's economy is the massive gap between the exorbitant interest rates of First World development loans to Third World nation states such as India and the increase in manufacturing of cheap commodities for export to the West. Such a gap continues to maintain the majority of India's population under conditions of illiteracy, unemployment and poverty. By placing this comment in parenthesis, Rushdie may seem to criticise the political spin of Nehru's economic policies that attempts to bracket and exclude materialist concerns about the impact of First world development loans and Third World poverty.

Yet in staging the exclusion of the people from Nehru's modernising rhetoric, Rushdie also risks perpetuating the dominant national fiction he seems to want to subvert. Indeed, this is further borne out later in the text, when Saleem tries to reconcile class divisions between Brahmins and untouchables in his public address to the Midnight's Children Congress (255). By appealing to the modernising rhetoric of the new postcolonial nation and the idealism of a Third World alternative between capitalism and communism, Saleem tries to unify the Midnight's Children congress and the imagined community of India. Yet, in doing so, Saleem also abstracts the nation, India, from the social and economic conditions of the emerging neocolonial world. Indeed, it is this abstraction that the working-class character Shiva, the biological son of Ahmed and Amina Sinai, opposes in his riposte to Saleem:

No, little rich boy; there is no third principle; there is only money and poverty, and have-and-lack, and right-and-left; there is only me-against-the-world! The world is not ideas, rich boy; the world is no place for dreamers or their dreams; the world, little Snotnose, is things. (255)

Even if *Midnight's Children* seems to focus primarily on the elite nationalist narrative of postcolonial India from its birth, the repressed symptoms of India's patriarchal and class-based society, as well as its colonial past, return to haunt the narrative and the nation itself. Indeed, this is further exemplified in Rushdie's use of the ghost as a narrative device to terrorise Mary Pereira into confessing the truth of Saleem's biological lineage in *Midnight's Children*. In book one, Mary Pereira switches the lower-class infant's name tag for that of the middle-class infant, who is later revealed to be Shiva. This subversive movement is described as a 'private revolutionary act' (117) which Mary committed as an act of solidarity with her lover, Joseph D'Costa, a revolutionary insurgent who declares that India's independence is 'for the rich only' (104). The ghost of Joseph subsequently haunts Mary for 11 years, until Joseph finally persuades her to confess this 'crime' to the Sinai family.

The grotesque appearance of Joseph's decaying body recalls Marx's descriptions of the worker as an apparition or a phantom, who returns to haunt the capitalist system in the early pages of *Capital Volume One*. Like Marx's spectral worker, the ghost of Joseph is a figure of insurrection rather than resurrection. That is to say Joseph's spectral presence in the text continues Mary's private revolutionary act by making public the buried secret of Saleem's illegitimate, mixed-race ancestry. Indeed, this supernatural moment of resistance in the text operates as a counterpoint to Saleem's feeling of being an active metaphor for postcolonial India and marks the beginning of Saleem's 'disintegration', or his social downfall within the Sinai family, and the class system.

Hyperbole and the Terror of Nationalist Rhetoric in *Midnight's Children*

By representing Saleem's body as a metaphor for the body politic, Rushdie transforms Saleem's body into a site of violent antagonism. Saleem elaborates on the significance of the metaphor of the body politic in 'The Kolynos Kid', a chapter in which he provides his audience with a scientific lesson in the modes of historical writing, and proceeds to outline a taxonomy to distinguish between the different ' "modes of connection" ' linking himself to the history of the nation (238):

> I must answer in adverbs and hyphens: I was linked to history both lit-
> erally and metaphorically, both actively and passively in what our
> (admirably modern) scientists might term 'modes of connection' com-
> posed of dualistically-combined configurations of the two pairs of
> opposed adverbs given above. This is why hyphens are necessary:
> actively-passively, passively-metaphorically, actively-metaphorically
> and passively-literally, I was inextricably entwined with my world. (238)

In the same passage, Saleem proceeds to provide examples to
support each of these categories: the 'manner in which [Saleem]
provided the language marchers with their battle cry' exemplifies
the active-literal because it is an act in which Saleem literally
'affected or altered the course of seminal historical events'; the
'unavoidable connection between the infant state's attempts at
rushing towards full-sized adulthood and [Saleem's] own explosive efforts at growth' exemplifies the passive-metaphorical
because it is an example of how socio-political events affected him
metaphorically; the 'freezing of [his] father's assets' exemplifies
the passive-literal mode because it constitutes a moment at which
a national event had 'a direct bearing upon the lives of [Saleem]
and [his] family'; and the 'mutilation of [Saleem's] middle finger'
instantiates the 'active-metaphorical' mode because it 'groups
together those occasions on which things done by or to me were
mirrored in the macrocosm of public affairs, and my private existence was shown to be symbolically at one with history' (238).

If these modes of connection between Saleem's autobiography
and the history of the nation seem hyperbolic, however, this is not
to suggest that Saleem's self-fashioning as one of the most articulate and important of the midnight's children is simply a sign of
Saleem's hubris. Rather, Saleem's use of hyperbole is significant
because it suggests a link between Saleem's narrative and the terror of postcolonial modernity. As Alex Houen has argued in
Terrorism and Modern Literature, one of the predominant tropes in the
rhetoric of terrorism is hyperbole: a trope which 'oversteps itself as
a term' (Houen 2002: 5–6). In Houen's account, hyperbole is an
exemplary metaphor for terrorism because it describes the ways in
which terrorism can produce material events and discursive practices that exceed a particular event of political violence (5). Houen's

observation is instructive for reading *Midnight's Children* as a novel concerned with the terror of postcolonial modernity because it provides a critical framework through which to read Rushdie's use of hyperbole. Yet this is not to say that Saleem's hyperbole is exactly the same as the hyperbole that Houen attributes to terrorism. For if hyberbole is used in the rhetoric of terrorism to sensationalise and exaggerate the significance of acts of political violence in order to increase television ratings or newspaper sales, or to garner public support for politicians to introduce authoritarian security measures and launch counter-terrorism offensives, in *Midnight's Children* Rushdie uses hyperbole to register how the excessive forces of history and the power of the postcolonial state terrorise Saleem's body. For Saleem's hyperbolic role, as a messianic figure who represents the nation, is unsustainable and ultimately leads to his physical destruction: 'my body is screaming, it cannot take this kind of treatment anymore … I am the bomb in Bombay, watch me explode, bones splitting beneath the awful pressure of the crowd' (462–463).

If Saleem's body is a metaphorical bomb, however, it is a passive-metaphorical bomb rather than an active-metaphorical bomb. That is to say, Saleem's body is more terrorised by the forces of history than actively terrorising the nation that his body purports to represent. Indeed, it is Saleem's blatant failure to represent the entire Indian population that mirrors the false universality of national independence and the terror that the postcolonial state unleashed on the people in the form of India's partition and the state of emergency declared by Indira Gandhi. As Saleem announces:

> I shall not describe the mass blood-letting in progress on the frontiers of the divided Punjab (where the partitioned nations are washing themselves in one another's blood …); I shall avert my eyes from the violence in Bengal and the long pacifying walk of Mahatma Gandhi. Selfish? Narrow-minded? Well, perhaps; but excusably so, in my opinion. After all, one is not born every day. (112)

Furthermore, it is significant that Saleem's hyperbolic and messianic claims to represent the nation lead to his bodily disintegration. For if Saleem's bodily life is read as a passive metaphor for the formation of India, his disintegration could be seen to literalise this metaphor and, in so doing, to expose the false universality of nationalist rhetoric and its propensity to terrorise the population at the very moment that nationalist rhetoric claims to unify the nation. The terror of such nationalist rhetoric is perfectly exemplified in Rushdie's representation of Prime Minister Indira Gandhi's Emergency suspension of civil law in 1975, about which this chapter will say more below.

For some of Rushdie's critics, Saleem's apparent indifference to partition and the violence in Bengal, as well as his satirical presentation of the communist characters in the novel as magicians clearly demonstrate Rushdie's bourgeois, anti-communist sensibility (Brennan 1989; Booker 1999). Yet in foregrounding the mistakes and omissions in Saleem's version of India's national narrative, Rushdie clearly encourages readers to question the credibility of Saleem's historical narrative. What is more, Saleem's bodily disintegration mirrors the fracturing of the nation by the multiple voices of the population. Indeed, Rushdie links Saleem's bodily disintegration as a figure of the nation to his failure to unify the 'many-headed multitudes' (462) who constitute the Indian nation: 'it is the privilege and the curse of midnight's children to be both masters and victims of their times, to forsake privacy and be sucked into the annihilating whirlpool of the multitudes' (462–463). Saleem's bodily disintegration is thus linked to the fragmentation of the postcolonial body politic. As Neil ten Kortenaar argues, the 'collective that Saleem imagines in his own image and in whose image he imagines himself resembles the figure of the sovereign in the original frontispiece of Hobbes' *Leviathan*: a giant towering over his dominions, his body composed of the lilliputian figures of his subjects' (ten Kortenaar 2004: 131). Rushdie's choice of the word multitude rather than people to describe the national population in *Midnight's Children* is significant, however, because it is opposed to Hobbes' idea of state control, epitomised in the image of the body politic described above by Kortenaar.

The Multitude and the State of Emergency in *Midnight's Children*

The term multitude derives from the Latin *multitudo*, meaning 'the character, quality, or condition of being many' (*OED*). As a category in political philosophy, the multitude was first elaborated by the philosophers Thomas Hobbes and Baruch Spinoza in the seventeenth century to denote a heterogeneous social group that could not be reduced to a singular political category, such as the People or the One. As Paolo Virno explains in *A Grammar of the Multitude*, Baruch Spinoza defined the *multitudo* as 'a plurality which persists as such in the public scene, in collective action, in the handling of communal affairs, without converging into a One' (Virno 2004: 21). In Spinoza's account, the multitude had a positive connotation, which was associated with freedom and civil liberties (Virno: 21). For Thomas Hobbes, however, the multitude was a hated concept because it was opposed to state authority and the 'state monopoly of political decision making' (Virno: 23). Hobbes attacked the multitude because he believed that it posed a threat to the political authority of the nation state in seventeenth-century Europe. In a discussion that echoes Thomas Hobbes, Jawaharlal Nehru in *The Discovery of India* describes India's population of 'four hundred million separate individual men and women' as 'multitudinous', and suggests at the same time that India is 'a cultural unity amidst diversity, a bundle of contradictions held together by strong but invisible threads' (Nehru 1946: 578). In contrast to Hobbes, Nehru's comments on the 'multitudinous' property of India's population seem to embrace the diversity of the population. Yet, by insisting that the 'diversity' of India's population is 'held together by strong but invisible threads', Nehru invokes the political authority of the state.

Saleem's assertion that it is the multitude that terrorises his body and brings about its disintegration might indicate that Rushdie, like Hobbes and Nehru, is opposed to the multitude and the political threat that it poses to the authority of the state. Indeed, Deepika Bahri has suggested that Rushdie figures the multitude as a terrifying mob that threatens the coherence of the nation state (Bahri 2003: 164–169). In a similar vein, Neil ten Kortenaar has noted how Rushdie compares the multitudes to insects (ten Kortenaar 2004: 84–85), a simile that would seem to reinforce the argument made by Deepika Bahri, M. Keith Booker and Timothy Brennan that *Midnight's Children* is a bourgeois novel that marginalises the working-class, subaltern characters it represents.

Yet, in his physical disintegration, Saleem allows for the structural possibility of a plural, heteroglot nation that is open to the 'inner monologues of all the so-called teeming millions, of masses and classes alike [who] jostled for space within [Saleem's] head' (168). Such an open vision of the nation is opposed to the Nehruvian model of 'unity in diversity', which seeks to contain and subordinate the voices of the multitude to the political will of the secular state. As Robert Bennett has argued in an essay on *Midnight's Children's* narration of Indian national identity, *Midnight's Children* 'dialogically rearticulates' traditional narratives of national identity 'as a heteroglot polyphony of multiple voices instead of a single, unified, collective voice' (Bennett 2000: 178). Bennett takes issue with what he sees as Fredric Jameson's reductive model of Third World literature as a national allegory, a critical model that defines all literary works produced in the third world as allegories of decolonisation and Third World politics. Against this reductive model, Bennett invokes the Russian literary theorist Mikhail Bakhtin's model of novelistic discourse as 'always "stratified and heteroglot"' and one which seeks to 'represent such an "actively heteroglot world"' (Bennett 2000: 183–184). In Bennett's argument, Bahktin's model of novelistic discourse offers a more appropriate critical framework through which to read *Midnight's Children* because *Midnight's Children* 'constructs a national allegory that is not only self-consciously fictional but also aggressively heteroglot and fragmentary' (Bennett 2000: 186).

Saleem's inability to contain the voices of the multitude within his head can be read as a mirror of Rushdie's failure to represent the nation as a totality in the novel. Moreover, by staging the disintegration of Saleem's body, and by implication the novel that he struggles to compose before his bodily disintegration, *Midnight's Children* satirises the very idea of a realistic national narrative that could accommodate all the voices, histories and languages of the Indian subcontinent. In so doing, *Midnight's Children* creates a rhetorical space for the multitude to contest the false universality of national independence. As Joseph D'Costa puts it 'this independence is for the rich only' (104).

For Rushdie in *Midnight's Children*, this false universality of national independence is nowhere more pronounced than in Prime Minister Indira Gandhi's Emergency suspension of civil law in 1975. The so-called Indian Emergency of 1975 can be seen to exemplify the sovereign power of the state and its techniques of biopolitical control. As Michel Foucault argues in *Society Must Be Defended*, biopolitics or the political control and regulation of human life, emerged in the nineteenth century as a strategy for controlling the multiplicity of the population: 'Biopolitics deals with the population, with the population as a political problem, as a problem that is at once scientific and political, as a biological problem and as power's problem' (Foucault 2003: 245). In the case of India's emergency from 1975–1977, the sovereign power of the state was exercised in and through the biopolitical control of Delhi's urban poor, which enforced the sterilisation of slum dwellers who had been displaced by the Emergency's slum clearances scheme in exchange for plots of land in Delhi's resettlement colonies. As a consequence, sterilisation became 'a medium through which people could negotiate their housing rights with officials of the DDA [Delhi Development Authority]' (Tarlo 2003: 88).

In book three of *Midnight's Children*, the biopolitical power of the state during India's state of emergency is foregrounded in Sanjay Gandhi's population control programme, the slum clearances in Delhi and in the forced sterilisation of the midnight's children. By giving voice to the state's violent repression of the people from the perspective of the people, Rushdie raises questions about the limitations of India's democracy in a way that echoes the rising tide of political opposition to Indira Gandhi's emergency government, during and after the Indian emergency. In an account of the Turkman Gate Clearance Scheme in Delhi on April 17 1976, for example, B. M. Sinha describes how the police fired indiscriminately at crowds of displaced slum dwellers, who protested the bulldozing of their homes (Sinha 1977: 151–153). A similar account of state repression is offered by The Communist Party of India, in a pamphlet published in 1977 that opposed the Delhi Development Authority's Family Planning programme on the grounds that it constituted 'an antipeople drive for coercive sterilization' together with the slum clearances in Delhi, which they described as 'the mass scale demolition of the residential premises of the common man' (CPI 1977: 3). The coercive character of this sterilisation programme is further borne out in a letter describing the family planning camps that were set up in Delhi:

> Hundreds of policeman were deployed in and around the camp from 7 pm onwards on the 15th April to round up the city-poor like riksha, thela, tonga drivers and jhalliwalas etc. from adjoining localities. Even poor labourers who usually stroll about in Edward Park or Parade

Ground to breathe fresh air in summer months were rounded up and brought under police escort to the Dujana House camp in batches, and detained there for the whole night. (CPI 1977: 13–14)

The CPI document proceeds to explain how the state threatened to withhold teachers' salaries if they did not bring poor people to the camps for sterilisation (CPI 1977: 19); how scooter drivers were threatened with non-renewal of their licences if they did not get sterilised (CPI 1977: 19); how slum dwellers in the Faridabad industrial complex 'are being threatened by the administration that their huts would be demolished if they do not get themselves sterilised' (21); how in 'one district in Punjab 60 applications for old age and widows pensions were held up in the office of the BDPO who told the applicants that their cases would be recommended only if they got sterilised' (20); and how in 'the various family planning camps where sterilisation was done deaths have taken place due to unhygienic conditions of operation' (31). Significantly, the pamphlet proceeds to link the government's policy 'of eliminating poverty through sterilisation' to its desire to 'curry favour with the World Bank and other neocolonialist agencies' (40).

In Rushdie's fictional representation of the Emergency, the forced sterilisation of Saleem Sinai takes place against the background of slum clearances and the incarceration of Indira Gandhi's political opponents. Moreover, in an imaginary conversation with the Widow's Hand, a synecdochal figure for Indira Gandhi, Saleem uses a demographic argument to question the detention and sterilisation of the midnight's children:

> There are four hundred and twenty of us; a mere 0.00007 per cent of the six-hundred million strong population of India. Statistically insignificant; even if we were considered as a percentage of the arrested thirty (or two hundred and fifty) thousand, we formed a mere 1.4 (or 0.168) percent!' (438)

In response to this argument, Saleem learns from the Widow's Hand that the incarceration and sterilisation of the midnight's children is not only an attempt to control the population, but also part of a struggle between gods:

> those who would be gods fear no one so much as other potential deities; and that only, is why we, the magical children of midnight,

were hated feared destroyed by the Widow, who was not only Prime Minister of India but also aspired to be Devi, the Mother-goddess in her most terrible aspect. (438)

Rushdie's characterisation of India's prime minister as the destructive Mother-goddess Devi in this passage reiterates the coexistence of the secular and the theological in postcolonial India. But this characterisation also foregrounds the sovereign power of India's political leader during the Indian emergency, and her tendency to act like a God. In this respect, *Midnight's Children* suggests that the biopolitical control of the population through Sanjay Gandhi's forced sterilisation programme was also an expression of his mother, Indira Gandhi's, sovereign power. Indeed, the political significance of Saleem's sterilisation is further borne out by his observation that Sanjay Gandhi's sterilisation programme leads to the midnight's children loss of faith or hope in the nation, and their position within it:

Not for us the simple vas- and tubectomies performed on the teeming masses; because there was a chance, just a chance that such operations could be reversed ... ectomies were performed, but irreversibly: testicles were removed from sacs, and wombs vanished for ever.

Test- and hysterectomized, the children of midnight were denied the possibility of reproducing themselves ... but that was only a side-effect, because they were truly extraordinary doctors, and they drained us of more than that: hope, too, was excised, and I don't know how it was done, because ... I was out for the count. (439)

In Saleem's account, the state's forcible excision of the midnight's children's reproductive organs and vital fluids simultaneously leads to a metaphysical draining away of hope, which Rushdie calls 'sperectomy' (437), a neologism derived from the Latin verb *sperare*, meaning to hope.

Saleem's loss of hope in the nation signifies his demise as a messianic figure in Nehru's modern, secular nation state. This draining away of hope also signals a clear split between the multitude, signified by Saleem and the midnight's children, and the increasingly authoritarian state that claims to represent the people. Yet this loss of hope or faith in the democratic promise of Nehru's modern, secular nation state is not a loss of hope in India's political future *per se*. For it is Saleem's storytelling that ultimately articulates the voice of the nation. In an interview with Alistair Niven, for example, Rushdie speaks of storytelling as a way of organising the multitude:

> [W]hen I wrote *Midnight's Children*, one of the ideas I had about it was that the simple fact about India is that the first thing to think about India is its multitude, its crowd, and I thought: 'how do you tell a crowd of stories?'. 'What is the literary equivalent of the multitude?' One strategy that was deliberately adopted in that book was deliberately to tell, as it were, too many stories, so that there was a jostle of stories in the novel and that your main narration, your main storyline, had to kind of force its way through the crowd .... (Rushdie in Chauhan 2001: 234)

For Saleem in his role of Scheherazade, the storyteller in *The Arabian Nights*, the proliferation of stories in *Midnight's Children* is an attempt to articulate the multiplicity of voices that constitute the nation rather than an attempt to subordinate those voices to the authority of a single narrative voice.

By exploding the myth of the body politic, Rushdie thus develops a more open and democratic narrative structure for articulating the multiple voices of the nation: a structure, which Ken Hirschkop has termed, in a study of the Russian literary theorist Mikhail Bakhtin, an aesthetic for democracy (Hirschkop 1999). In Hirschkop's argument, Bakhtin's criticism was a product of his social and political milieu in post-revolutionary Russia. What is more, Hirschkop argues that for Bakhtin, political concepts such as democracy and equal rights are constituted by linguistic dialogue, a dialogue which finds its apotheosis in the vernacular codes of the European novel: 'In the concept of novelistic style one finds an intersubjectivity which depends on a historical sense, irony, a literate print culture, an eye and ear for social differentiation, and much else characteristic of modern social life' (Hirschkop 1999: 48). Just so for Rushdie, the explosion of Saleem's body at the end of *Midnight's Children* is not simply a sign of Rushdie's opposition to the multiple voices of the nation, which threaten to destroy him. Rather, Saleem's body, like Rushdie's novel, is a site of dialogue and debate. It is in this sense that *Midnight's Children* is an appropriate aesthetic form for India's democracy.

POSTCOLONIAL GOVERNMENTALITY AND THE PUBLIC SECRET OF STATE TERROR IN *SHAME*

If the epic, hyperbolic, encyclopaedic and digressive structure of Saleem's narrative in *Midnight's Children* is an appropriate aesthetic form for the democratic principles of postcolonial India, Rushdie's third novel *Shame* seems to be its diametric opposite, both in style and subject matter. As Timothy Brennan argues in *Salman Rushdie and the Third World*:

> If *Midnight's Children* was a novel whose key historical events involved huge and nebulous activities – Gujaratis, Kashmiris, Dravidians, Sikhs and Bombay Christians with Portuguese names, in *Shame* those events are seen strictly in the higher echelons. Their differences have as much to do with the direction from which they analyse political power, as with the fact that they focus on different nations. (Brennan 1989: 121)

For Brennan, one of the crucial differences between *Midnight's Children* and *Shame* lies in its representation of political power. Whereas *Midnight's Children* analyses political power from the standpoint of the people, *Shame* represents political power from the perspective of the ruling elite. As a consequence, the people are largely absent in Rushdie's *Shame*. As Syed Mujeebuddin puts it:

> Unlike the 'teeming', crowded, quality of the plurality of Indian life that Saleem in *MC* symbolises – the multitudes that jostle inside him and eventually break him up – *Shame* is riddled with images of empty, labyrinthine houses in remote places and frontiers surrounded by nothingness. (Mujeebuddin 2003: 132)

Rushdie's fictional representation of Pakistan's political history in *Shame* certainly implies a value judgement about the authoritarian form of government that underpins Pakistan's political history. By framing events in Pakistan's history such as the rise of Zulfiqar Ali-Bhutto, his subsequent execution and the succession of Zia Ul-Haq as a grotesque fairy tale, Rushdie foregrounds the constraints placed on writers in a repressive authoritarian society. Such constraints on the position of the writer in society are further borne out in the narrator's account of a poet who 'had spent many months in jail for social reasons' (28). This personal anecdote functions as a metafictional device in the text, which draws attention to the stance of the writer as a migrant writing about Pakistan from the West. Rushdie's negative portrayal of Pakistan had led some critics such as Aijaz Ahmad and Inderpal Grewal to argue that Rushdie's representation of Pakistan in *Shame* conflates the state and civil society, downplays the significance of popular movements and thereby forecloses the agency of the people (Ahmad 1992; Grewal 1994).

Rushdie's rather bleak vision of Pakistan in *Shame* can be linked to the partial and fragmentary knowledge of the narrator, who is a self-confessed migrant. In the novel, the narrator asserts that he has never lived in Pakistan 'for longer than six months at a stretch' and that as a consequence he 'learned Pakistan in slices' (69). While the narrator acknowledges that this fragmentary and partial perspective might be seen to undermine his right to speak about Pakistan (28), he attempts to answer this charge by claiming that the idea of Pakistan was 'originally thought up in England by a group of Muslim intellectuals' before it 'was born-across or trans-lated, and imposed itself on history; a returning migrant, settling down on partitioned land, forming a palimpsest on the past' (87). This claim is subsequently conflated with the experience of the *mohajirs*, the migrant population of Indian Muslims who moved to Pakistan during the partition of the Indian subcontinent. The origin of the noun *mohajir* in Urdu, as Hima Raza explains, is 'derived from the Arabic word meaning "emigrant, evacuee, or refugee" ' (Raza: 55). What is more, a '*mohajir* refers to one who has performed the act of *hijrat*', a word that also comes from Arabic and which connotes 'separation, migration, flight, specifically the flight of the prophet Mohammad from Mecca to Medina' (Raza: 55). If the *hijrat* is 'an exalted form of migration' which tests the faith of an individual *mohajir*, as well as defining his identity (Raza: 55), in the context of Pakistan the *mohajir* refers specifically to the 'Muslim migrant/ refugee/ exile' who was displaced during India's partition: 'More than fifty years after the Partition the *mohajir* population in Pakistan still sees itself as being displaced' (Raza: 55). In Raza's account, this 'insecurity is rooted in the perception of the *mohajir* as an outsider by the native population of the country' (Raza: 55).

This is not to suggest, however, that the narrator's experience of migrancy is identical with that of the *mohajir* characters in the novel, such as Bilquis Hyder. Certainly, the narrator is a migrant

54 SALMAN RUSHDIE

who describes himself as a 'translated man'. The narrator then proceeds to suggest that he 'like all migrants' is 'a fantasist' who builds 'imaginary countries' and tries 'to impose them on the ones that exist' (87). One of the problems with Rushdie's representation of the migrant in *Shame* is that it conflates his own experience as a metropolitan migrant with the experience of the refugees who were forced to move to Pakistan during India's partition. This generalized metaphor of migrancy as part of a palimpsest, which the state attempts to erase, prevents Rushdie from specifying the differences between the experiences of metropolitan migrancy and the *mohajir* experience of Indian Muslims who migrated to Pakistan after India's partition.

Such criticisms of Rushdie's migrant sensibility in *Shame*, like the comparisons of his representation of Pakistan's civil society in *Shame* with that of India in *Midnight's Children*, are helpful in identifying the limitations of Rushdie's political satire about Zulfikar Ali Bhutto and General Zia's repressive governments in Pakistan. Yet they do not take account of the ways in which both *Midnight's Children* and *Shame* use literary devices to publicly articulate the violence of the postcolonial state. Whereas Rushdie uses satire in *Midnight's Children* to describe the slum clearances in Delhi, and Sanjay Gandhi's sterilisation programme during India's state of emergency from 1975–1977, in *Shame* Rushdie combines the generic conventions of the fairy tale and magical realism to articulate the public secret of state repression in Pakistan.

If, as Timothy Brennan has suggested, the fairy tale genre is 'the genre of subversives' and the fairy tale writer is 'a covert satirist operating under conditions of intense repression' (Brennan 1989: 135), Rushdie in *Shame* suggests that the art of governmentality in Pakistan is a form of magic, in which people mysteriously vanish in a puff of smoke. Like the Latin American writer Gabriel Garcia Marquez, Rushdie uses the generic conventions of magical realism in *Shame* to articulate the excesses of state terror, as they are publicly understood. As Michael Taussig has argued in a discussion of state terror in Columbia, a law of silence operates in authoritarian states, in which people dare not speak about state violence in public. Instead, the people are forced to adopt alternative forms for speaking about state terror. Taussig describes such forms of articulating the unspeakable as public secrets, or 'that which is generally known but cannot be spoken' (Taussig 1999: 50).

In *Shame*, the fairy tale performs an analogous function to the public secret in Columbia: to expose the excesses of state terror. One example of this public secret is the 18 shawls stitched by Rani Harappa during the six years she was placed under house arrest. In each of these shawls, Rani depicts her husband's various acts of corruption and repression during the term of his political leadership. Neluka Silva has described the stitching of these shawls as Rani's 'single but powerful act of defiance' in the novel, an act that 'intricately captures the debaucherous, violent and inhuman acts of her husband's career' (Silva 2003: 156–157). Rani Harappa's shawls certainly serve to publicly articulate the terror of Iskander Harappa's governmental authority. Yet, in *Shame*, it is Raza Hyder's daughter, Sufiya Zinobia, who performs the role of the public secret. Many critics have argued that Sufiya Zinobia's first name contains a morphemic allusion to Sufism, the branch of Muslim heterodoxy with which Rushdie is most closely identified. As Timothy Brennan explains, 'It was the practice of the Sufis to appeal directly to the masses and to reject the dogmatism of the clerical scholars (the "*ulama*")' (Brennan 1989: 127). In the fictional world of Raza Hyder's Islamic theocracy, Sufiya Zinobia can thus be seen as a part of what Rushdie calls the palimpsest of Pakistan's history; she embodies the cultural histories which are repressed by the state, but cannot be articulated. Significantly, some critics have also suggested that Sufiya's destructive potential is a Muslim version of the Hindu goddess, Kali, a reading which seems to support the narrator's claim that 'Indian centuries lay just beneath the surface' of Pakistan (Clark 2001; Fletcher 1994; Van der Veer 1989).

Yet such a reading elides the precise significance of Sufiya Zinobia's violent reign of terror vis-à-vis the state. As the narrator asserts at one point in the novel, Sufiya 'had discovered in the labyrinths of her unconscious self the hidden path that links *sharam* to violence' (139). On one level, Sufiya's violence is a symptom of her family's repressive and abusive treatment on the grounds that she is mentally retarded. This symptom initially manifests itself in Sufiya's blushing (121–123), a physical sign of repression which the narrator terms a 'psychosomatic event' (123). By describing Sufiya's blushing as an event, the narrator underlines the exterior, public manifestation of a private repressed feeling. Yet this embodied manifestation of Sufiya's shame is also a synecdoche for the affect of state repression on the people. This characterisation of Sufiya's blushing is a symptom of what Michael Taussig calls the nervous system of the state: a system which depends on the terror that it is bent on eliminating (Taussig 1992: 13).

Sufiya Zenobia and the Nervous System of the Body Politic

The idea of Sufiya Zenobia as a public sign of the affect of state repression on the body politic is developed further during Sufiya's monstrous reign of terror at the end of the novel. Significantly, the random beheadings committed by Sufiya's beastly double against animals and villagers in Pakistan are blamed on a terrorist group based in Afghanistan called Al-Iskander, a group 'which was being given Soviet arms and Palestinian training' (256). By inventing this fictional terrorist group as a scapegoat for Sufiya's atrocities, Raza Hyder and General Raddi attempt to displace the violent foundations of state terror onto an external terrorist threat.

In *A Thousand Plateaus*, the French philosophers Gilles Deleuze and Felix Guattari have suggested that external threats to the sovereignty of the nation state, such as terrorist attacks, operate as war machines, which the state attempts to appropriate for its own political ends: 'One of the fundamental problems of the State is to appropriate this war machine that is foreign to it and make it a piece in its apparatus' (Deleuze and Guattari 1987: 230). In *Shame*, however, the state fails to contain the destructive power of the war machine, which the state has itself produced. The random 'Murders of animals and men' that take place across the fictional landscape of Rushdie's Pakistan mirrors the public secret of state terror in Pakistan. And it is the monstrous alter ego of Sufiya Zinobia who functions as this secret war machine. Sufiya is described as 'a rumour, a chimera, the collective fantasy of a stifled people, a dream born of their rage' (263). In this way, Rushdie establishes a clear connection between the monstrous fantasy of Sufiya Zenobia and the violent excesses of state power. Like the fictional terrorist group, Al-Iskander, the monstrous alter ego of Sufiya Zenobia is a 'collective fantasy' (263), which allows the people to articulate publicly 'that which is generally known but cannot be spoken' (Taussig 1999: 50).

Significantly, it is the killings perpetrated by the monstrous alter ego of Sufiya Zenobia that are responsible for bringing down

Raza Hyder's Islamic government. Sufiya's monstrous double is a fairy tale of pure violence that demystifies the violent foundations of Hyder's government:

> It seemed to [Hyder] once again that the years of his greatness and of the construction of the great edifice of national stability had been no more than self-delusory lies, that this nemesis had been stalking him all along, permitting him to rise higher and higher so that his fall might be greater; his own flesh had turned against him, and no man has a defence against such treason. (257)

In ancient Greek mythology, a nemesis was a goddess, who was conventionally portrayed as an agent of divine punishment for wrongdoing or hubris. By characterising Sufiya Zinobia as Hyder's 'nemesis' Rushdie thus attributes a moral logic of divine retribution to Sufiya's reign of terror.

The representation of Sufiya as a divine figure is developed further in Rushdie's characterisation of Sufiya as 'a person who suffers in our stead' (141). This characterisation of Sufiya recalls the Sufi belief, articulated by the medieval mystic Al-Hakim Al-Tirmidhi, that the spirit is a medium for feeling both shame and pain (Al-Hakim Al-Tirmidhi 1996: 139). Yet Sufiya's gradual transformation from a saintly embodiment of the spirit into a beastly figure of death and destruction at the end of the novel implies a logic of martyrdom that clearly transgresses the Sufi ethic of love and generosity.

In Rushdie's novel, Sufiya's acts of violence cannot be understood without reference to Raza Hyder's attempt to establish a Muslim theocracy in Pakistan. Like Saleem Sinai in *Midnight's Children*, Raza Hyder is plagued by voices in his head. Yet, in contrast to Saleem, these voices are not the voices of the multitude; rather, they are the voices of the Muslim cleric Maulana Dawood and Hyder's political antecedent, Iskander Harappa. Significantly, Hyder attempts to block out the voice of Harappa and concentrate on the voice of Maulana Dawood.

Maulana Dawood and the Political Theology of the State in *Shame*

Maulana Dawood is a fictional caricature of the Islamic scholar and founder of the Islamic Party, Maulana Mawdudi, but the name

Dawood is also an allusion to an English translator of the *Qur'ān*, N. J. Dawood. By conflating these names, Rushdie suggests that the literalist and ahistorical reading of the *Qur'ān*, which he implicitly attributes to Mawdudi, is flawed because it denies the fact that the *Qur'ān* is always interpreted in history. Indeed, Mawdudi's Islamic revivalism took place in the context of India's partition and the marginalisation of Muslims by the dominant Hindu majority in India (Nasr 1996: 49). Mawdudi, in contrast to the Ayatollah Khomeini of Iran and Sayyid Qutb, never really advocated radical social and political transformation as the means to achieve what he called Islamic revolution, and he was opposed to the idea of an Islamic nation on the grounds that nationalism was a secular, western concept; instead, his 'Islamic revolution was to be a gradual and evolutionary process of cultural, social and political reform' (Nasr 1996: 76). What is more, Mawdudi's 'demand that society first be educated in Islam and prepared for the Islamic revolution and the Islamic state stood in clear contrast to the approaches of Ayatollah Khomeini and General Zia ul-Haq, both of whom used state power to carry out Islamization and therefore placed primary importance on the struggle for political power' (Nasr 1996: 78). As a consequence, Zia ul-Haq's use of state power to achieve an Islamic revolution in Pakistan seems to depart from Mawdudi's reformist vision of Islamic revolution through culture and education.

If Raza Hyder and Maulana Dawood are read as the fictional equivalents of Zia ul-Haq and Maulana Mawdudi, Rushdie's suggestion that Raza Hyder's Islamisation of Pakistan is influenced by Maulana Dawood's religious teachings would seem to be a case of careless listening on Hyder's part since Maulana Mawdudi was opposed to Islamic revolution at the level of the state on the grounds that he believed such a politicisation of Islam was un-Islamic. Be that as it may, Zia ul-Haq's introduction of Martial Law Regulations based on a rigid interpretation of the tenets of Islam following the military coup of 1977 was praised by the leader of the *Jamaat-i-Islami* (the Islamic party of Pakistan) and the *Jamat-ul-Ulema-i-Islam* (Kaushik 1993: 35); and it is Zia's attempt to politicise Islam that Rushdie lampoons in *Shame*. By listening to Maulana Dawood's speeches, Raza Hyder institutes a repressive theological law in Pakistan by prohibiting the sale of alcohol; he broadcasts theological lectures on national television, and makes it a legal requirement for Pakistan's citizens to attend the mosque on the Prophet's birthday (247). During a television interview with an English news reporter, in which the reporter invites Raza Hyder to refute the allegation that his 'institution of such Islamic punishments as flogging and cutting-off of hands might be seen in certain quarters as being … barbaric', Hyder argues that because these laws are 'the holy words of God, as revealed in sacred texts … they cannot be barbaric' (245).

Despite Hyder's attempt to establish an Islamic state, the narrator directly questions the religious foundations of Pakistan by contrasting it with postrevolutionary Iran under the Ayatollah Khomeini (250–251), and by arguing that Islam and the Muslim State were for Jinnah, the founder of Pakistan, 'political and cultural ideas; the theology was not the point' (251). In a similar vein, the narrator proceeds to question whether the authoritarian imposition of a fundamentalist interpretation of Muslim law is the most effective form of government: 'In the end you get sick of it, you lose faith in the faith, if not *qua* faith then certainly as a basis for the state' (251). The narrator's questioning of what he regards as the theological foundation of the Pakistani state under Raza Hyder implies a secularist belief in the separation of religion and the state. Yet, this is not to say that there is a necessary correlation between Islamic law and political violence, or that secularism offers a solid guarantee that the cultural, political and human rights of minorities will be protected. Rather, what Rushdie illustrates in *Shame* is the way in which political leaders have used religion as well as law in strategic ways to justify the exercise of political violence and the repression of the population. In this respect, *Shame's* depiction of Zia's repressive military government like *Midnight's Children's* depiction of Indira Gandhi's state of emergency is concerned to highlight the limitations of democracy and the violence of the state's sovereign power in a divided, postcolonial South Asia.

In his four lectures on *Political Theology* (first published, 1922), the German political thinker Carl Schmitt argued that all 'significant concepts of the modern theory of the state are secularized theological concepts not only because of their historical development … but also because of their systematic structure' (Schmitt 1985: 36). Perhaps one of the clearest examples of Schmitt's claim is the way in which political leaders of the modern state act as if they are sovereign figures with a divine right to rule. Salman Rushdie's fictional portraits of Indira Gandhi in *Midnight's Children* and General Zia in *Shame* certainly highlight the way in which these political leaders act and rule as if they are Gods. Yet, at the same time, by imagining what Schmitt calls the 'state of emergency', in which civil law is suspended and the state can exercise repressive measures against its own people, Rushdie, in both *Midnight's Children* and *Shame*, also gestures towards the dialectical antithesis of the state of emergency, in which the people are given a voice. As I have suggested in this chapter, Rushdie's use of hyperbole and the grotesque in *Midnight's Children* to register the multitudinous voices of his fictionalised Indian subcontinent, and his employment of the fairy tale in *Shame* to articulate the repressed voices of the people through a fragmented, migrant's-eye view of Zia's Pakistan offer an important and progressive counterpoint to the more coercive forces of postcolonial modernity, such as neo-colonialism and political repression.

4

THE SATANIC VERSES, HAROUN AND THE SEA OF STORIES AND *EAST, WEST*

The angry response of some Muslim leaders around the world to the publication of 12 cartoons depicting the Prophet Muhammad as a terrorist in the Danish newspaper *Jyllands-Posten* in September 2005 might at a first glance seem to echo the critical response to Salman Rushdie's fourth novel *The Satanic Verses* (1988). For just as the *Jyllands-Posten* cartoons seemed to deliberately provoke protests and anger from a community identifying itself as Muslim by presenting the Prophet Muhammad using racist caricatures that equate Islam with terrorism, so, at least for some readers, Salman Rushdie's novel *The Satanic Verses* desacralised a religious text by questioning the theological basis of revelation, presenting the Prophet Muhammad as a human being with sexual desires, and suggesting that the *Qur'ān* itself was written by Satan.

Yet, as the political theorist Mahmood Mamdani has argued, there is an important distinction to be made between an act of bigotry or hate speech, which he defines as a dominant culture deliberately misrepresenting a minority culture, and an act of blasphemy, or criticism from within the historical and cultural traditions of that culture, which seek to bring about social and cultural reform (Mamdani 2007). While it is clear that the *Jyllands-Posten* cartoons can be read as an act of bigotry or hate speech (in Mamdani's definition) since they malign and caricature the Prophet Muhammad from a secular, European tradition outside Islam, it is not clear whether Rushdie's 1988 novel *The Satanic Verses* represents an act of blasphemy or bigotry. For even though the novel conforms to the conventions of the European novel as a secular cultural form, it also borrows from Arabic and Urdu literary forms and the narrative conventions of Bombay cinema. With close reference to *The Satanic Verses* and its intertextual sources, the main part of this chapter considers how the complex narrative structure of Rushdie's novel renders Mamdani's distinction between blasphemy and bigotry indeterminate in order to question (1) the secular values of Britain's post-imperial culture from the standpoint of a South Asian migrant, and (2) the authoritative claims of Islamic fundamentalists such as Maulana Mawdudi and Ayatollah Khomeini to define and normalise the Islamic faith as a political ideology. The chapter then proceeds to consider how Rushdie engages with Islamic literature and history in *Haroun and the Sea of Stories* and 'The Prophet's Hair'. In so doing, the chapter argues that Rushdie's fictional engagement with Islam and its history takes the epistemological claims of religion seriously in order to make sense of political and historical events in the postcolonial world at the end of the Cold War.

ORIENTALISM AND THE HISTORICAL SOURCES OF *THE SATANIC VERSES*

Rushdie's journalistic response to the London bombings of July 7 2005 published in *The Washington Post* certainly implies that he believed *The Satanic Verses* to make an important contribution to what Mamdani calls the social and political reform of Islam. In this response, entitled 'The Right Time for An Islamic Reformation', Rushdie argues that a reformation of Islam would allow Muslims to 'study the revelation of their religion as an event inside history, not supernaturally above it'. Such an argument clearly reiterates Rushdie's defence of *The Satanic Verses* in his essay 'In Good Faith' (1990), in which he says that the point of his fictional reworking of 'the satanic verses incident' was meant to encourage critical discussion and debate about the 'human event of revelation in the Islamic faith' (408–409).

For many critics of *The Satanic Verses*, however, what was particularly offensive about the text was its tendency to rehearse Orientalist caricatures of Islam. One instance of such a caricature was Rushdie's use of the name Mahound to describe the Prophet

Muhammad. This was deemed particularly offensive because it evoked a history of Western cultural representations of Islam that can be traced back to medieval Europe. As the journalist Malise Ruthven explains: 'Mahound … is a medieval European version of Muhammad, whom Christians presumed the infidel Muslims worshipped as God. For poets from Langland to Burns, Mahound is synonymous with the devil – an expletive by which people swear, or a false God' (Ruthven 1990: 35). Furthermore, the title of Rushdie's novel alludes to an apocryphal verse that was recorded by the ninth-century commentator, Abu Ja'far Muhammad b. Jarir al-Tabari (839–923 CE). For some commentators, the apocryphal verses follow a passage in the *Qur'ān* entitled 'The Star' (Sura 53: 19–20), in which the Prophet Muhammad sought to convert the people of Mecca to the Islamic faith. In this passage, Muhammad asserts: 'Have you thought on Al-Lat, Al-Uzza, and, thirdly on Manat?' (113). These three names refer to three female goddesses who the pagans of Mecca believed to be daughters of Allah (113). In Dawood's English translation of the *Qur'ān*, the Prophet Muhammad refuted this belief by arguing that these are the names of false idols and that 'Allah has vested no authority in them' (113).

According to the ninth-century historian al-Tabari, however, when Muhammad had uttered these lines, Satan then 'put upon [Muhammad's] tongue' the following verse: ' "these are the exalted *Gharaniq* [cranes or beautiful women] whose intercession is approved"' (al-Tabari cited in Ibn Hisham 1967: 166). In doing so, Satan attempted to undermine the religious authority of God. Once these verses were identified as a mistake by the angel Gabriel, al-Tabari reports that God annulled 'what Satan had put upon the prophet's tongue' (al-Tabari cited in Ibn Hisham 1967: 166).

Qur'ānic scholars such as Ibn al-Athir have disputed the veracity of this story, and some Western Orientalist scholars have invoked the story to question the coherence and divine authority of the *Qur'ān* (see Ahsan 1991: 131–41 and Kuortti 2007: 134). Indeed, it was the British oriental scholar William Muir who described these verses as 'the satanic verses' in chapter 5 of his *Life of Mohammad* (Muir 1912: 82). Muslim scholars, by contrast, tend to regard the omitted apocryphal verses as the *gharaniq* ("birds") verses (Erickson 1998: 141). This is significant because in borrowing the title used to describe the verses in Western Orientalist scholarship, Rushdie also runs the risk of reinforcing Orientalist stereotypes of Islam.

Indeed, it was partly Rushdie's use of a name borrowed from Western Oriental scholarship on the history of Islam that prompted some scholars and readers to discredit his novel.

Such a criticism of Rushdie's use of the name Mahound is partly anticipated by the narrator's assertion that the character Gibreel Farishta deliberately chooses to adopt this derisory label as a rhetorical strategy: 'To turn insults into strengths, whigs, tories, Blacks all chose to wear with pride the name they were given in scorn; likewise our mountain-climbing, prophet-motivated solitary is to be the medieval baby-frightener, the Devil's synonym: Mahound' (93). The use of Mahound as a sign of political identification may make sense as a rhetorical strategy in the context of late-twentieth-century social movements, such as the anti-racist movement in Rushdie's fictional London district of Brickhall. Yet the social movements that Rushdie represents in *The Satanic Verses* are not exclusively Muslim and neither, for that matter, is Mahound a prominent character in the Brickhall chapters of *The Satanic Verses* (rather he is an imaginary figure who appears in Gibreel Farishta's dreams). Indeed, it is the secular migrant Saladin Chamcha who is first demonised by the British authorities and subsequently celebrated as a political icon by the black community in the fictional London district of Brickhall. Moreover, the fact that Mahound is represented as a monotheistic tyrant in *The Satanic Verses* seems to reinforce Orientalist stereotypes of Islam rather than challenging them (as the narrator insists). On the other hand, it may be possible to read Gibreel's performance of Mahound as a non-secular form of political identification with the rioting and anti-racist protests against the British police and the right-wing political establishment that form the centrepiece of the novel.

RUSHDIE'S DEFENCE OF *THE SATANIC VERSES*

In his essay 'In Good Faith', which was published in the collection *Imaginary Homelands*, Rushdie defended his novel *The Satanic Verses* by arguing that the point of the story of Mahound and the fictional reconstruction of the episode in which Satan added two lines to the Prophet's speech was to 'try to understand the human event of revelation' (Rushdie 1991: 408). Similarly, in an interview with David Frost, Rushdie argued that he wanted to present Muhammad as a more human figure,

> [t]o show [Muhammad] as a human figure wrestling with the political
> and social realities of his prophesy and of his revelation flirting with
> compromise, rejecting it and renewing the strength of his message, in
> my mind that doesn't make him a lesser figure. It makes him a more
> human and understandable and comprehensible figure. (Rushdie in
> Chauhan 2001: 147)

Such a defence of Rushdie's representation of the Prophet
Muhammad in *The Satanic Verses* might seem like a rational defence
of the novel. Yet, as the anthropologist Talal Asad argues in
Genealogies of Religion, Rushdie's representation of the Prophet
Muhammad as a human not only devalues his status as a sacred
figure in the *Qur'ān* but also assumes a culturally specific meaning
of what it means to be human that can be universally applied to all
cultures:

> Several commentators have suggested that the sexual episodes in the
> novel's account of the Prophet serve to humanize him. This may
> indeed be so. But the assumptions constituting that humanity are
> themselves the product of a particular history. Thus, in the Christian
> tradition, to sexualize a figure was to cut him off from divine truth, to
> pronounce him *merely* (sinfully) human; in the post-Christian tradition
> of modernity, to 'humanize' a figure is to insist on his sexual desire, to
> disclose in it, by a discursive stripping of its successive disguises, his
> essential human truth (Asad 1993: 292).

In Asad's argument, what is particularly problematic about *The
Satanic Verses* is not the novel's criticism of Islam *per se*, but that the
'*force* of [Rushdie's] criticism depends on the fact that he is situated
in a Western liberal tradition and is perceived to be addressing an
audience that shares it' (Asad: 295). In this respect, Asad suggests
that *The Satanic Verses* is a form of what Mahmood Mamdani calls
bigotry, or hate speech, because it criticises Islam using the cultural codes and secular values of European literature.

THE RECEPTION OF THE SATANIC VERSES
IN THE ISLAMIC PUBLIC SPHERE

Talal Asad's criticism of *The Satanic Verses* on the grounds that it
mocks the religious beliefs of British Muslims from a position

within the post-Christian cultural and literary traditions of the British liberal intelligentsia are insightful, but in focusing on Rushdie's rhetorical stance as a writer who is addressing an educated, secular, liberal and middle class British readership, he overlooks the way in which *The Satanic Verses* also became the site of a global political debate about the relationship between Islam and Western modernity. Such a reading has been developed by the literary critic Aamir Mufti, who situates *The Satanic Verses* in terms of a broader debate about the meaning and role of Islam as a political ideology as well as a religious ethos in the years since the Iranian revolution of 1979 (Mufti in Booker 1999: 51). In Mufti's argument, *The Satanic Verses* raises questions about the role of women in modern Islamic communities; the place of secular political concepts, such as nationhood, citizenship, democracy and social justice in Islam; and the role of Islam in the struggle against the economic, political and cultural imperialism of the West (Mufti: 51). In doing so, Rushdie seems to challenge the revolutionary Islam of conservative intellectuals such as Maulana Mawdudi, Sayyid Qutb and Ayatollah Khomeini to define revolutionary Islam as a 'revolt against history' (Rushdie 1991: 384). For Rushdie, Islamic revivalism is not 'a religious event', but rather 'a political event that is almost always nationalist in character' (380). By demonstrating that the birth of Islam was an event that took place in history, *The Satanic Verses* clearly challenged the conceptual premises upon which Khomeini's Islamic revivalism was based. Indeed, as one commentator put it, the "death sentence" pronounced by Iran's Ayatollah Khomeini 'has as much to do with Khomeini's sense of his role in the larger Islamic community' and his aspiration to 'the leadership of the Islamic world' as it does with 'the content of Rushdie's book' (Bakhash 1988: 236). And within the context of Iran, almost ten years after the revolution, Khomeini used the '*fatwa*' against Rushdie to rekindle the 'fervour of the revolution', to 'shift the balance of power, ensure a "radical" successor, and unite disparate Muslim sects and communities' (Ranasinha 2007: 46).

The reception and translation of *The Satanic Verses* among some Muslim readers may in some cases differ significantly from the reception of the novel amongst Muslim and non-Muslim readers familiar with the conventions and values of modern European literature. Indeed, the novel's circulation in what Mufti calls 'the Islamic public sphere' involved the public relations officer of the Islamic foundation in Leicester photocopying and mailing the offending passages in the novel to the embassies of 45 Islamic countries, including Iran (Mufti 1999: 70). Further, the fact that the 'militant opposition to the novel' was based on 'a realist and fragmented reading' (Mufti: 66) suggests that the reception of the novel within the Islamic public sphere framed *The Satanic Verses* in terms of the hermeneutic codes of Qur'ānic exegesis rather than the cultural codes of modern literature, in which the fictional allusions to the life of the Prophet Muhammad are one part of a more complex narrative.

To read *The Satanic Verses* as a work of literary fiction would thus seem to be to read the novel in terms of a secular cultural tradition, which is imbricated in the history of European colonial modernity. For the secular category of imaginative literature in English has its provenance in the civilising mission of nineteenth-century British imperialism (Asad 1993: 290). Yet the assumption that the secular category of literature and the non-secular category of Qur'ānic interpretation are mutually exclusive is to reinforce the opposition between the secular and the religious that *The Satanic Verses* calls into question. In this respect, the British government's defence of Salman Rushdie's *The Satanic Verses* as a work of imaginative literature or culture is no more objective than the angry response of some readers to the novel's depiction of the Prophet Muhammad.

The so-called Rushdie affair, in which the Ayotollah Khomeini called upon Muslims around the world to kill Rushdie on February 14 1989, and the British government defended Rushdie's right to free speech by offering him state protection against this death threat, could be seen to exemplify what the conservative Harvard political scientist Samuel Huntingdon called the 'clash of civilisations' between the West and the Islamic world (Huntingdon 1996). For the conventions and meanings of Western civilisation and its literary culture, which *The Satanic Verses* assumes, are not shared by *some* of the novel's readers.

Yet *The Satanic Verses* also seeks to interrogate this reductive dichotomy between the civilisations of the West and the so-called Islamic world by exploring the experience of the postcolonial migrant in the Western metropolis. The novel does this by juxtaposing the fictional experiences of South Asian migrants in 1980s London with episodes from the life of the Prophet Muhammad, references to Bombay cinema, popular culture and world literature. This juxtaposition of South Asian migration to Britain with the Prophet's exile in seventh-century Medina suggests that the novel decentres – or, to use Gibreel Farishta's term, 'tropicalises' – London's status as an imperial metropolitan centre. By satirising characters such as Mahound and the Imam, however, *The Satanic Verses* also seems to criticise traditional scholastic and literal interpretations of the *Qur'ān*. Rushdie's critical engagement with Islam may make sense if it is situated within the tradition of Urdu and Persian poetry; but, as suggested below, the literary form of *The Satanic Verses* as an Anglophone novel also locates it within a European literary tradition. The hybrid literary form of *The Satanic Verses* may imply that it is a work of global fiction, which aspires to synthesise different cultural traditions. But the danger of this hybrid literary form is that it transforms the scriptural foundations of Islam into an aesthetic object, and thereby subordinates Rushdie's fictionalised version of Islam to the secular values of the West.

PROVINCIALISING EUROPE AND READING THE NON-SECULAR IN *THE SATANIC VERSES*

If we take Rushdie's suggestion in 'In Good Faith' seriously, and read *The Satanic Verses* as an examination of revelation as an event that takes place inside history, however, it is possible to read Rushdie's treatment of miraculous events in the novel as an attempt to make sense of historical events through a non-secular epistemological framework. Such an approach to Rushdie's magical realism corresponds with what the South Asian historian Dipesh Chakrabarty calls provincialising Europe, or the process by which the social, economic and political legacies of European colonialism are negotiated and translated in different postcolonial societies (Chakrabarty 2000). Crucial to Chakrabarty's definition of provincialising Europe is the process by which secular concepts such as democracy, capitalism, citizenship and history are translated and understood in radically different non-secular epistemological paradigms. By applying this term to *The Satanic Verses*, I want to consider how the novel negotiates and translates the histories of South Asian migration and race politics in 1980s Britain through the non-secular framework of Islamic history, literature and culture. In doing so, I want to suggest that Rushdie's magical realism in *The Satanic Verses* emphasises the importance of religion as an epistemological framework for making sense of postcolonial modernity from the diasporic standpoint of a secular British Indian Muslim. This is not to say that Rushdie's representation of religion as a system of knowledge in *The Satanic Verses* is always progressive; on the contrary, in the case of Gibreel Farishta's dreams and delusions, religious understanding is presented as a form of paranoia/schizophrenia. Yet, as the chapter proceeds to argue, Rushdie's representation of the Ayesha pilgrimage in *The Satanic Verses* offers a counterpoint to the dogmatic interpretations of the Qur'ānic scriptures advocated by Mahound/Gibreel and the anti-historical Imam in the novel. By doing so, Rushdie stresses a more open, subjective approach to Islam that recognises the co-existence of the secular and the religious in the modern postcolonial worlds of his fiction.

Migration and Postcolonial Modernity in *The Satanic Verses*

One of the central ways in which postcolonial modernity is thematised in *The Satanic Verses* is through the idea of migration. As discussed in Chapter 3, Rushdie's *Shame* uses the experience of the *hirjat*, or an exalted form of migration that has its roots in the flight of the Prophet Muhammad from Mecca to Medina (Raza 2003: 55), to register the experience of migrant characters who were forced to move from India to Pakistan after partition. In a similar vein, *The Satanic Verses* re-writes passages from the life of the Prophet Muhammad to register the experience of migration from India to Britain in the late twentieth century. In doing so, Rushdie parallels the Prophet's search for his identity during his exile in Medina with the identity crisis experienced by the novel's two protagonists, Gibreel Farishta and Saladin Chamcha, during and after their fantastical migration to London (see Jussawalla 1999: 88). In some respects, the identity crisis of the two protagonists in *The Satanic Verses* mirrors the novel's preoccupation with migration as an ontological condition of postcolonial modernity. If migration is understood as a particular kind of ontological condition – a way of inhabiting a place one does not feel entirely at home in while also nostalgically imagining a homeland somewhere else – *The Satanic Verses* stages this condition through the figure of the double, a figure which the psychoanalyst Sigmund Freud described as *unheimlich*, or unhomely, in his essay on 'The Uncanny'. This doubleness is exemplified in part seven of the novel, where the narrator asserts that Chamcha and Gibreel are 'conjoined opposites ... each man [is] the other's shadow' (426). Whereas Gibreel wishes to remain 'continuous' (427) with the imaginary homeland he left behind, Chamcha embraces his impure, hybrid identity as a British South Asian.

Gibreel and Chamcha's opposing responses to the unhomely condition of their migration are played out through a struggle for recognition in the post-imperial metropolis of 1980s London. Indeed, Jaina C. Sanga has characterised 'the relationship between Chamcha and Farishta' as 'dialectical' (Sanga 2001: 81). Such a reading implies that the relationship between these two characters is equivalent to a Hegelian struggle for recognition between two antithetical concepts of identity: one based on continuity, homogeneity and purity, the other based on discontinuity, heterogeneity and impurity. In Sanga's reading, the resolution or synthesis of this dialectical struggle comes with the revelation 'that survival for the migrants [in *The Satanic Verses*] depends on making connections between things, realizing that the world is not homogenous, and believing that they are not ultimately, exclusively, Western or Eastern' (81). Sanga's reading here points to an interesting tension in *The Satanic Verses*. For if the struggle between Chamcha and Farishta represents an epic, dialectical struggle between two different ideas of migrant identity, it does so in the historical context of 1980s Britain, at a time of great social, political and economic turbulence for many Black Britons.

The opening chapter of the novel represents Saladin Chamcha and Gibreel Farishta falling from Air India flight 420 – a symbol of postcolonial modernity – after it has been blown up by a Sikh terrorist group above the English Channel. For the critic Srinivas Aravamudan, the number 420 alludes to both the Indian Penal Code and the section of the Indian Code of Criminal Proceedings, which punishes fraud and corruption (Aravamudan in Fletcher 1994: 191). Aravamudan also ventures to suggest that Indira Gandhi may have used section 420 during the state of emergency to contain her political opponents.

That the terrorists who hijack Air India flight 420 in *The Satanic Verses* are Sikhs also seem to be significant in that it alludes to the tragic crash of Air India flight 182 off the coast of Ireland in June 1985, which was believed to be the work of Sikh separatists. The crash also alludes to Indira Gandhi's involvement in the killing of 20,000 Sikh civilians at the Golden Temple, Amritsar in June 1984 and the assassination of Indira Gandhi by her Sikh bodyguards in October of the same year. Yet this reading is complicated by the description of the female leader of the terrorist group, Tavleen, who blows herself and the aeroplane up above the English Channel. While the male members of the group are described as being 'too squeamish, too narcissistic, to want blood on their hands' (78), Saladin Chamcha recognises from Tavleen's introspective demeanour that she 'was here on business', 'she became quiet, her eyes turned inwards, and she scared the passengers stiff' (Rushdie 1988: 78). Chamcha's suspicions are later confirmed when Tavleen reveals her denuded body to the passengers, 'so that they could all see the arsenal of her body, the grenades like extra breasts nestling in her cleavage, the gelignite taped around her thighs' (Rushdie 1988: 81). Rushdie's representation of Tavleen as a sexualised yet destructive female figure recalls his representation of Indira Gandhi in *Midnight's Children*, who is herself figured as a version of the Hindu goddess, Devi. In this respect, Tavleen's act of terror as a Canadian Sikh can be seen as a response to the state terror Indira Gandhi perpetrated against Sikhs in 1984.

For the narrator, however, the political cause of the terrorist group is less significant than the performance of the hijack and its representation in the global media. The male members of the terrorist group were motivated by a desire 'to be on television' and their political demands for 'An independent homeland, religious freedom, release of political detainees, justice, ransom money, a safe-conduct to a country of their desire' (78–79) are described as 'Nothing new' (78). In the narrator's account, the political demands of the hijackers are a symptom of life in the twentieth century: 'If you live in the twentieth century you do not find it hard to see yourself in those, more desperate than yourself, who seek to shape it to their will' (79). Thus, for the narrator, the motivation for the hijack and the destruction of Air India flight 420 has more to do with philosophical questions about human will and agency in the twentieth century than with the violence committed against the Sikh community by the state in late twentieth-century India.

The destruction of the plane and the miraculous survival of Saladin Chamcha and Gibreel Farishta develop this philosophical dimension of the novel further by raising questions about the possibility of reincarnation or life after death. For, as Saladin and Gibreel fall from the plane, Gibreel's body is taken over by an invisible force that commands him to fly and sing a song in 'a language he did not know to a tune he had never heard' (9), and as he does so, both Gibreel and Saladin 'began to slow down' (9). The responses of Gibreel and Saladin to this apparently miraculous event are significant because they represent two different ways of thinking about religion in the novel. Whereas 'Gibreel never doubted the miracle', and 'never stopped saying that the gazal had been celestial', Saladin Chamcha 'tried to reason it out of existence' (9). Chamcha's secular and sceptical approach to their survival seems to be supported by the narrator's subsequent description of Gibreel as an Indian movie star, whose 'big break arrived with the coming of the theological movies' (24). This reference to theological movies is significant because it draws attention to the novel's artifice, and suggests that the story of Saladin and Chamcha's survival is itself a fictional construct, which could be part of a movie script. Such a reading of this episode may appear to be consistent with Talal Asad's argument that *The Satanic Verses* is a work of postmodern literary fiction, and as such it is a product of Western culture and its secular values. Yet Gibreel's belief in the miracle also implies a way of understanding his survival of the aeroplane crash and his migration through a non-secular epistemological paradigm.

The Satanic Verses and its Arabic and Urdu Literary Precursors

Gibreel's reference to 'the gazal' in the passage cited above also suggests an alternative reading of the novel, which situates *The Satanic Verses* in a Persian and Urdu literary tradition. The 'gazal' or ghazal is a form of lyric poetry written in couplets with a regular metre and rhyme scheme. Each of these couplets encapsulates a complete theme, such as romantic love or the love of a mystic for his God (Russell 2003: 297); as a consequence, the ghazal seems to lack a unified theme (Russell 287). Bedouin poets originally developed the ghazal in Arabic during the late sixth century; it was later adopted in Persian, and was disseminated to North India by Sufi mystics in the twelfth century; subsequently, the ghazal was developed in Urdu during the period of the Mughal Empire (Schimmel 1975: 127–130). During the twentieth century, the Urdu ghazal came to symbolise Muslim decadence within India and 'an imperial culture in decline' (Mufti 2004: 254). By alluding to this poetic form and its cultural history within India, Rushdie thus locates his engagement with the Islamic world in terms of India's Muslim cultural inheritance.

In a commentary on the celebrated Urdu poet Ghalib, Ralph Russell argues that 'the love between two human beings' expressed in ghazals is sometimes used as a metaphor of 'the similar love of the mystic lover for his God' (Russell 2003: 297). In *The Satanic Verses*, Rushdie suggests a similar parallel between Gibreel Farishta's love for Alleluia Cone and his belief that he is a messenger of God. In the post-Christian context of late-twentieth-century London, however, Gibreel struggles to separate his material, embodied love for Alleluia and his transcendent love for God. During an argument with Alleluia, for example, Gibreel experiences a revelation in which 'the spirits of the world of dreams flooded through the breach into the universe of the quotidian [and] Gibreel Farishta saw God' (318). By literalising the symbolic relationship between Gibreel's material love for Alleluia and his divine love for God, Rushdie collapses the boundary between the secular and the non-secular.

If the song that Gibreel Farishta is prompted to sing as he falls from Air India flight 420 is a celestial 'gazal', it is the Persian and Urdu literary genre of the *dastan* that provides a rich intertextual resource for the narrative structure and geographical location of *The Satanic Verses*. As the literary critic Feroza Jussawalla explains, the *dastan* is characterised by 'a long-winded stream of consciousness tale that incorporates many related and sometimes loosely strung-together frame tales and assorted humorous anecdotes' (Jussawalla 1999: 95). Furthermore, the plot of the *dastan* covers ' "a broad geographical area including most of the world known to the medieval geographers [and] takes place in an indefinite time, generally said to be long in the past" ' (Hanaway cited in Jussawalla 1999: 96).

As well as being a long-winded narrative, *The Satanic Verses* certainly takes place across a 'broad geographical area' and in 'an indefinite time'. While the novel begins with a plane crash above the English Channel in the late twentieth century, chapters 2 and 6 of *The Satanic Verses* are situated in seventh-century Jahilia; and chapters 4 and 8 (the Ayesha chapters) are located in late-twentieth-century India. Rushdie's framing of the Jahilia chapters and the Ayesha chapters within the dream sequences of Gibreel Farishta is also consistent with the framing devices and stream of conscious-ness style that Jussawalla associates with the *dastan*.

Moreover, if Gibreel's dream sequences are read as an extended interior monologue, it is possible to situate Rushdie's use of Islamic history in terms of the migrant experience in late-twentieth-century British society. In Jussawalla's account, Rushdie's satirical representation of historical events from the life of the Prophet Muhammad is part of a 'long tradition of Indian Islamic writers who both criticized Islam and yet were deeply part of the post-Mughal literary/religious tradition' in India (Jussawalla 1999: 94). The imperative behind Rushdie's satirical representation of Islam is, however, different from that of other writers in this tradition such as the nineteenth-century Indian writers 'Ghalib and his stu-dent Altaf Husain Hali, Bahadar Shah Zafar and Dagh' (Jussawalla: 94) in that Rushdie uses the form of the Anglophone novel to rein-terpret the *Qur'ān* rather than the poetic forms conventional to the Persian and Urdu literary traditions that Jussawalla invokes. In so doing, Rushdie violates what Homi K. Bhabha calls 'the poetic license granted to critics of the Islamic establishment' (Bhabha 1994: 226).

Gibreel's dream work in *The Satanic Verses* is certainly an attempt to make sense of his identity both as a migrant and a Muslim in postcolonial British society. Yet, the crucial question is whether, by re-inscribing the *Qur'ān* within the context of postcolonial British society, Gibreel's dream work 'places the authority of the Koran within a perspective of historical and cultural relativism', as the postcolonial theorist Homi K. Bhabha suggests (Bhabha 1994: 226), or whether this dream narrative interprets the post-Christian liberal values of twentieth-century British society within a non-secular frame of reference by defining modern British society as a contemporary form of Jahilia?

The Satanic Narrator of
The Satanic Verses

The section of the novel entitled 'Mahound', which is set in sev-enth-century Jahilia, is reported from Gibreel's point of view as a migrant in twentieth-century Britain. Gibreel's dream narra-tive of the story of Mahound is represented as a theological film: 'Gibreel: the dreamer, whose point of view is sometimes that of the camera and at other moments, spectator' (108). While the story of Mahound is represented as a Bombay film adaptation, in which Gibreel is both the audience and the central character, he is, nonetheless, afraid of the 'self his dream creates' (109). Gibreel's fear is initially articulated as a form of stage fright – 'the kind of fear you feel when you're on a film set for the first time' (109) – but it is subsequently described as a fear of not having the authority to communicate the words of God: '*Mahound comes to me for revelation, asking me to choose between monotheist and henotheist alternatives, and I'm just some idiot actor having a bhaenchud nightmare, what the fuck do I know, yaar, what to tell you, help. Help*' (109). Gibreel's pleas for help in this passage point towards a recognition of a tradition of Qur'ānic interpretation, about which he feels unqualified to comment.

Later in the novel, the role that Gibreel plays takes over his psyche, and he begins to speak 'verses in Arabic, a language he did not know' (340). That these verses are a repetition of the *gharaniq* or 'birds' verses cited in Al-Tabari's *Annals* is significant because it suggests that the voice that possesses Gibreel is that of the Devil rather than God. This is not to suggest, however, that Gibreel's dreams and visions simply confirm or deny the existence of God or the Devil. Indeed, as Roger Y. Clark has persuasively argued, the voice that possesses Gibreel is that of Rushdie's satanic narrator, whose manipulative behaviour recalls that of the character Iago in Shakespeare's *Othello* as well as the figure of Satan in al-Tabari's *Annals*: 'Rushdie inserts key elements of the satanic verses incident into this Shakespearean drama when the possessed Chamcha whispers doggerel satanic verses over the telephone, thus driving Gibreel into a monstrous green-eyed jealousy' (130). For Clark, the 'satanic narrator's mode of operation' in *The Satanic Verses* is a diabolical form of indeterminacy, which 'moves in and out of the text in order to insinuate that there is no such thing as a single, transcendental Meaning and Unity' (Clark 2001: 131). Such a reading of the satanic narrator in *The Satanic Verses* is premised on the view that 'critics have focused on the worldly politics of the Rushdie Affair rather than the otherworldly politics in the text itself' (Clark 2001: 129). What Clark implies but does not explicitly say is that the narrator's movement 'in and out of the text' also juxtaposes the worldly and otherworldly dimensions of the novel. In this respect, the narrative structure of *The Satanic Verses* represents what the deconstructive literary theorist Paul de Man calls an allegory of reading, in which the rhetorical organisation of a literary text draws attention to the necessity of the text's misunderstanding (de Man 1983: 136). For in combining the worldly and otherworldly dimensions of the novel, Rushdie prevents readers from deciding with any certainty whether a satanic narrator has possessed Gibreel Farishta, or whether Gibreel is a Prophet, or whether he is suffering from mental illness. Yet, as Rushdie has frequently suggested, this textual indeterminacy has a political purpose: to expose the invention and interpretation of Islam in and through history, while also creating a fictional space for exploring the structure of belief.

The narrative juxtaposition of the worldly and otherworldly dimensions of the novel, which contributes to the textual indeterminacy of *The Satanic Verses*, is perhaps most clearly exemplified in Gibreel Farishta's attempt to bring moral and religious redemption to 1980s London. Like Jahilia in the seventh century, London is presented as an ungodly metropolis of 'masks and parodies' (320), a city that Gibreel attempts to 'redeem ... all the way from A to Z' (322). This geographical mapping of Gibreel's religious mission in London is later rendered futile as Gibreel realises that 'the city in its corruption refused to submit to the dominion of the cartographers, changing shape at will and without warning' (327). In order to control the moral 'corruption' that he perceives in London's shifting urban space, Gibreel sets on a path of destruction with a flame-throwing trumpet, which he calls *Azraeel, the Last Trump, the Exterminator of Men!* (448). Gibreel uses this trumpet as an instrument of divine judgement to execute a group of sex workers and their pimps outside Kings Cross station, whom he confuses with the 12 sex workers behind the curtain at Jahilia. In this juxtaposition of the worldly space of 1980s London and the otherworldly space of Jahilia, Rushdie highlights the way in which Islam is produced in and through history. Whether Gibreel's violent rampage is a figment of his deluded imagination or a brutal act of murder committed in the name of religious judgement, his actions reinforce the narrator's characterisation of Gibreel as an 'untranslated man' (427), or a migrant who refuses to assimilate to the liberal and secular values of late-twentieth-century British society.

Gibreel Farishta and the Identity Formation of British Muslims

Rushdie's characterisation of Gibreel Farishta as an untranslated man, who 'has wished to remain, to a large degree, *continuous* – that is, joined to and arising from his past' (427) also raises an important question about his identity as both a South Asian migrant and a former actor who believes he is one of the fictional characters in a Theological feature film. Such a question corresponds with debates about British Muslim identity in contemporary Islamic studies. In the introduction to *Islams and Modernities* (1993), Aziz Al-Azmeh argues that the angry responses of British Muslims to the representation of the Prophet in *The Satanic Verses* are based on a coherent cultural identity that had to be invented. In Al-Azmeh's argument, this fictional identity was based on a 'sentimentalist view of a spurious, unsullied reality prior to the corruption of the present', which

> is neither 'real' nor old, but is a recherché cluster of modes of visible behaviour which are said by certain Islamist authorities to represent the 'true prior reality' – one that British Pakistani Muslims had never known until recently, for it is not only traditions that are invented, but also collective memories. (Al-Azmeh 1993: 8)

The Problem of History in *The Satanic Verses*

Al-Azmeh's critique of the idea that Islam is a coherent and unified culture and religion outside of history also seems to echo Rushdie's fictional re-invention of the life of the Prophet Muhammad in *The Satanic Verses*, and his characterisation of the Imam as a figure who is against history and the measurement of time (211–215). While some of Rushdie's critics take issue with *The Satanic Verses* on the grounds that the novel fails to present an accurate historical account of the life of the Prophet Muhammad, *The Satanic Verses* stages the impossibility of recovering such a coherent history by exposing the lacunae, contradictions and multiple meanings embedded in early historical sources such as al-Tabari's *Annals*.

One example of this staging is seen in chapter 5 of the novel, in which the Prophet's scribe, Salman, alters the words of God as the angel Gibreel dictates them to the Prophet:

> Here's the point: Mahound did not notice the alterations. So there I was, actually writing the Book, or re-writing, anyway, polluting the word of God with my own profane language. But, good heavens, if my poor words could not be distinguished from the Revelation by God's own Messenger, then what did that mean? What did that say about the quality of the divine poetry? (367)

In this passage, Salman al-Farsi draws attention to the material and textual basis of the Prophet's revelation, which is also at the same time a 'recitation' (364). By incorrectly transcribing this recitation, Salman not only questions the reliability and authenticity of primary historical sources but also starts to question his faith in God. This fictional account of Salman al-Farsi's incorrect transcription of the Prophet's words may correspond with a similar passage in al-Tabari's *Annals*, in which Abdullah ibn Sa'ad, one of the Prophet's scribes, temporarily lost his faith after an incorrect transcription of the Prophet's words went unnoticed (see Ruthven 1990: 39). But this assumes that *The Satanic Verses* is a realistic representation of Islamic history rather than a fictional representation of the way in which Islamic law has been invented and interpreted *in history*. Such a fictional representation may encourage further reflection on the ambivalence and multiple meanings of Islamic history, but this representation not only presupposes a readership familiar with the codes of contemporary European literature but it also takes for granted that readers will be willing to accept the claim that the history of the Prophet Muhammad is an invented narrative.

In this respect, Gibreel's revelations in *The Satanic Verses* may seem antithetical to and discontinuous with the novel's representation of postcolonial migrants in the fictional district of Brickhall in 1980s London. The literary critic Ian Baucom contends that Gibreel's attempts to 'tropicalise' or reclaim the streets of London mirror the riots in Brickhall (Baucom 1999: 208–216). Yet this is to collapse Gibreel's desire to punish the moral corruption that he perceives in 1980s British society as an avenging angel and the genuine political grievances of black Britons against racist discrimination and social exclusion.

Rushdie's representation of Saladin Chamcha's experience of police brutality and racism as an illegal South Asian migrant who washes up on the shores of Hastings; his depiction of Dr Uhuru Simba's death in police custody; and the subsequent riot that erupts in Brickhall in response to Dr Simba's death certainly suggest that *The Satanic Verses* is sympathetic to the political cause of anti-racism and the riots in Brixton of 1981. This sympathy is, however, complicated by a distinction that the narrator of *The Satanic Verses* makes between the secular, hybridised idea of the self exemplified by Saladin Chamcha and the coherent, essentialist idea of the self embodied by Gibreel Farishta: as 'homogenous, non-hybrid, [and] "pure" ' (427). Rushdie's narrator asserts that the idea of the self that Saladin Chamcha symbolises, is false and, therefore, evil, while Gibreel, 'to follow the logic of our established terminology, is to be considered "good" by virtue of *wishing to remain*, for all his vicissitudes, at bottom an untranslated man' (427). The narrator also inverts this distinction by claiming that the idea of cultural purity is itself insufficient. In so doing, Rushdie's narrator seems to valorise the hybridised, secular migrant over the non-secular migrant who refuses to assimilate to the cultural values of the host nation.

Hybridity and Purity in *The Satanic Verses*

Rushdie's apparent valorisation of the hybrid, secular migrant character of Saladin Chamcha, who abandons his youthful Anglophilia, suggests that cultural hybridity allows Chamcha to transgress the essentialist fiction of a pure cultural identity. That the idea of hybridity has its provenance in nineteenth-century biology would seem to complicate if not undermine the emancipatory claims that *The Satanic Verses* makes about hybridity. As Robert J. C. Young has argued, late-twentieth-century theories of cultural hybridity are more bound up with the categories of nineteenth-century racial thought than the critique of biological essentialism is prepared to allow (Young 1995: 26–27). Indeed, Young argues that it became increasingly common for Englishmen in the nineteenth century to invoke Daniel Defoe's account of 'that Het'rogenous Thing, an Englishman' as a national virtue to rival the self-regarding purity of the Germans after unification in 1871 (Young: 17).

The Satanic Verses may seem to rehearse the nineteenth-century discourse of cultural hybridity identified by Young. As Sabina Hassumani has argued, by questioning ideas of cultural purity Rushdie represents Islam in *The Satanic Verses* 'as a rigid, male-dominated myth' (Hassumani 2002: 75). In so doing, Hassumani implies that Rushdie's inversion of binary oppositions such as the sacred and the profane or purity and hybridity are calculated to expose Islam as a myth. Certainly, *The Satanic Verses* is critical of the ideas of divine authority and revelation, which underpin some traditional scholastic and literalist readings of the *Qur'ān* (see Ramadan 2004: 24–25). Yet this is not to say that *The Satanic Verses* simply discredits Islam as a male-dominated myth. Rather, the novel seeks to provoke dialogue and debate about the relationship between the historical context in which the *Qur'ān* was written and the position of South Asian immigrants in 1980s Britain.

The Coexistence of the Secular and the Religious in the Ayesha Chapters

In the chapter titled 'Return to Jahilia' the satirical poet, Baal, nails his poetry to the prison door after his capture by Mahound, an act that recalls Martin Luther nailing his 95 theses on the Castle Church door at Wittenburg in 1517. This act might suggest that it is the figure of the writer in *The Satanic Verses* who is instrumental in the reformation of Islam that Rushdie calls for in 2005. But this would be to overlook the significance of Mahound's statement, which he makes as Mahound's soldiers lead Baal to his execution: 'Writers and whores. I see no difference here' (392). For Mahound, 'Writers and whores' are identical in so far as they both transgress social rules and conventions. As a consequence, both groups are regarded as a threat to the social and political order. Indeed, the 12 sex workers at the curtain threaten Mahound's authority by pretending to be his wives. As Rushdie has suggested in an interview, this strategy of inversion serves to exemplify the way in which 'women have been bought and sold' as both wives and sex workers (Rushdie in Chauhan 2001: 222). Moreover, as suggested below, it is through the female character Ayesha that a rethinking of Islam is most clearly articulated in *The Satanic Verses*.

Rather than merely criticising the commodification of female sexuality, *The Satanic Verses* suggests that it is women who offer an alternative vision of Islam to that offered by Gibreel Farishta and the Imam. Indeed, it is Ayesha and Mirza's pilgrimage from the Indian village of Titlipur to Mecca that offers a more progressive model of Islam. In 'the two sections [of the novel] that mirror and transform the Mahound sections', Ambreen Hai argues that Ayesha 'becomes the female migrant leader of archetypal postcolonial migrants and of believers in a prominent future' (Hai in Booker 1999: 37). Further more, Ayesha is the sworn enemy of the Imam, who during his exile in London broadcasts radio messages calling for a revolution against Ayesha and against history. If the anti-historical Imam in *The Satanic Verses* is a fictional caricature of the Ayatollah Khomeini, and his period of exile in Paris before the Iranian Revolution in 1979 (Brennan 1989: 156), Ayesha seems to offer a more progressive approach to Islam. Ayesha's diagnosis of Mishal Akhtar's cancer and her encounter with the Angel Gibreel, who encourages her to lead the villagers of Titlipur on a pilgrimage to Mecca, suggests that she is herself a prophet. What is more, Ayesha's ability to persuade the villagers to follow her on the pilgrimage contrasts strikingly with the coercive and destructive methods of Mahound and the Imam.

The tragic ending of this pilgrimage, in which many of the pilgrims die in the attempt to cross the Arabian Sea, might seem to discredit both Ayesha's promise of a miraculous parting of the Arabian Sea, and the religious faith that such a promise represents. Yet this tragic ending is less significant than the rational debate that the pilgrimage provokes. Like Gibreel Farishta and Saladin Chamcha's fall from the Air India aeroplane, aptly named the *Bostan* (the Arabic word for garden or heaven), Ayesha's pilgrimage across the Arabian Sea is a test of the pilgrims' faith. Moreover, it is Mirza Saeed's persistent scepticism and arguments against the pilgrimage – to save his dying wife, Mishal – that offers a counterpoint to Ayesha's religious belief. While Mirza accuses Ayesha of being a 'God-bothered type from ancient history' (238), Mishal criticises Mirza's 'imported European atheism' (238). And, in response to Ayesha's assertion that the waters of the Arabian Sea will part in order to allow the pilgrims to travel to Mecca from Titlipur, Mirza asserts that the 'mystical experience is a subjective, not an objective truth'. As a consequence of this scepticism, he predicts that the 'waters will not open' (239).

Mirza's secular view that the mystical experience is subjective would seem to be confirmed by the way in which the pilgrimage is perceived as it proceeds to the Arabian Sea. For the police and some extremist religious elements the pilgrimage is regarded as a 'sectarian demonstration' (474); it is subsequently branded the Ayesha Haj and denounced as an attempt to 'incite communal sentiment' (488). Furthermore, some of these extremist groupings distribute leaflets arguing that ' "Padyatra, or foot-pilgrimage, is an ancient, pre-Islamic tradition of national culture, not imported property of Mughal immigrants" ' (488). Such a communalist reading of the pilgrimage is, however, undermined by the Brahmin toy merchant Sri Srinivas' perception of Ayesha as having the 'identical, same-to-same face' as the Hindu goddess Lakshmi (476). Srinivas' misrecognition of Ayesha as Lakshmi thus implies that the religious identity of the pilgrims is less significant than their belief in the prophet Ayesha.

While the narrator appears to reinforce Mirza Saeed's assertion that 'mystical experience is a subjective not an objective truth' (239), Mirza's experience of being-towards-death following the drowning of Mishal and the other pilgrims in the Arabian Sea implies that Mirza has himself lost the argument with Ayesha and Mishal about the parting of the Arabian Sea. For as Mirza drifts towards unconsciousness, he has a vision of the sea pouring over him, and Ayesha stepping miraculously out of his wife's body (506). As the pilgrims start to struggle underwater, Ayesha repeatedly commands Mirza to 'Open', an order that he stubbornly refuses to obey until he realises that Ayesha is drowning:

> She was drowning, too. He saw the water fill her mouth, heard it begin to gurgle inside her lungs. Then something within her refused that, made a different choice, and at the instant that his heart broke, he opened.
>
> His body split apart from his adam's-apple to his groin, so that she could reach deep within him, and now she was open, they all were, and at the moment of their opening the waters parted, and they walked to Mecca across the bed of the Arabian Sea. (507)

Ayesha's appeal to the secular landlord Mirza to 'open' is on one level a demand for Mirza to recognise the co-existence of the theological and the secular in an era of postcolonial modernity. But, as Sara Suleri has argued, Ayesha's injunction to 'open' from the standpoint of a woman and a Muslim is also a sign of Rushdie's feminisation of Islam (Suleri 1992: 202–206). Against the dogmatic monotheism of Mahound and the anti-historicism of the Imam, Ayesha embodies a more open and inclusive approach to Islam, which encourages dialogue and debate rather than foreclosing it. In this respect, The Satanic Verses seems to parallel the attempts by Muslim women writers such as Assia Djebar, Leila Aboulela and Fatima Mernissi to articulate the position of women in Islam.

REWRITING ISLAMIC LITERATURE AND CULTURE IN *HAROUN AND THE SEA OF STORIES*

If Ayesha's injunction to 'open' mirrors The Satanic Verses' attempt to read the history of the Prophet Muhammad as an open text, or a text that is open to different readings, Rushdie's subsequent novella Haroun and the Sea of Stories (1990) might seem to register the impossibility of such a project. As many critics have suggested, Haroun and the Sea of Stories appears to be an allegory of Rushdie's own predicament as a writer living under the threat of the death sentence issued by the Ayatollah Khomeini on February 14 1989. Catherine Cundy, for example, describes how 'one cannot help but make connections between Khattam-Shud and Rushdie's own chief persecutor, Khomeini, the voice of the fatwa that seeks to impose the most final of silences on Rushdie's utterances' (Cundy in Fletcher 1994: 338). Yet, as suggested below, Haroun and the Sea of Stories also complicates the binary opposition that structures the narrative between free speech and its foreclosure.

Written from the narrative point of view of a young boy, Haroun Khalifa, the story recounts Haroun's father's silencing as a storyteller after his wife leaves him, and Haroun's attempt to redeem his father's storytelling power through a fantastic journey to an imaginary world called Kahani (the Arabic word for story). During his imaginary visit to Kahani, Haroun discovers that the leader of the Chupwalas, Khattam-Shud, has polluted the Ocean of the Streams of Story. In an effort to save the Ocean of the Streams of Story, the source from which his father draws his stories, Haroun becomes involved in a war against the Chupwalas.

The imaginary geography of *Haroun and the Sea of Stories* bears some relationship to the South Asian subcontinent. The Valley of K, which is also referred to as 'Kache-Mer' and 'Kosh-Mar', is an obvious reference to Kashmir, and the division between the Land of Gup and the Land of Chup across the Twilight strip implies a partition of Kahani that resembles India's partition. If Haroun seems to take the side of the Land of Gup in the conflict with the Land of Chup, the narrative complicates the dichotomy between these two places by showing how the Land of Gup represents the Land of Chup as a space of perpetual darkness and alterity. During an encounter with the Chupwala shadow warrior Mudra, however, Rashid learns to read *abhinaya*, the shadow warrior's gesture language. By translating the language and culture of the Chupwalas for Haroun and the Guppees, Rashid Khalifa thus encourages Haroun and the Guppees to see how 'silence had its own grace and beauty' (Rushdie 1990: 129).

Haroun and the Sea of Stories also develops Rushdie's engagement with literary and cultural texts from the Islamic world such as Farid Ud-Din Attar's twelfth-century epic poem *The Conference of the Birds* and *The Arabian Nights*. In this respect, as Roger Y. Clark has argued, 'the novel works more like *Grimus*, in that it is a masterful fusion of cosmological and mystical paradigms' (Clark 2001: 186). Haroun is transported from the Valley of K to Kahani on a mechanical hoopoe, the bird in Attar's epic poem that leads the other birds on a journey to find God. As Iff, the water genie, explains to Haroun, ' "Perhaps you know that in the old stories the Hoopoe is the bird that leads all other birds through many dangerous places to their ultimate goal" ' (61). Similarly, the proper names Rashid and Haroun allude to the eighth-century Abbasid caliphate Harun al-Rashid, who also features in many of the stories that constitute *The Arabian Nights*. The court of Harun al-Rashid in Baghdad was noted not only for its opulence but also for its patronage of poets, men of letters, religious scholars, singers and musicians (Meisami and Starkey 1998: 274). Like Harun al-Rashid's court, Gup City displays similar grandeur with its pleasure garden, fountains and pleasure domes.

Rushdie's engagement with Islamic history and culture is also figured in the narrator's account of the 'Pagination and Collation' of the Guppee army or library. This complicated process involves a number of pages – or 'thin persons in rectangular uniforms that did, in fact, rustle exactly like paper' (116) – attempting to arrange themselves into chapters and volumes, even though some of the pages contain the same page number. This process recalls a scene from *Midnight's Children*, in which Ahmed Sinai attempts to re-arrange the *Qur'ān* in chronological order.

Like the pages of the Guppee army, the individual chapters or *suras* in the *Qur'ān* are not arranged in a coherent, linear fashion. Yet the *suras* can be read in a different order depending on the context of the reading. In this respect, the interpretation of the *suras* resembles the interpretation of the story streams in *Haroun and the Sea of Stories*. As Aron R. Aji puts it: 'each reading of the *suras* is not unlike the Plentimaw's re-creation of new narratives from the existing ones, in which the existing ones are neither destroyed nor undermined but brought together in new, harmonious and compatible wholes' (Aji 1995: 124). If the ocean of the sea of stories resembles the pages of the *Qur'ān*, it is significant also that the authoritarian dictator Khattam-Shud attempts to poison the sea of stories, the implication here being that Khattam-Shud's interpretation of the stories corrupts the stories' fluidity and polysemic quality.

Rushdie's magical resolution of the conflict between the land of Gup and the land of Chup, the destruction of the Cultmaster Khattam Shud, and Rashid Khalifa's rediscovery of his story-telling voice at the end of the novella may be consistent with the conventions of children's fiction. But, as Roger Y. Clark has pointed out, this ending can also 'hide' what he regards as a 'shift in Rushdie's *oeuvre*, away from a serious and problematic use of other worlds' (Clark 184). Certainly, one can see how Rushdie in *Haroun and the Sea of Stories* uses what Clark calls the other worlds of Kahani, Gup and Chup in 'an intensely idealistic fashion' in order to project 'them as an escape from the real-world threats of dogma and fatwa' (Clark 183). Yet in carefully plotting such an escape through intertextual allusions to *The Conference of Birds*, *The Arabian Nights*, and the *Qur'ān*, Rushdie in *Haroun and the Sea of Stories* offers an image of postcolonial modernity that is based on a dynamic synthesis of the secular and the religious. Such an image of postcolonial modernity is perhaps best illustrated in Rushdie's juxtaposition of Butt the

Hoopoe, a mechanical version of the bird in Attar's epic poem *The Conference of Birds*, who transports Haroun and his father to the fictional world of Kahani; and the bus driver, who takes Haroun and his father on a white-knuckle trip around the hairpin bends of the valley of K.

RELIGIOUS CAUSALITY AND THE SACRED SIGNIFIER IN 'THE PROPHET'S HAIR'

Whereas *Haroun and the Sea of Stories* expands and develops Rushdie's preoccupation with literary and cultural texts from the Islamic world, his next book, a collection of short stories entitled *East, West* (1994), contains a range of stories that seem to echo Rushdie's social and political concerns in novels such as *Midnight's Children* and *The Satanic Verses*, as well as his essay collection, *Imaginary Homelands*. In 'The Free Radio', for instance, the state vasectomy of the protagonist, a rickshaw driver named Ramani, in return for the thief's widow hand in marriage and the false promise of a free radio recalls the forced sterilisation of Saleem Sinai by the widow, Indira Gandhi, in *Midnight's Children*. The manner is which Ramani cups his hand to his ear in order to mimic the sound of a radio is also reminiscent of Saleem's telepathic power to broadcast the multitude of voices that constitute the Indian nation. 'At the Auction of the Ruby Slippers' is based on the ruby slippers in Frank Zappa's film *The Wizard of Oz*, a film that has inspired some of Rushdie's critical writing about the significance of home in writing from the South Asian diaspora. And the mental breakdown and eventual suicide of Eliot Crane, the author of a book on the occult, in 'The Harmony of the Spheres' parallels the mental illness of Gibreel Farishta, and the suggestion that he might be possessed by the devil. The parallels between these short stories and Rushdie's fiction are perhaps not surprising when one considers that 'six of the nine stories had been published earlier and at different times' (Goonetilleke 1998: 125).

Of all the stories published in the short story collection *East, West*, it is 'The Prophet's Hair' that most explicitly develops Rushdie's engagement with Islamic history and culture. The story is based on an incident that occurred in the 1960s when the holy relic of the Prophet's hair was stolen from a mosque in Kashmir, and subsequently returned to its shrine by the thieves who originally stole the relic. 'The Prophet's Hair' was first published in 1981 in the journal *Atlantic*, and was subsequently republished as a special edition, together with 'The Free Radio' in 1989 following the death sentence issued by the Ayatollah Khomeini of Iran (Rushdie 1989). This special edition took the form of 72 signed copies, which were hand printed on Arches Vélin paper and included five woodcuts and three linocuts by the artist Bhupen Khakhar. The timing and the exclusive, luxury quality of the publication made it an object whose meaning was not simply contained within the words of the story, but in its appearance and form. As a material object, the book was a defiance of the attempt by the Ayatollah Khomeini to silence Rushdie. Moreover, for Rushdie, the subsequent re-publication of 'The Prophet's Hair' in *East, West* signified his defiance of the death sentence. As Rushdie asserts in an interview with Alistair Niven, ' "The Prophet's Hair" is the answer to the intimidation question. If I was being scared off writing about Islam it wouldn't be in the collection, would it?' (Rushdie in Chauhan 2001: 238). Rushdie's re-publication of the story not only could be interpreted as a defiance of the attempt by the Ayatollah Khomeini to silence him, but it could also be seen as an attempt to capitalise on his notoriety since the so-called Rushdie affair.

The narrative structure of 'The Prophet's Hair' also foregrounds the foundations of religious authority by removing a holy icon (The Prophet's Hair) from its sacred location in a shrine and replacing it in the secular space of the money lender's safe. The theft of the hair could be interpreted as an act of sacrilege, blasphemy or wilful irreverence against the purity and stability of a religious icon. By removing the hair from its proper, sacred site, in other words, the theft of the hair threatens the stability of its religious meaning. So instead of a metonym, or a part of the Prophet Mohammed's body, which stands in for the whole sacred body of the Prophet, the icon is exposed as an empty signifier once it is removed from its sacred site. Or to put it another way, the theft of the hair could be seen to demystify the meaning of the hair as a religious icon. Outside of the shrine, the hair is merely a material object, an insignificant piece of human hair, which is denuded of any reference to the Prophet Muhammad.

The sacred location of the hair in a shrine at Hazratbal, in the valley of Kashmir may also seem to connect with certain narratives of religious nationalism. That is to say, the location of the hair at a holy shrine in Kashmir could be interpreted as a justification for the presence of Muslims in India, and the artificiality of the national boundary between India and Pakistan, which was drawn by the British colonial administration before India's independence in 1947. Yet, at the same time, the imprecise historical context of the story at some point in the twentieth century makes it difficult to determine whether the text is offering some commentary on the several wars that have raged across the Kashmir border between India and Pakistan since the partition of India and Pakistan in 1947. Despite the imprecise historical context of the story, it is clear that the site of Kashmir is an important symbolic space in Rushdie's fictional work. As one critic has observed, Kashmir operates as a personal myth for the source of story telling in Rushdie's work (Hogan 2001). In *Midnight's Children*, for example, the narrator contrasts his grandfather's idyllic, rural life in the valley of Kashmir in the early twentieth century with the state of Kashmir after India's independence, partition and the subsequent evacuation of Kashmir by Indian Muslims to Pakistan. So as an Indian Muslim, Rushdie could be seen to have a somewhat vexed relationship to the history of partition, ethnic conflict and the rhetoric of Indian nationalism.

Like *The Satanic Verses* and *Haroun and the Sea of Stories*, 'The Prophet's Hair' engages with an Islamic tradition that is specific to India's cultural history. The transformation of Hashim from a secular Muslim moneylender at the beginning of the story into an extremely orthodox Muslim could be interpreted as a satirical representation of Muslim orthodoxy from Rushdie's standpoint as a secular Indian Muslim. At the start of the story, Hashim is depicted as a secular Muslim. The third-person narrator asserts that Hashim is not 'a godly man', but ' "makes a point of living honourably in the world" ' (41). This principle of honour is complicated by Hashim's blatant extortion of his debtors, but it does make the point that morality and hypocrisy are often bound together. As the narrator states:

> In that spacious lakeside residence, all outsiders were treated with the same formality and respect, even those unfortunates who came to negotiate for small fragments of Hashim's great fortune, and for

whom he naturally asked an interest rate of 71 percent, partly, as he told his Kirichi-spooning wife, "to teach these people the value of money: let them only learn that, and they will be cured of this fever of borrowing, borrowing all the time – so you see that if my plans succeed, I shall put myself out of business!"

In their children, Atta and Huma, the moneylender and his wife had sought, successfully, to inculcate the virtues of thrift, plain dealing, perfect manners and a healthy independence of spirit. (41–42)

This description of Hashim's money-lending practices works to undermine his appearance as an honourable and tolerant Muslim man, before his subsequent magical transformation into a patriarchal tyrant. Indeed, the narrator suggests that it is Hashim's conscious decision to keep the 'famous relic of the Prophet Muhammad' on the grounds that it is 'a secular object of great rarity and blinding beauty' (44) that causes a strange transformation in Hashim's religious faith and in his behaviour towards his family. By adopting some of the more stringent moral laws described in the *Qur'ān*, Hashim declares an 'end to hypocrisy', and reveals to his family the existence of a mistress and his regular visits to sex workers; he orders his daughter to enter purdah; burns every book in the house except the *Qur'ān*; forces his family to rise for prayers at 5 am and forbids them from going to the cinema.

Hashim's mysterious adoption of religious rituals and disciplinary practices also seems to undermine his earlier assertion that the Prophet's Hair is a 'secular object' with no 'religious value' (44). Furthermore, Huma's decision to repeat the theft of the Prophet's Hair – in order to negate the effects of the curse upon Hashim's household – follows the logic of inversion that underpins *Shari'ah* law. As Fiona Richards explains:

The story presents and exceeds a simple inversion of morality. The inversion is begun by the misappropriation of the relic. The 'good' family of the moneylender is forced, by the disruption signalled by the intrusion of a holy object into the profane world, into contact with the 'bad' family of Sheikh Sin in an attempt to restore order. The original transgression which brought the sacred object out of the shrine and abandoned it in the secular world must be repeated in order to reverse it. The relic must be stolen, because an illegal act is the only kind which is effective in transporting the relic over the line from the holy place to the profane and vice versa. Religious transgression can only be effected by transgression of the moral and religious laws against stealing, and of course in Islam religious, legal and moral laws are closely bound, deriving from the same source, the *Shari'ah*. (Richards 2000: 14)

For Richards, the narrative's inversion of the binary oppositions between legality and illegality, the sacred and the profane is consistent with the structure of the *Shari'ah*. In Richards' account, the *Shari'ah* is not just a simple prescription of laws and rules; but is also based on a simple inversion, emphasised through the necessity of repetition. This logic of inversion and repetition is repeated in the story, when Atta attempts to return the story to its 'proper' place. When he tries to return the phial to a mosque, Atta finds that there is a hole in his pocket, and subsequently learns that his father has recovered the phial from the mosque. After a severe beating by her husband, Huma begins to understand that the only way out of their troubles is to repeat the theft of the hair:

> The hair … was stolen from the mosque; so it can be stolen from this house. But it must be a genuine robbery carried out by a bona-fide thief, not by one of us who are under the hair's thrall – by a thief so desperate that he fears neither capture nor curses. (50)

So the precise repetition of the crime could be seen to be consistent with the structural logic of inversion and repetition underpinning *Shari'ah* law.

But what are the implications of this reading? By reading Rushdie's text alongside the structure of Islamic law, one might conclude that the text itself does not simply subvert or challenge *Shari'ah* law; rather 'The Prophet's Hair' follows the structural logic of *Shari'ah* law in order to question some of its more conservative rules. Alternatively, Hashim's attempt to re-locate the hair in a secular context could be interpreted as an allegory of India's national condition, and its final failure to cohere. The room where Hashim collects his objects contains religious and military treasures from different cultures within India, including a spear belonging to a Hindu sect from Jaipur called the Naga, swords which were probably taken from Sikhs, as well as the hair of the Prophet. The attempt to appropriate these symbols from different cultures and to replace them in the single setting of Srinigar may seem to highlight the problems of trying to unify a national culture in secular terms, an idea that recalls Nehru's attempt to modernise India after independence. So the tragic consequences of Hashim's actions for the rest of his family could be read as a sign of the tragic failure of Nehru's attempt to modernise and unify the Indian nation after independence. And, following Hashim's unwitting murder of his daughter, and subsequent suicide, the restoration of the Prophet's hair to its proper place at the Hazratbal mosque, which is described as being 'closer than any other place on earth to Paradise' (57), could be read as an ironic statement on the structures of violence that are associated with religious nationalism in the Western Orientalist imagination.

Like *The Satanic Verses* and *Haroun and the Sea of Stories*, 'The Prophet's Hair' continues Rushdie's preoccupation with the place of Islamic history in the postcolonial world. While Rushdie may seem to satirise Islam from the perspective of an educated, secular, Indian Muslim, he does so in order to question secular ways of reading historical events such as terrorist attacks, aeroplane crashes and religious conversion with determinate and rational historical causes. If *The Satanic Verses* challenges the political authority of Islamic fundamentalists such as the Ayatollah Khomeini by questioning the truth claims of religious ideas such as revelation and encouraging readers to see the birth of Islam as an event within history, 'The Prophet's Hair' interrogates the political arguments that were made about the Prophet's Hair to strengthen Pakistan's territorial claims on Kashmir. Yet the question of whether Rushdie's political challenge to the authority of certain forms of Islamic fundamentalism is a form of bigotry or blasphemy is rendered indeterminate by the hybrid literary form of his writing. For if we read *The Satanic Verses* as a straightforward appeal for the reformation of Islam in the late twentieth century, the postmodern literary medium of Rushdie's message and his rhetorical stance as a secular British Indian Muslim writer would seem to confuse and distort the communication of this appeal. But if we read Rushdie's framing of Islamic history in terms of the magical realist conventions of his writing, then it becomes possible to read *The Satanic Verses* as a way of understanding events – such as the Ayesha pilgrims attempting to cross the Arabian Sea, the migration of Gibreel Farishta and Saladin Chamcha from Bombay to London or the historical emergence of Islam – through a critically secular lens that facilitates a serious intellectual and historicised engagement with the epistemological claims of religious texts such as the *Qur'ān*.

5

THE MOOR'S LAST SIGH

If Saleem Sinai's narrative in *Midnight's Children* mirrors Nehru's cosmopolitan vision of a secular Indian nation, the narrator of Rushdie's sixth novel *The Moor's Last Sigh* (1995) is much less optimistic about this cosmopolitan, secular vision of India's postcolonial future. Written from the first-person perspective of Moraes 'Moor' Zogoiby, the novel traces the downfall of the Zogoiby family, as well as the rise of right-wing Hindu politics in Bombay during the 1990s. Like Saleem Sinai and Rashid Khalifa, Moraes is likened to Scheherazade, the narrator of the *Arabian Nights*, who is under pressure to complete the narrative of his family's history. This recurrent narrative motif in Rushdie's fiction not only situates his writing in relation to a literary tradition that has its roots in eighth-century Baghdad but it also serves to establish Rushdie's concern with the precarious position of the writer's relationship to political power and authority in the twentieth century.

The narrative starts at the end of the story, with Moraes recounting his escape from incarceration by his mother's former lover and rival, Vasco Miranda, and Vasco's demand that Moor write a story about his life or face death. In this respect, as some critics have suggested, *The Moor's Last Sigh* could be read as an allegory of Rushdie's own position as a writer living in exile and under house arrest after the Ayatollah Khomeini's death sentence.

Yet such a reductive biographical reading would be to ignore the multiple histories of diaspora, hybridity, modernity and violence that inform and inflect *The Moor's Last Sigh*. Like *Midnight's Children*, *The Moor's Last Sigh* is concerned with the position of the minority in a postcolonial nation state that promises to respect the rights of minority groups through its secular principles. But, whereas *Midnight's Children* is concerned with the position of the

93

Indian Muslim before and after independence and partition, *The Moor's Last Sigh* traces the crisis of Prime Minister Nehru's secular ideology from the Emergency period (1975–1977) to the riots that followed the destruction of the Babri mosque, a major Muslim mosque in Ayodhya, in December 1992. And where Saleem Sinai is born into an Indian Muslim family, with a Christian ancestry, Moraes Zogoiby is the son of Christian and Jewish parents. Moraes is, as he explains at the end of the novel using a compound noun that recalls James Joyce's description of the protagonist Leopold Bloom as a jewgreek in *Ulysses*, a 'cathjew' (428).

'CHRISTIANS, PORTUGUESE AND JEWS ... CAN THIS REALLY BE INDIA?' COSMOPOLITANISM AND FUNDAMENTALISM IN *THE MOOR'S LAST SIGH*

Rushdie's choice of an Indian protagonist with both a Jewish and Catholic background is significant, then, because that protagonist symbolises the experience of the minority in a postcolonial nation state that claims to tolerate cultural difference. As Jawaharlal Nehru argued in *The Discovery of India*, 'ideas of cultural and religious toleration were inherent in Indian life' (Nehru 1946: 387). Just as Jewish experience of anti-Semitism in Europe reveals the limitations of European modernity vis-à-vis its claims to human freedom, so the experience of communal violence in India for minority groups such as Muslims reveals the limitations of India's secular modernity, and its claim to recognise the rights of minority groups. If the holocaust signifies the failure of European modernity, and its liberal principles of freedom, equality and tolerance, Rushdie in *The Moor's Last Sigh* suggests that events such as the Emergency and the destruction of the Babri mosque by Hindu groups signals the failure of Nehru's liberal vision of postcolonial modernity, particularly his promise to recognise the equal rights of all religious communities within India.

As well as being the son of the Zogoiby family, a family that descends from the fifteenth-century Portuguese colonist Vasco da Gama, Moraes Zogoiby is an Indian Jew, and as such he represents a minority within Indian society. By invoking the history of the Jewish diaspora to India, Rushdie also draws a parallel between the experience of other minority groups in India, such as

Muslims, and the experience of the Jews in twentieth-century Europe.

Moraes' father Abraham Zogoiby is a 'family employee' (69), and a descendent of what his mother calls the 'White Jews of India, Sephardim from Palestine [who] arrived in numbers (ten thousand approx.) in Year 72 of the Christian Era, fleeing from Roman persecution' (70–71). Indeed, it is Abraham's identity as a Cochin Jew that prompts his mother's resistance to his marriage to Aurora da Gama. For while the Jewish population of Cochin have historically co-existed with other ethnic groups in India, such as the majority Hindu population, they have also defined their ethnic identity as separate. One of the ways in which Cochin Jews attempted to define their identity as separate, as Nathan Katz explains, is to become accepted as a caste within mainstream Indian society (Katz 2000: 60). This attempt has involved not only the observation of strict moral and social codes, regarding diet and the use of a sacred language but also compulsory endogamy (Katz 2000: 72). Such strict moral codes would certainly account for Flory Zogoiby's resistance to her son's marriage to Aurora da Gama. Yet, as Abraham subsequently discovers from reading an old Spanish manuscript, the Zogoiby family is itself the product of an exogamous relationship between the exiled Sultan of Boabdil and an ejected Spanish Jew: 'two powerless lovers making common cause against the power of the Catholic Kings' (82). This act of miscegenation, as Abraham describes it, might seem to valorise hybridity and cosmopolitanism. But, as suggested below, Rushdie's use of the history of the Cochin Jews also reveals something about the limitations of Nehru's secular, cosmopolitan vision of India's postcolonial modernity.

In a speech delivered at the Cochin synagogue at the celebration of its quarter centenary on December 15 1968, the then prime minister of India, Indira Gandhi, is quoted as saying that 'Secularism in India does not mean animosity towards religion … It implies equal respect for all religions … It is a matter of pride for us in India that all the great religions in the world are respected in our country' (cited in Katz 2000: 57). It is precisely this liberal ideology of secularism and tolerance that Rushdie subjects to scrutiny in *The Moor's Last Sigh*, a novel that was written in the aftermath of the destruction of the Babri mosque in Ayodyha on December 6 1992, and the subsequent riots and bombings that happened in

January 1993. Rushdie locates the origins of the crisis in India's secularist discourse in the Indian Emergency. Following Indira Gandhi's emergency suspension of civil law in 1975, Moraes declares 'Before the Emergency we were Indians. After it we were Christian Jews' (235). Moreover, by tracing India's history through the genealogy of the Zogoiby family and Aurora Zogoiby's paintings, Rushdie draws a parallel between the disintegration of Moorish Spain, and the expulsion of Jews and Moors by the Catholic monarchs Isabella and Ferdinand in the fifteenth century, and the sweeping away of Nehru's secular pluralist vision of India by the right-wing ideology of Hinduvata. As Aamir Mufti puts it:

> The political rise of violent Hindu nationalism in Bombay and Maharashtra in the form of the Shiv Sena, which reappears here as 'Mumbai's Axis' or the M.A., is thus figured as a sort of *Reconquista*, with the 'mongrel' Bombay of the Nehruvian decades consumed by the violent religious, ethnic, and linguistic rigidities of 'Maharashtra for Mahrashtrans'. (Mufti 2007: 246)

Against this *Reconquista* in postcolonial South Asia, it is Aurora Zogoiby's paintings that continue to idealise Bombay as a cosmopolitan space (Mufti 246–247). Of all Aurora Zogoiby's paintings, it is perhaps her paintings of Mooristan and Palimpstine that evoke the Nehruvian ideal of India as a secular, cosmopolitan nation. In these paintings, Moraes asserts that Aurora was 'seeking to paint a golden age' in which 'Jews, Christians, Muslims, Parsis, Sikhs, Buddhists, Jains' coexisted (227). The paintings are described as 'polemical' in the attempt to 'create a romantic myth of the plural, hybrid nation' and the use of 'Arab Spain to re-imagine India' (227). Yet this didacticism is offset by the paintings' aesthetic quality:

> with the vivid surrealism of her images and the kingfisher brilliance of her colouring and the dynamic acceleration of her brush, it was not easy to feel preached at, to revel in the carnival without listening to the barker, to dance to the music without caring for the message in the song. (227)

By establishing a connection between the surreal aesthetics of Aurora Zogoiby's paintings and the hybrid politics of a postcolonial nation state based on the liberal principles of secularism and tolerance, Rushdie thus implies that *The Moor's Last Sigh* – like Aurora's art – is a mirror of India's postcolonial future.

If Aurora Zogoiby's paintings stand as a mirror image of Nehru's secular vision of postcolonial India, they also reflect the elitism of his nationalist project. During the naval strike in Bombay of 1946, for example, Aurora directs the driver of her imported American motor car to

> the heart of the action, or, rather, of all that grand inaction, being set down outside factory gates and dockyards, venturing alone into the slum-city of Dharavi, the rum-dens of Dhobi Talao and the neon fleshpots of Falkland Road, armed only with a folding wooden stool and sketchbook. (129)

Aurora is able to efface her class position as an independently wealthy, upper middle class visual artist during the industrial action. However, once the Congress Party leadership calls off the strike – a decision that prompts the anger of the sailors – Aurora realises that her position as an artist is untenable: 'Aurora was not a sailor ... and knew that to those angry boys she would look like a rich bitch in a fancy car – as, perhaps, the enemy' (133).

Moraes' analysis of the bourgeois character of Aurora's artwork is further hinted at in his account of her painting of Mooristan and Palimpstine in chapter 13. In this painting, the 'real-life Bombayites on the beach' are described as 'a cavalcade of local riff-raff – pickpockets, pimps, fat whores, hitching their saris up against the waves ...' (226). By incorporating the masses into her painterly evocation of late-twentieth-century Bombay, Aurora could be seen to offer a transparent representation of Bombay society. Yet the description of these different social characters as 'local riff-raff' suggests that these characters are criminalised and subordinated to the artist's survey of the city. Such a representa-tion might suggest that the painter inhabits an elite position in relation to the working-class subjects depicted in the painting. Yet the fact that these characters are painted from the vantage point of the 'Mughal palace-fortresses in Delhi and Agra' (226) complicates this reading somewhat by suggesting that the painter identifies with the minority subject position of an Indian Muslim.

Aurora's juxtaposition of Moorish Spain in the fifteenth century and late-twentieth-century Bombay is significant also because it traces the destruction of two cosmopolitan societies, whose culture and economy have benefited from migration. Just as the Spanish Catholic monarchy expelled Moors and Jews from Alhambra in the fifteenth century, so groups such as the Shiv Sena attempted to expel Muslims from Bombay in the early 1990s. Moreover, if Aurora's paintings embody the golden age of Bombay's cosmopolitanism and Nehruvian secularism, Moraes' stuffed dog on wheels Jawaharlal (an allusion to the former Indian prime minister Jawaharlal Nehru) signifies the obsolescence of Nehru's secular democratic ideal in late-twentieth-century India. As Rustom Bharucha puts it, 'Rushdie's critique of contemporary India is cast in a time warp, and as such, is almost as redundant as that stuffed old dog-on-wheels Jawaharlal, who is trundled through the last pages of the novel, an object of pathos rather than derision' (Bharucha 1998: 4).

Like Aurora Zogoiby's early paintings, *The Moor's Last Sigh* may at times seem nostalgic for a golden age of secularism, which never really existed. Indeed, the end of secularism that Rushdie in both *Midnight's Children* and *The Moor's Last Sigh* attributes to the 1975 state of emergency declared by Indira Gandhi overlooks the way in which secularism conceals a structure of intolerance towards populations deemed to be minorities from the foundation of the Indian nation state. For the principle of toleration, as the South Asian historian Partha Chatterjee points out 'is the willing acceptance of something of which one disapproves' (Chatterjee 1997: 256). Tolerance in this definition conceals a power relationship between the dominant and the subaltern, or the majority and the minority. In the contemporary United States, the political theorist Wendy Brown argues that tolerance is part of a 'discourse that identifies both tolerance and the tolerable with the West and marks non-liberal societies and practices as candidates for an intolerable barbarism that is itself signaled by the putative intolerance ruling these societies' (Brown 2006: 6). This discourse of tolerance was also implicit in Jawaharlal Nehru's attempt to separate religion and the state in the foundation of the Indian nation state. One of the problems with this state discourse of secularism, as Ashis Nandy contends, is that 'the modern nation state has no means of ensuring that the ideologies of secularism, development, and nationalism themselves do not begin to act as faiths intolerant of others' (Nandy 1998: 333). Nandy is right to emphasise that secularism offers no guarantee of protection against intolerance towards minority groups. For in the aftermath of the destruction of the Babri mosque, the Supreme Court of India 'not only failed to recognize the profound threat that the Hindu Right presents to Indian secularism, but actually endorsed their vision of Hinduvata as secular' (Cossman and Kapur 1999: xvi). Yet the problem is not exactly with secularism, development or nationalism *per se* (as Ashis Nandy suggests), but the historical context in which the discourses of secularism and tolerance came into being during the partition of India. As Aamir Mufti puts it, 'The abstract, "secular" citizen has its *Enstehung*, its moment of emergence, in a violent redistribution of religious identities and populations' (Mufti 1998: 119). Historians estimate that up to a million people were killed, and millions displaced, in acts of communal violence that were committed by both the Hindu and Muslim populations during the partition of India and Pakistan in 1947. What the event of South Asian partition revealed was that the apparently universalist notion of secularism underpinning India's constitution was based on a tacit assumption that the majority Hindu population were natural citizens of India, whereas the minority Muslim population had to demonstrate their loyalty to the Indian nation (Pandey 2006: 132–133). As a result, it was the Muslim population who were marked as a minority group that should be tolerated in Nehru's secular nationalist discourse.

The vulnerable position of minorities such as Muslims, Jews and Christians is prophesied in Vasco Miranda's drunken diatribe on the eve of India's independence. Against Nehru's promises of secular socialism, Miranda roundly criticises the Zogoiby family for being 'Minority group members' and 'Macaulay's minutemen', whom Nehru duped into buying the idea of secular socialism 'like a cheap watch salesman' (166). This metaphor of the cheap watch salesman is significant because it suggests that secular socialism is an inferior imitation of a concept imported from Europe; a concept that is belated, out of joint, and therefore has no relevance in post-independence India. As such it is also an apt counterpoint to the temporal motif of the countdown to independence signified by Mountbatten's 'ticktock' in *Midnight's Children*. Further, Vasco's reference to 'Macaulay's minutemen' alludes to Lord Macaulay's 1835 'Minute on Indian Education', in which Macaulay argued that it was necessary to educate an elite class in Indian society who could act as interpreters between the English and the non-English speaking Indian population: 'a class of persons, Indian in blood and colour, but English in taste, in opinions, in morals and in dialect' (Macaulay 359). By describing the Zogoiby family as 'Macaulay's minutemen' because of their gullible belief in Nehru's promises of equality to migrants, Vasco Miranda implies that Nehru's ideology of secularism, and its blind adherents, signify a continuation of European colonial rule in a different guise.

In this respect, Vasco's critique of secularism resembles Ashis Nandy's argument that Indian secularism is a discourse of the middle-class political elite, who regard religion as 'an ideology in opposition to the ideology of modern statecraft' (Nandy 1998: 324) and a 'hurdle to nation building and state formation' (Nandy: 341). The problem with this criticism of secularism is that it assumes that secularism is part of the dominant discourse of the state, rather than a discourse that can be shaped and determined by minority groups. By doing so, Nandy runs the risk of playing into the hands of right-wing Hindu movements, such as the Shri Ram Janmabhumi Liberation movement, who attacked the 'partisan-ship of the secularism professed by the Indian state and by the national and provincial governments' on the grounds that this sec-ularism constituted a 'pseudosecularist pacification of the Muslims and other minorities' (Pandey 2006: 83). Against this pseudosecu-larism, movements such as the Shri Ram Janmabhumi Liberation movement called upon Hindus to take back their country through actions of communal violence such as the destruction of the Babri mosque.

Instead of secularism, Vasco Miranda argues that bribery and corruption are the only means of opposing communal violence towards religious minorities such as Muslims and Jews in post-colonial India. Such a view is borne out by Rushdie's subsequent account of Abraham Zogoiby's secular empire of corruption, which he describes as 'the only force ... that could defeat fanati-cism' (332). Corruption is also central to the economy of Rushdie's Bombay in The Moor's Last Sigh. Indeed, it is only when Moraes is sentenced to imprisonment for narcotics smuggling in a prison, which is ironically named Bombay Central that he begins to under-stand how the city is dependent on an informal economy. As the inmate whom Moraes calls the elephant man explains, '[Bombay Central] ... is the stomach, the intestine of the city' (287). This grotesque metaphor reflects what the sociologist Jayant Lele describes as 'the underside of state sponsored capitalist development' in late-twentieth-century Bombay, that is an ' "underworld" of extortion, smuggling, drug trafficking and contraband peddling' (Lele in Patel and Thorner 1995: 186). As a spatial metaphor for the circulation of capital in the city, Bombay Central mirrors the source of Abraham Zogoiby's business empire in the criminal underworld. Bombay is also central in Rushdie's geographical imagination in the sense that it is a synecdoche for the nation: 'Bombay was central; had always been. Just as the fanatical 'Catholic Kings' had besieged Granada and awaited the Alhambra's fall, so now barbarism was standing at our gates' (372).

If, as Jayant Lele suggests, Hindu fundamentalist groups such as the Shiv Sena demonised migrants from South India as the cause of such corruption, Abraham Zogoiby would seem to reinforce this stereotype as a South Indian businessman with interests in prostitution, drug smuggling and arms dealing. Yet, rather than simply repeating the right-wing discourse of Hindu fundamentalism, Moraes also interrogates the rhetoric and political theology of Raman Fielding, leader of the fictional right-wing Hindu fundamentalist group, the Mumbai axis. Fielding, as many critics have noted, is a fictionalised version of Bal Thackeray, the leader of the Maharashtra fundamentalist group, the Shiv Sena. In Moraes' account, Fielding is not the pure Hindu he makes himself out to be, but a political opportunist. Despite his public opposition to the immigration of non-Marathi speakers to Bombay, his support for sati, strike breaking, and the destruction of Muslim mosques that were supposedly built on sacred Hindu sites (298–299), Fielding is revealed to have 'many non-Hindu tastes': he 'loved meat' and applauded the 'non-veg cuisine' of 'Bombay's meat-eating Parsis, Christians and Muslims' (297); he would also 'sing ghazals and recite Urdu poetry' (299). By exposing the contradiction between Raman Fielding's public persona as the advocate of a right-wing Hindu fundamentalist ideology and his private persona as a bourgeois figure with a cosmopolitan appreciation for India's hybrid culture, Rushdie suggests that Fielding's right-wing ideology is motivated by a political desire for power rather than a strong sense of religious belief. In this respect, Rushdie implies that Raman Fielding's fanaticism is no different from Abraham Zogoiby's corrupt business enterprise.

At stake in Rushdie's satirisation of Bal Thackeray and the Shiv Sena is not simply a critique of Hindu fundamentalism, but the failure of a certain idea of secularism, a failure which is also embodied in Abraham Zogoiby's capitalist ambitions to rebuild Bombay as a centre of (corrupt) business (Trousdale 2004: 107–108). Abraham's building of skyscrapers in Bombay with the sweated labour of migrant workers, whom Moraes describes as 'phantoms' (186), confirms the Marxist Joseph D'Costa's suspicion in *Midnight's Children* that India's independence is for the rich only. And like Ahmed Sinai in *Midnight's Children*, Abraham Zogoiby would seem to betray the socialist ideals epitomised in Nehru's five-year plans by pursuing his own private business interests.

Rushdie's representation of communal violence in *The Moor's Last Sigh* also interrogates the moral logic that was used to justify the violent Muslim response to the Hindu destruction of the Babri mosque in Ayodhya:

> Violence was violence, murder was murder, two wrongs did not make a right … There comes a point in the unfurling of communal violence in which it becomes irrelevant to ask, "Who started it?" The lethal justifications of death part company with any possibility of justification, let alone justice. (365)

In Moraes' analysis, communal violence exceeds a moral explanation precisely because this violence is embedded in the political foundations of the Indian postcolonial nation state. In a related discussion, the South Asian historian Gyanendra Pandey has argued that violence in India is often represented as an aberration to the secular norms of tolerance and peaceful coexistence, which are exemplified in the representation of communal violence as a riot, or a spontaneous uprising. Yet this representation 'deflects attention away from the way the construction of a normal India sets different populations – the Muslims and sometimes other communities – against the authentic nation' (Pandey 2006: 14). In Pandey's account, violence in India is not an aberration, but a total social fact, which is 'implicit in the insistent construction of permanent majorities and minorities, based usually on supposedly immutable racial, religious, or ethnic differences' (14).

Moraes Zogoiby's self-reflective account of the communal violence, in which he also participates, squarely locates the source of communal violence in Bombay *within* the nation rather than attributing it to an external, foreign enemy: 'the barbarians were not only at our gates but within our skins … the explosions burst out of our very own bodies. We were both the bombers and the bombs. The explosions were our own evil – no need to look for foreign explanations' (372). The grotesque metaphor of explosions bursting 'out of our very own bodies' registers the responsibility of Moraes Zogoiby and his cadres for the violence that follows the razing of the Babri mosque in 1992. Moraes' refusal to adopt a partisan or communalist explanation for the violence may seem surprising given his implication in it. Yet, in refusing to justify the use of violence by blaming Bal Thackeray's group the Shiv Sena, Moraes suggests that violence is inherent to the social body of postcolonial India rather than an exception or an aberration.

Furthermore, Moraes' refusal of Vasco Miranda's accusation that he and his family are Macaulay's minutemen – or elite foreigners, who have no stake in the nation – refuses the majoritarian rhetoric of Hindu nationalism that underpins Vasco's drunken diatribe: 'Vasco was wrong. We were not, had never been, that class' (376). Moor's refusal of Vasco's derisory label is predicated on his identity as *both* an Indian and a hybrid minority. Indeed, at one point in the novel, Moraes claims his Jewish identity in order to refuse his father's demands to help him build technology to support a nuclear weapons programme. In response to his father's request, Moraes asserts, 'I guess you must know who-all this bomb is meant to blow into more bits than poor Rajiv and where?' (336). Although the interrogatives 'who-all' and 'where' in this statement are not tethered to a determinate referent, the historical context of Abraham's illegal arms technology dealing in 1990s Bombay/Mumbai suggests that this episode can be linked to the Indian military's proliferation of nuclear weapons in its ongoing war with Pakistan. In this reading, the 'who-all' and the 'where' Abraham Zogoiby refers to in his conversation with Moraes implicitly denotes the population of Pakistan, and suggests that Abraham's statement is a caution that the weapons technology he wishes his son to help build will be utilised by the Indian nation state in its ongoing war with Pakistan. If Abraham's corrupt business practices and his involvement in nuclear arms dealing epitomise everything that is wrong with the dominant values of liberal secularism in late-twentieth-century India, Moraes' identification as a Jew can be read as a gesture of solidarity with other minorities, such as Indian Muslims, even though Moraes also describes this ethnic identification as 'involuntary' and 'unconscious' (335).

Moraes' identification as a Jew, nevertheless, complicates the dichotomy between the secular and the religious that Rushdie seems to posit elsewhere in his fictional and non-fictional writing. At one point in *The Satanic Verses*, for instance, the character Swatilekha refers to the Supreme Court of India's ruling on the Shahbano case of 1985, in which a divorced Indian Muslim woman attempted to claim alimony from her husband after he divorced her. The Shahbano case is sometimes invoked as a test case of the Indian government's official policy of secularism because the Supreme Court undermined the authority of the Muslim Personal Law to legislate on matters relating to the family by ruling that Shahbano's husband should pay his divorced wife regular monthly maintenance. In Swatilekha's account of the Shahbano case, the counsel for Shahbano's husband attempted to rule that 'alimony payments were contrary to the will of Allah' (Rushdie 1988: 535) according to its interpretation of Shari'ah law. In response to this judgement, Swatilekha exclaims ' "Battle lines are being drawn up in India today," ... "Secular versus religious, the light versus the dark. Better you choose which side you are on" ' (536).

Swatilekha's assertion certainly highlights the way in which Shahbano's demand for maintenance became a broader site of political struggle over 'the liberal discourse of secularism and constitutional rights in India' (Pathak and Rajan 1992: 261). Yet this liberal discourse was ultimately subordinated to the exigencies of electoral politics. For, as Zakia Pathak and Rajeswari Sunder Rajan have argued, 'when the sizable Muslim vote turned against the ruling party (the Congress-I) partly because it supported the judgement [referring to the Supreme Court's ruling on the Shahbano case]' the ruling party responded by reversing its earlier position and passing a bill to save Muslim person law, which was known as 'the Muslim Woman (Protection of Rights in Divorce) Act' (Pathak and Rajan 1992: 257–258).

If Swatilekha defends the democratic principle of secularism in order to counter the rise of Muslim fundamentalism in India, Moraes foregrounds the way in which the constitutional discourse of secularism in India has paradoxically aided and abetted the rise of the Hindu right. By aligning himself with a minority group in

postcolonial India, Moraes challenges the dominant political discourse of secularism for two principle reasons: first, because the
Nehruvian discourse of state secularism is increasingly regarded
by both Moraes and Vasco as an outdated legacy of the ruling liberal ideology of British colonialism, which as mentioned above,
was adopted by Nehru to recognise the cultural rights of Muslims
and other minorities during the transition to independence and
the framing of India's constitution; and second, because the rhetoric of secularism masks the corrupt business practices of
Bombay's criminal underworld, of which Abraham Zogoiby is
both a principle agent and a beneficiary. Yet, rather than simply
rejecting secularism as a progressive social and political principle,
Moraes' identification as a minority – that is, his declaration to his
father that he finds himself to be a Jew – re-defines the secular as a
minority position from which to contest the spurious use of secularism by the criminal underworld (represented in the novel by his
father), as well as its discrediting by the Hindu right (represented in
the novel by Raman Fielding). In this respect, Moraes' identification as a Jew corresponds with the postcolonial theorist Homi K.
Bhabha's plea in his essay 'Unpacking my Library ... Again' for a
'subaltern secularism that emerges from the limitations of "liberal" secularism and *keeps faith* with those communities and individuals who have been denied, and excluded, from the egalitarian
and tolerant values of liberal individualism' (Bhabha 1996: 209).
For when Moraes asserts that he is a Jew, he is not only making a
statement about the singularity of his hybrid ethnic identity as a
'cathjew' (428); he is also claiming affinity with the different subaltern and minority groups that have been excluded from participation in India's state discourse of ' "liberal" secularism' (as Bhabha
defines it above). In this respect Moraes Zogoiby, like Saleem Sinai
in *Midnight's Children*, adopts the rhetorical stance of the minority
in order to question whether liberal political concepts such as secularism, which are overdetermined by the histories of British
colonialism and communal violence, can be reinvented in such a
way that might transform the democratic grounds of the modern
postcolonial nation state.

6

THE GROUND BENEATH HER FEET

In an essay titled 'Talking about our Modernity in Two Languages' (1997) the South Asian historian Partha Chatterjee diagnoses the condition of Indian modernity. Writes Chatterjee, 'Somehow from the very beginning, we had made a shrewd guess that given the close complicity between modern knowledge and modern regimes of power, we would for ever remain consumers of universal modernity; never would we be taken seriously as its producers' (Chatterjee 1997: 275). It is precisely this assumption that Indian modernity is somehow belated or backward that Salman Rushdie seeks to challenge in his seventh novel *The Ground Beneath Her Feet* (1999).

POSTCOLONIAL MODERNITY IN *THE GROUND BENEATH HER FEET*

One of the most striking instances of Rushdie's challenge to the idea that Indian modernity is somehow belated in this novel lies in the narrator, Rai's account of how Bombay invented rock 'n' roll music before it was arguably invented by Elvis Presley in the United States:

> Rock music ... was allegedly first revealed to a Parsi Indian boy named Ormus Cama, who heard all the songs in advance, two years, eight months and twenty-eight days before anyone else. So according to Ormus and Vina's variant version of history, their alternative reality, we Bombayites can legitimately claim that it was in truth our music, born in Bombay like Ormus and me, not 'goods from foreign' but made in India, and maybe it was the foreigners who stole it from us. (96)

Against the prevalent historical narrative that rock music is an American product, which was subsequently exported to the rest of the world, Rai recounts how Ormus Cama first overhears his ghostly brother Gayomart singing vowel sounds in a dream, which he subsequently hears again 'two years, eight months and 28 days later', when he listened to Elvis Presley's 'Heartbreak Hotel' in a listening booth in Bombay (90). This fictional re-writing of the history of rock 'n' roll could be understood as an example of what Rushdie calls disorientation in *The Ground Beneath Her Feet* because it decentres the importance of American and British culture in the history of global modernity. Yet Rai's attempt to posit the Indian rock 'n' roll music of Ormus Cama's fictional band VTO as an alternative to the *cultural* dominance of the West in the twentieth and twenty-first centuries does not in itself address the global political and economic dominance of the United States, or the way in which contemporary South Asian music has been packaged as World Music or Asian cool: an exotic commodity for Western consumer society. As Ashwani Sharma argues in *Dis-Orienting Rhythms: The Politics of the New Asian Dance Music* (1996), the 'rise of World Music in the 1980s is undoubtedly part of the emergence of a notion of "ethnicity" as a master-signifier of marketing and advertising' (Sharma 1996: 22). Moreover, this master-signifier can 'too easily mask the exploitative labour relationship of the very powerful transnational corporations with the "Third World" musicians, let alone with those of the Third World with only their photogenic poverty to sell' (22). In this sense the Indian rock 'n' roll music of VTO, which forms the subject of *The Ground Beneath her Feet*, draws attention to the process by which Indian culture is commodified for a global market through cultural forms such as popular music and the novel. In doing so, *The Ground Beneath her Feet* refuses the straightforward commodification of Indian culture.

To be sure, Rushdie's representation of the legal battle between Yul Singh, the head of Colchis Records, and Mull Standish, the manager of VTO, over the rights to produce VTO's music reveals the economic agenda of the global music industry. And Vina Apsarda's fear of the music business is precisely a more general fear of the alienation and short life expectancy associated with the contemporary cultural phenomenon of the celebrity (370). Furthermore, Rai suggests that the success of Ormus and Vina's music is precisely a response to the failure of American imperialism in Indochina during the Vietnam war:

> The U.S. Army (and its rock songs) went into one East and came out
> with a bloody nose. Now Ormus's music has arrived like an affirmation
> from another East to enter the musical heart of Americanness ...
> America, disoriented, seeking a new voice, succumbs to theirs.
> (378–379)

Yet the feeling of disorientation that Rai attributes to the rock
music of VTO is itself a part of the exotic packaging of VTO as a
global commodity for mass consumption. The success of VTO in
Britain and the United States during the 1960s and 1970s may seem
to recall the success of the sitar player Ravi Shankar, who played at
rock festivals such as Monterey and Woodstock in the 1960s
alongside artists such as the Jimi Hendrix Experience, the Who
and Janis Joplin (Hyder 2004: 59). As Rehan Hyder suggests,
Shankar's success in the Western rock music world was part of a
broader tendency within Western rock 'n' roll music to borrow
' "surface" elements of Indian music to provide Western pop bands
with an exotic frisson aimed at achieving a short-lived novelty
appeal' (Hyder 60). For Western bands from the Beatles to
Madonna, Kula Shaker and Oasis have variously appropriated
'Indian instruments and sounds as adornments for Western tunes
in a tokenistic way' (Hyder : 61). Such an appropriation of the sitar
and Sanskrit verse by Western popular culture exemplifies the
way in which Indian music and culture has provided an exotic and
mystical backdrop to Western consumer culture rather than the
syncretic transformation of Western rock 'n' roll music and 'traditional Indian' music that is sometimes claimed. In *The Ground
Beneath Her Feet*, such a superficial engagement with Western
music is exemplified by Ormus's musical director Mull Standish,
whose reverence for a Tantric master symbolises '*the curious posses-
sive fascination of the hedonistic West with the ascetic East*' (266). This 'fascination' is subsequently described as a form of corruption or
confusion, in which 'This England is addled by mysticism' (287),
and Ormus is fetishised by 'girls on their scooters and motorbikes,
the girls in their bubble cars and Minis, the girls in their false eye-
lashes and high boots' for being 'spiritual' (291).

Given the history of Western rock 'n' roll music's selective and
superficial appropriation of Indian music, it is perhaps difficult to
see how Rushdie's fictional Indian rock group VTO challenges the
regressive stereotypes of Indian culture as mystical that continue

to circulate in late twentieth-century Western society. At one point, the narrator asserts that Vina Apsarda enjoyed 'the music of India, from northern Sitar ragas to Southern Carnatic melodies' and 'could listen to recordings of ghazals for hours at a stretch, and was entranced, too, by the complex devotional music of the leading *qawwals*' (Rushdie 1998: 123). Yet Rai offers an already articulated response to the suggestion that Vina's interest in Indian music is a search for 'an "authentic Indianness" that she could never attain', by suggesting instead that Vina's proclivity for Indian music is motivated by a desire for a 'glimpse of the unknowable': 'The music offered the tantalising possibility of being borne on the waves of sound through the curtain of *maya* that supposedly limits our knowing, through the gates of perception to the divine melody beyond' (123). Such a speculative account of Vina's search for transcendence in different musical forms associated with South Asia may be consistent with Rushdie's re-writing of Virgil's version of the Orpheus myth, in that Vina, like the character of Eurydice in book four of Virgil's *Georgics*, descends to the underworld and dies. And, despite Vina's love of Indian music, Rai stresses that Vina never actually used these musical forms in her rock 'n' roll music: 'Sometimes I try to imagine how she would have sounded singing ghazals. For even though she dedicated her life to another music entirely, the pull of India, its songs, its languages, its life, worked upon her always, like the moon' (124). Yet Vina's search for transcendence seems to fall back on the very orientalism that Rai attempts to disavow. By juxtaposing Indian musical forms with ancient Roman myths and Asian rock 'n' roll music, the narrator – in the manner of a disinterested anthropologist or a surrealist collage artist – suggests that these myths are structurally equivalent. In so doing, Rai re-inscribes an orientalist representation of musical forms such as Sitar ragas and ghazals, and divests these very different musical forms of their specific cultural significance.

Rai's observation that Vina 'dedicated her life to another music entirely' (124), while continuing to listen to different Indian musical forms as a source of inspiration for her own practice as a musician may seem to circumvent the pitfalls of orientalism. Indeed, the narrator seems to focus on VTO's lyrics and their self-fashioning as rock stars rather than the non-verbal acoustic signs of the percussion, bass and guitar conventionally associated with rock 'n' roll. He details, for instance, how Ormus Cama anticipated Bob

Dylan's 'Blowing in the Wind' with a song entitled 'The Ganja is growing in the tin' (141); how Vina performs in clubs in London and New York, and becomes a figure of controversy after describing one of her audiences as dead Kennedys after the assassination of President John F. Kennedy (224–226); how Ormus's lyrics – which prophesy 'doom' to 'the New World' for squandering its 'privileges' – appeal to the sentiments of U.S. anti-war protestors during the Vietnam war, and prompt an FBI investigation into Ormus's inadvertent use of LSD (380–391); and how, later in his career, Ormus Cama's 'self-hating, deracinated music has long been at the service … even at the heart, of the arrogance of the West, where the world's tragedy is repackaged as youth entertainment and given an infectious, foot-tapping beat' (556).

While the music of VTO seems to participate in the left-wing liberal opposition to US foreign policy during the Vietnam War and the secular culture of consumerism with which the late-twentieth-century Western world has become associated, Rushdie also suggests that the music of VTO is complicit in that secular consumerist culture. In this respect, the music of VTO would seem to contrast with South Asian bands of the 1990s such as Cornershop, Fun^Da^Mental, Voodoo Queens, and Asian Dub Foundation, who have invented new musical forms to articulate the diasporic histories and experiences of Asians in Britain: 'Fun^Da^Mental mix samples of sitars onto their hip hop beats, Black Star Liner fuse tablas and tambours with heavy dub bass-lines and Cornershop juxtapose a whole panoply of "Indian" sounds with distorted guitars, funky beats and country rhythms' (Hyder 2004: 172). By contrast, the music of VTO seems to erase any trace of traditional musical forms associated with South Asia, in an attempt to challenge the claim that Elvis and the Beatles invented rock 'n' roll, and the assumption that contemporary popular culture was invented and defined by the West.

FICTIONS OF GLOBAL CRISIS IN *THE GROUND BENEATH HER FEET*

If the success of VTO as a rock 'n' roll band in America and Britain signifies the symbolic reversal of a global world system in which American popular culture is often regarded as dominant (Appadurai 1996; Tomlinson 1999), it is the narrator who documents the crisis inherent to that global world system through his photographic practice. Significantly, Rai's photographic practice oscillates between political photojournalism and the celebrity photography associated with the paparazzi and magazines such as *Life*, which his French mentor M. Hulot describes as 'the danger of mannerism' (222). Such a danger parallels Rushdie's own practice as a writer who, in his more recent fiction, wavers between a preoccupation with American commodity culture and the figure of the celebrity on the one hand and a more explicit political criticism of neoliberal globalisation and American foreign policy on the other.

One of Rai's crowning achievements as a photojournalist is his exposé of the right-wing Indian entrepreneur Piloo Doodhwala's fraudulent business practice as a goat farmer in a remote village in Madhya Pradesh. In doing so, Rai likens himself to the early-nineteenth-century French photographer Louis Daguerre (209). For just as Daguerre usurped the position of his collaborator, Joseph Nicéphore Niépce, by claiming to have taken the first photograph (209), so Rai claims to expose Doodhwala's 'great goat scam' – in which 'huge sums of public money' are spent on 'one hundred million wholly fictitious goats' (232–233) – by developing a film concealed in the hiking boot of another photojournalist, who is apprehended and executed by Doodhwala's henchmen before Rai's arrival in the Indian village where the goats are supposedly located, and presenting this film as his own work. As the narrator explains:

> The hanged man and I were alone for a long time. His feet swung not far from my revolted nose and yes I wondered about the heels of his boots yes when I got the ropes off I made myself approach him yes in spite of his pong … yes I twisted the left heel it came up empty but the right heel did the right thing the film just plopped down in my hand and I put an unused film in its place from my own boot … and I made my escape with Piloo's fate and my own golden future in my hand yes and to hell with everything I said yes because it might as well be me as another so yes I will yes I did yes. (244)

In an echo of Molly Bloom's monologue at the end of James Joyce's *Ulysses*, Rai's repeated affirmations, and the absence of punctuation or subordination in this quoted passage recall the risk and danger of Rai's retrieval of the photographic film from the heel of the dead photographer, as well as registering the emotional affect of his guilty secret, that his entire career as a famous photographer was built on his passing off the work of another photographer as his own. As Rai puts it, 'Piloo Doodhwala had his scam; and as you see, I had mine. He made four million dollars. I just made my name' (245).

Rushdie's suggestion that Rai is a fraud or a fake may be interpreted as a commentary on the status of the author in an age of mechanical reproduction, or as a criticism of the romantic idea that art or writing is autonomous from the 'scam', or the corruption associated with the market. Yet, it is perhaps more productive to consider the photograph in *The Ground Beneath her Feet* as a mode of conceptualising historical events. Such a parallel between photography and the process of historical understanding has been developed further by the critical theorist Eduardo Cadava in his rethinking of Walter Benjamin's 'Theses on the Philosophy of History' through the medium of photography: 'Like the camera that seeks to fix a moment of history, thought wishes to bring history within the grasp of a concept' (Cadava 1997: xviii). In *The Ground Beneath her Feet*, it is Rai's photograph of Vina (entitled *The Lady Vanishes*), taken moments before her death in a Mexican earthquake, which renders the event of the earthquake meaningful as a historical event (466). Indeed, Rai compares this image of Vina to 'that small stock of photographic images – Monroe's flying skirt, the burning girl in Indochina, Earthrise – which actually become experiences, part of the collective memory of the human race' (467).

Rai's photograph of Vina moments before her death in an earthquake also becomes a symbol of disaster or catastrophe. Throughout the novel, Rushdie suggests a parallel between the earthquake and global crisis. During Ormus's visitation by the spectral figure of Maria, for example, Maria argues that 'Earthquakes … are the means by which the earth punishes itself and its population for its wrongnesses' and that 'Human faults cause earthquakes too' (327). In a similar vein, Rai suggests that earthquakes are part of a 'military-industrial megaconspiracy' that protects America's financial interests in the Middle East and pulls the rug out from under the feet of its enemies (501–502). As a sign of global crisis, in other words, Rushdie suggests that earthquakes reveal the fault lines in the world economic system. Rai's suggestion that earthquakes are political signs also recalls the use of phenomena from the natural world to explain the rise of revolutionary nationalism in colonial India. In the June 1908 edition of the London-based newspaper of Indian nationalism *The Indian Sociologist*, for instance, Shyamaji Krishnavarma described how one of the newspaper's correspondents justified the 'explosive assassinations' of leading British officials in colonial India by arguing that they were the natural results of tyrannical pressure in the same way that earthquakes or the eruptions of volcanoes are 'the natural results of pressure applied to underground forces' (*Indian Sociologist* June 1908: 23).

In *The Ground Beneath Her Feet* the narrator's reference to the response of philosophers and writers to the Lisbon earthquake in 1755 also situates Rushdie's writing on catastrophe and shock to a tradition of aesthetic representations of disaster, a tradition that is linked to the idea of the sublime as an encounter with human finitude or death. As Gene Ray observes of the German philosopher Immanuel Kant's *Critique of Judgement*, published over 30 years after the Lisbon earthquake,

> we can feel the memory of Lisbon in Kant's metaphor and word choice: the sublime moves the mind like the tremors or deep shudders of an earthquake. Amidst all the vibrating, gushing and shaking, this natural object that defeats the imagination opens up like an abyss; registration of threat, reason to the rescue. (Ray 2005: 29)

In Rai's account of the 1755 Lisbon earthquake, however, the response of philosophers such as Kant and Voltaire – who saw 'that catastrophe … as an irrefutable argument for the tragic view of life and against Leibnizian optimism' (457) – is subordinated to an account of how the locals executed the 'celebrated philosopher Pangloss' and his associate 'Herr Candide of Thunder-ten-tronckh' (457). What lies behind this representation of the Lisbon locals' response to the 1755 earthquake is both a critique of human sacrifice and its religious justification. For Rai – like Rushdie in some of his interviews on *The Satanic Verses* – argues that when 'we stop believing in the gods we can start believing in their stories' (458).

Embedded in this sentence is a clue to reading Rushdie's use of the Orpheus/Eurydice myth in *The Ground Beneath her Feet*. For just as Rai offers a secular criticism of the Lisbon locals' response to the 1755 earthquake, so Rushdie uses the story of Orpheus and

Eurydice in Virgil's *Georgics* to question the onto-theological claims made in this classical poem. Virgil's story of Orpheus and Eurydice may appear to provide an archetype for the secular romantic tragedy of Ormus and Vina in *The Ground Beneath her Feet*, because Vina – like Eurydice – is transported to the underworld by an earthquake (rather than a Roman god) and Ormus – like Orpheus – is left to endure the pain of mourning the loss of his beloved.

Yet this is to ignore the way in which Rushdie uses the Virgilian archetype of Orpheus and Eurydice to construct a myth of Vina and Ormus as quasi-theological rock 'n' roll celebrities. Such myth making is reinforced by Rai's photograph of Vina at the precise moment of her disappearance from the world of the living. Indeed, this photograph could be interpreted both as an example of what the literary critic Roland Barthes has called 'shock photography' and as an example of the celebrity photojournalism associated with the paparazzi. In Barthes' analysis, many of

> the photographs exhibited to shock us have no effect at all, precisely because the photographer has too generously substituted himself for us in the formation of his subject: he has almost always *overconstructed* the horror he is proposing, adding to the *fact*, by contrasts or parallels, the intentional *language* of horror. (Barthes 1997: 71)

In consequence, the photograph 'introduces us to the scandal of horror, not to horror itself' (Barthes 73). Rai's photograph 'The Lady Vanishes' is precisely an example of the way in which horror – in the form of an encounter with death – is mediated through the photographer's lens. Such mediation is an example of what Rushdie, in an essay on the death of Princess Diana, has described as 'the lethal voyeurism' of contemporary celebrity culture. By documenting Vina at the moment of her passage to the underworld, in other words, Rai's photograph visually enacts the relationship between death and celebrity culture. As the cultural critic Elizabeth Bronfen explains:

> Rushdie allows this narrator, a news photographer ... to reflect upon how he, when faced with situations of catastrophe like the earthquake he and Vina find themselves in, passes into the trance so typical of the paparazzi. The scene in which he describes how he is caught in the pas-

sion of photographing rather than feeling compassion for the victims of the disaster, explicitly invokes the case of Diana. For he compares himself to photographers for whom the medical team trying to reach a dying woman were nothing other than an obstacle to their work. (Bronfen 2002: 182)

Bronfen's reading of Rushdie's articulation of death and celebrity culture is certainly compelling in its ethical criticism of the contemporary media's obsession with the image of the celebrity.

Yet such a reading also elides the political fault lines of the contemporary globe into which Vina Apsarda disappears. In the first chapter of *The Ground Beneath Her Feet*, for instance, Rai makes a passing reference to 'the unclaimed newspapers, whose headlines about French nuclear tests in the Pacific and political unrest in the southern province of Chiapas smudged the bare soles of Vina's feet with their shrieking ink' (4) just before her death. This marginal reference to the Zapatistas' uprising against the Mexican government in the Southern Mexican state of Chiapas – an uprising that provided many global justice movements in Europe and North America in the late 1990s and early twenty-first century with a source of inspiration – is literally erased in this passage by the body of a rock 'n' roll celebrity. In staging the erasure of this 'political unrest', Rushdie may appear to draw attention to the political unconscious of the contemporary celebrity culture, of which Vina is a part. Yet this passage could also be read as an allusion to the means by which the Zapatistas successfully marketed their demands for ' "work, land, housing, food, health care, education, independence, liberty, democracy, justice, and peace" ' (Bob 2005: 118) to the rest of the world. As Clifford Bob explains:

> [T]he Zapatistas received moral, tactical, and material support from diverse sources around the world. They attracted transnational NGOs in the indigenous rights, human rights, social justice, and peace sectors. They became heroes of leftist intellectuals, academics and activists, spurring many to visit Chiapas to aid the rebels. They galvanized one of the world's first Internet solidarity networks, including numerous listservs and Web sites carrying Zapatista communiqués. And their masked spokesman, Subcomandante Marcos, won celebrity, inspiring many in the emerging antiglobalisation or global justice movement that made itself known later in the 1990s in Seattle, Genoa, and elsewhere. (Bob 118)

In Clifford Bob's analysis, it was the Zapatistas' ability to communicate their political demands to an international civil society using a public relations strategy that targeted mainstream left-wing newspapers in Mexico and abroad that made their political campaign so successful. Such an analysis is illuminating in what it tells us about the relationship between political movements and the global media in the late twentieth and early twenty-first centuries, a relationship that also informs Rushdie's representation of globalisation in *The Ground Beneath Her Feet*. Rather than offering a straightforward political counterpoint to the superficial media representation of Vina as a celebrity, Rushdie's marginal reference to the news of the Zapatistas' political uprising in the Southern Mexican state of Chiapas in the Mexican newspaper headlines draws attention to the role of the media in communicating the message of political struggle internationally. By imprinting the 'shrieking' Mexican newspaper headlines on the feet of his celebrity–protagonist, Rushdie may appear to efface rather than amplify its political message. Yet, in so doing, Rushdie also gestures towards a global political disaffection with American foreign policy and neoliberal globalisation, a disaffection that is cryptically registered in the seismic metaphors that structure the novel.

7

FURY AND *SHALIMAR THE CLOWN*

The sentiment expressed by the third-person narrator of Salman Rushdie's eighth novel *Fury* (2001) that anti-Americanism reinforces the authority of America's global hegemony at the end of the twentieth century may suggest a withdrawal from the political in Rushdie's later fiction. As the narrator puts it, 'Even anti-Americanism was Americanism in disguise, conceding, as it did, that America was the only game in town and the matter of America the only business at hand' (Rushdie 2001: 87). If *The Satanic Verses* and many of Rushdie's essays of the 1980s offered a critique of Margaret Thatcher's Conservative government and the racism of the British state towards Britain's migrant population, his recent fiction and essays seem to suggest a resignation to, and even at times a tacit approval for, America's unilateralist foreign policy in the early twenty-first century, and in particular the Bush administration's war on terrorism.

ANTI-AMERICANISM IN *FURY*

Many commentators have noted how anti-Americanism is as old as the foundation of the US republic and its constitution (see Ross and Ross 2004: 1; Rubin and Rubin 2004: 21–43). In a historical study of anti-Americanism, Barry Rubin and Judith Culp Rubin argue that 'most members of Europe's governing and intellectual elite' (Rubin and Rubin 2004: 5) regarded America's democratic experiment as a threat to the social hierarchies of Europe, and the ruling monarchies on which many European nation states were based. In the early nineteenth-century, many European

117

anti-Americans 'concluded that the United States was to be ridiculed, not feared. Its ludicrous political system was a clear failure and might well collapse of its own weight' (Rubin and Rubin 42–43). With the subsequent emergence of America as a major industrial economy at the end of the nineteenth century, however, the European discourse of anti-Americanism shifted from the prediction of its political failure to a belief that 'its modernization was innately inimical to culture' (Rubin and Rubin: 59). Moreover, the success of America as a major industrial power in the world economy at the end of the nineteenth century prompted many left-wing critics of America, such as the leader of the Soviet Union, Vladimir Lenin, to declare that 'the United States embodied "the most rabid imperialism" ', and that 'U.S. participation in the [First World] war was only due to 'the interests of the New York Stock Exchange' (cited in Rubin and Rubin: 80).

The Soviet Union's main argument against America that it 'was seeking global political and cultural domination' (Rubin and Rubin: 90) is significant not only for what it reveals about the politics of Soviet anti-Americanism during the Cold War but also because it prefigures the criticism of the US adoption of a unilateral imperialist project after the attacks on America of September 11 2001. As this chapter contends, Salman Rushdie's liberal defence of America's democratic values and its foreign policy at the beginning of the twenty-first century is linked to the current phase of anti-Americanism, in which 'U.S. domination, both as a great power and as a terrible model for civilization (as the centrepiece of globalisation, modernization and Westernization) is taken to be an established fact' (Rubin and Rubin x). In this respect, the current phase of anti-Americanism would seem to confirm Lenin's fears of America's imperialist ambitions almost a century ago. For the war on terrorism, as the social geographer Neil Smith argues, is not a ' "war on terrorism" so much as a war to finish off a larger and longer term project' of US imperialism which can be traced back to the foreign policies of Woodrow Wilson and Franklin D. Roosevelt (Smith 2005: viii).

In the case of the US-led war that began in Afghanistan after 7 October 2001, Smith argues that this 'represents not a war on terrorism in any meaningful sense but a war for a US-centred globalism representing the apex of the third moment of US global ambition' (Smith 2003: 264). If the first moment of US imperialism was exemplified by Woodrow Wilson's Monroe doctrine, which sought to assert American control over the world's economy through diplomacy rather than direct territorial rule; and the second moment of US global ambition was characterised by Franklin D. Roosevelt's recognition that it was 'economic control of markets, labor and resources that motivated US interests' rather than 'political control of territory' (Smith 2003: 255); the third moment of US global ambition refers to the struggle for sovereignty over the economy and natural resources of the Middle East.

Such a view of the so-called war on terrorism is echoed in Neil Lazarus's recent observation that the Iraq war revealed 'the unmistakable and unmistakably brutal face of US globalism: the power of the American state, now frankly projected and bent on world domination' (Lazarus 2006: 11). Against this bleak image of American economic and military dominance, Lazarus recalls the 'energy, dynamism and optimism of the decolonising and immediate post-independence era' (Lazarus: 13). Much of Salman Rushdie's fiction – from *Midnight's Children* to *Shalimar the Clown* – seems to write this post-independence era off as an idealistic illusion, which was shattered by the global economic crisis of the late 1960s and early 1970s, the Third World debt and the corruption of many Third World governments, including that of Indira Gandhi. Yet Rushdie's fiction is, nonetheless, informed by a historical consciousness of the end of European imperialism and the optimism of the post-independence era that Lazarus invokes. Moreover, it is this historical consciousness of the end of European imperialism which partly informs Rushdie's reflections on contemporary American foreign policy, even when he seems to defend it.

The predominant idea that America's neoliberal democracy provides an economic and political model for the rest of the work, and has sought to assert global hegemony over the world's economic and natural resources in the aftermath of the collapse of the communist bloc partly underpins Rushdie's account of anti-Americanism in *Fury* and his recent editorials. Yet, in contrast to critics of the current phase of US imperialism, Rushdie seems to defend contemporary American foreign policy in the Middle East. In an article that was first published in *The New York Times* on February 4 2002, and reprinted in his collection of non-fiction, *Step Across this Line*, Rushdie seems to expand on the narrator's reflections on anti-Americanism in *Fury* quoted in the epigram to this chapter. In this article, entitled 'Anti-Americanism', Rushdie argues that the American military's campaign against the Taliban in Afghanistan, following the attacks on America of September 11 2001, was a success, but he adds that this campaign has reinforced feelings of anti-Americanism elsewhere in the world. As Rushdie puts it:

> America did, in Afghanistan, what had to be done, and did it well. The bad news, however, is that these successes have not won new friends for the United States outside Afghanistan. In fact, the effectiveness of the American campaign may have made some parts of the world hate America more than they did before. Critics of the Afghan campaign in the West are enraged because they have been shown to be wrong at every step: no, American forces weren't humiliated the way the Russians had been; and yes, the air strikes did work; and no, the Northern Alliance didn't massacre people in Kabul; and yes, the Taliban did crumble away like the hated tyrants that they were, even in their Southern strongholds; and no, it wasn't that difficult to get the militants out of their cave fortresses; and yes, the various factions suc-ceeded in putting together a new government that is surprising people by functioning pretty well. (Rushdie 2002: 399)

For Rushdie, however, these feelings of anti-Americanism are either a 'smokescreen for Muslim nations' many defects', or in the case of Western anti-Americanism, a 'personalized' attack on the 'American citizenry' for 'American patriotism, obesity, emotionality, [and] self-centredness' (Rushdie 2002: 399–400). While acknowl-edging that America is perceived as a global superpower by the rest of the world, Rushdie also tacitly supports the secular, demo-cratic values of American society as against what he regards as the non-secular, extremist values associated with so-called Islamic fundamentalism.

Many of Rushdie's articles on the Bush administration's war on terrorism and so-called Islamic fundamentalism in *The New York Times* and *Washington Post* were published after *Fury*'s publication in August 2001, and the early-twenty-first century context of Manhattan in which most of the novel is set. By invoking the col-lapse of the Nasdaq in April 2000 (3); the murder of Amadou Diallo by four New York Police officers in February 1999 (6); and the run up to the US presidential elections in November 2000, Rushdie clearly situates the novel in New York at the turn of the last century. For this reason, it may seem anachronistic to read *Fury* in relation to Rushdie's post-9/11 editorials. Yet, to the extent that Rushdie's novel is preoccupied with the global perception of America's liberal democratic rhetoric, consumer culture and foreign policy, the novel seems to anticipate Rushdie's ambivalent sentiments towards America expressed in some of his post-9/11 editorials.

For Rushdie's protagonist, Professor Malik Solanka, the visual opulence of Manhattan's street merchandise exemplified how 'America insulted the rest of the world ... by treating such bounty with the shoulder-shrugging casualness of the inequitably wealthy' (6). Yet, as the narrator proceeds to explain, such an insult masks the fact that 'New York in this time of plenty had become the object and goal of the world's concupiscence and lust, and the "insult" only made the rest of the world more desirous than ever' (6). Nevertheless, it is clear from a subsequent conversation with Solanka's friend Jack Rhinehart that it is US foreign policy that provokes Solanka's rage. As Rhinehart explains, 'you can't not know how hard your friends try to avoid certain subjects in your company. U.S. policy in Central America, for example. U.S. policy in Southeast Asia. Actually, the U.S.A. in general has been pretty much an off-limits topic for years' (68).

Solanka's anger against US foreign policy in the aftermath of the Cold War and the collapse of the communist bloc is also a sign that the United States operates as a dominant imperial power in the late twentieth century. Such a view is reinforced by the 'cartographic imperatives of the neo-conservative "Project for the New American Century" ', a project led by many key figures in the Bush administration, such as Richard Cheney, Donald Rumsfeld, Paul Wolfowitz and John Bolton, and which sought to expand US military presence in order to 'secure American global hegemony' (Gregory 2004: 51). This imperialist project was aided and abetted by the attacks on America of September 11 2001, which provided George Bush's neoconservative administration with the moral and political justification it needed to implement its imperialist foreign policy in the Middle East. As the social geographer David Harvey explains, the Project for the New American Century recognized in a 1999 report that it would 'take a catastrophic and catalyzing event, like a new Pearl Harbour' to make a military strike [on Iraq] acceptable internationally and domestically. 9/11 provided the opportunity, if only they could make a connection between Saddam and al Quaeda (Harvey 2003: 15).

In *Fury*, however, what Rushdie's character Jack Rhinehart identifies in his conversation with Solanka is an apparent contradiction between Solanka's anger about contemporary US foreign policy and his desire to migrate to America. Such a contradiction between an opposition to the global expansion of US military control and economic sovereignty on the one hand and a desire to find social justice under American capitalism on the other is precisely the double bind facing many new immigrants from different class backgrounds in the contemporary United States. As the anthropologist Arjun Appadurai explains:

> For the 'wretched' of the world who come to make their lives in the United States, a curious split has emerged. As Americans, they have a powerful sense of their rights and freedoms, which they seek and enjoy to the fullest extent possible. As non-Americans, they retain the sense of revulsion, alienation, and distance that they have always had. (Appadurai 2006: 122)

Appadurai goes on to distinguish between those immigrants of 'modest means and lower class backgrounds … who have chosen to enter the United States through the Statue of the Yellow Cab' (121) and those 'higher up the class ladder' who 'run companies, advise mayors and cabinets, run major journals and publishing houses, patent new bio and cyber technologies, and teach at most of the elite universities in the United States' (123). While this elite transnational migrant class pursue careers within the United States, they also share with 'the third-world cab driver' 'the right to be anti-American in matters of culture, politics, even lifestyle' (125). For Appadurai, the anti-Americanism of many South Asian and African migrants living in the United States is not a simple sign of hypocrisy but a simultaneous desire for a good life, and a 'deep moral resentment of American polity and the American government as global forces' (126).

It is precisely this double bind that Malik Solanka embodies in *Fury*. The narrator's account of Solanka as an Indian-born Oxford graduate and professor of philosophy clearly situate his social identity within the elite transnational migrant class Appadurai describes. Solanka seems to share a hatred of American foreign policy in the Middle East with an Urdu-speaking New York taxi driver from either India or Pakistan – who 'blamed all New York road users for the tribulations of the Middle East' – even though Solanka recoils in moral disgust from the vitriolic, anti-Semitic rhetoric in which the taxi driver's opposition is voiced:

> Islam will cleanse this street of godless motherfucker bad drivers,' the taxi driver screamed at a rival motorist. 'Islam will purify this whole city of Jew pimp assholes like you and your whore roadhog of a Jew wife too.' All the way up Tenth Avenue the curses continued. 'Infidel fucker of your underage sister, the inferno of Allah awaits you and your unholy wreck of a motorcar as well.' 'Unclean offspring of a shit-eating pig, try that again and the victorious jihad will crush your balls in its unforgiving fist.' Malik Solanka, listening in to the explosive, village-accented Urdu, was briefly distracted from his own inner turmoil by the driver's venom. (65)

While the references to Islam and Allah in this verbal outburst suggest that the taxi driver is a devout Muslim and an anti-Semite, the narrator proceeds to explain that the taxi driver behaved this way because it was 'the boy's first day at work in the mean streets and he was scared witless' (66). Furthermore, the narrator attempts to contextualise the taxi driver's anti-Semitic diatribe by relating it to President Bill Clinton's attempt to rescue the Oslo Agreement between Israel and the Palestinian territories at Camp David in 2000: 'as the Middle East process staggered onward and the outgoing American president, hungry for a breakthrough to buff up his tarnished legacy, was urging Barak and Arafat to a Camp David Summit conference, Tenth Avenue was being blamed for the sufferings of Palestine' (66). The sincerity of the taxi driver's outburst would appear to be undermined by his final disclaimer 'Me, I don't even go to the mosque. God bless America, okay? It's just words' (66). Yet the driver's vitriolic speech also points to what Arjun Appadurai terms the 'the right [of immigrants] to be anti-American in matters of culture, politics, even lifestyle' (125).

Malik Solanka's migration to the United States also seems to resemble the middle-class aspirations of the transnational elite migrant class described by Appadurai. For Solanka, as the third-person narrator explains, 'had come to America as so many before him to receive the benison of being Ellis Islanded, of starting over' (51). The quasi-religious noun 'benison', meaning a blessing given by God (*OED*), and the verb form 'to be Ellis Islanded' in this sentence registers an unmistakable undertone of irony in its account of American citizenship. Such an ironic undertone is made more explicit in the narrator's subsequent parody of Emma Lazarus's 1883 poem 'The New Colossus', the poem devoted to the erection of the Statue of Liberty on Bedloe's Island off the Southern tip of Manhattan in 1886:

> Give me a name, America, make of me a Buzz or Chip or Spike. Bathe me in amnesia and clothe me in your powerful unknowing. Enlist me in your J. Crew and hand me my mouse-ears! No longer a historian but a man without histories let me be. I'll rip my lying mother tongue out of my throat and speak your broken English instead. Scan me, digitize me, beam me up. (51)

In contrast to Emma Lazarus's suggestion in her 1883 poem that the Statue of Liberty stands as symbol of America's democratic promise to recognise the rights and freedoms of poor, working class immigrants from Ireland, Germany, Eastern Europe, Russia and Asia – or the 'huddled masses yearning to breathe free' – Rushdie's narrator in this passage compares the process of becoming American to that of an amnesiac, who is subjected to the state's digital surveillance of its migrant population: 'No longer a historian but a man without histories let me be' (51).

Solanka's desire for forgetfulness is not, however, motivated by the experiences of political oppression or impoverished economic circumstances that Emma Lazarus associated with immigration in her 1883 poem. His desire to leave Britain for the US is motivated instead by a manifest fear of his pathological fury, a fury which almost led to him murdering his wife and child with a kitchen knife in their London home. Such fury might suggest that the novel is more of a psychological thriller than a political critique of recent American foreign policy. Yet, as suggested below, Solanka's fury is ultimately subordinated to the collective fury of the Filbistani Resistance Movement.

The fury to which the title of the novel refers evokes a history of anger as a significant moral and political as well as psychological emotion. Indeed, for writers such as Aristotle and Thomas Hobbes, anger advances the 'redressing of perceived injustices through retaliation' (Ngai 2005: 27). In a similar vein, the literary historian Andrew M. Stauffer has argued in *Anger, Revolution and Reaction* (2005) that the unbounded rage of the public in revolutionary France at the end of the eighteenth century led to a democratisation of anger in the press, and a shift in attitude towards anger (Stauffer 2005: 1). English Romantic writers such as William Blake, Percy Shelley and Lord Byron regarded indignation as a 'moral stance detached from the emotion of anger as such, which is firmly identified as a loss of self control', and there was a similar tendency in 'legal discourse during the period whereby provocation law defines angry outbursts as transports of rage during which the rational self is abandoned' (Stauffer 2005: 4).

But after T.S. Eliot's famous declaration of a 'disassociation of a sensibility' in early-twentieth-century European modernist writing and Fredric Jameson's suggestion that postmodern culture is characterised by a 'waning of affect', it may be tempting to read Salman Rushdie's turn to fury in his eponymous novel as an early-twenty-first-century structure of feeling as a belated form of the affective fallacy, a fallacy which reinforces its protagonist's lack of agency. Such a reading is reinforced by the narrator's comparison of Solanka's fury to the existential questions evoked by Edward Munch's painting 'The Scream' (1893): 'In the tormented flames and anguished bullets, Malik Solanka heard a crucial, ignored, unanswered, perhaps-unanswerable question – the same question, loud and life-shattering as a Munch scream, that he had just asked himself: is this all there is? What, this is it? This is it?' (184)

Moreover, if, as Fredric Jameson has suggested, contemporary postmodern culture is characterised by a waning of the emotions that were powerfully evoked in early modernist paintings such as Munch's 'The Scream' (1893), why does Rushdie structure his eighth novel around a discourse of angry feelings or emotions? This seems particularly surprising when one considers that many of Rushdie's fictional protagonists have suggested that the foreclosure or repression of affect is an appropriate (if unethical) defence mechanism against the adverse psychological effects associated with political violence. In *Midnight's Children*, for instance, Saleem Sinai describes how, during his involvement in the war between East and West Pakistan, he suffers from amnesia and becomes 'anaesthetized against feelings as well as memories' (353). Similarly, in *The Moor's Last Sigh*, Moraes Zogoiby recounts how 'feeling itself was blown apart' (374) after the communal riots following the destruction of the Babri mosque. And in *Shame*, the monstrous other of Sufiya Zenobia, who engages in the beheadings of young men, is figured as the repressed rage of the people against the state.

In *Fury*, however, Professor Malik Solanka's rage has political, psychological and aesthetic dimensions: 'Fury – sexual, Oedipal, political, magical, brutal – drives us to our finest heights and coarsest depths. Out of *furia* comes creation, inspiration, passion but also violence, pain, pure unafraid destruction, the giving and receiving of blows from which we are never to recover' (Rushdie 2001: 30–31). By invoking the 'sexual' and 'Oedipal' connotations of fury in this passage, Rushdie's narrator suggests that Malik Solanka is in the grip of a childhood trauma of which he remains unconscious. Indeed, the narrator later suggests that Solanka's episodes of blind rage, in which he attempts to kill his wife and child, is a symptom of something that 'was bubbling inside him [which] defied all explanations' (128).

But Solanka's fury is also linked etymologically to the furies of ancient Greek tragedy, especially that of Aeschylus, in which violence had a political dimension. As Arno J. Mayer explains,

> in the time of Aeschylus' Greece, intense foreign and civil war, fear and disorder were entwined with an endless cycle of spiralling violence in defense of rupture and (re)foundation. The transmutation of the 'raging' female divinities Erinyes into the kindly Eumenides marked the termination of a difficult transition from a crescendo to a diminuendo of violence. This mutation was symbolized by the establishment of the Council of the Areopagus, which concluded the struggle between chaos and cosmos. (Mayer 1999: xvi–xvii)

Rushdie's allusion to the furies of Aeschylus is apposite here in the sense that the transmutation of the female divinities in Aeschylus' play parallels Solanka's sublimation and control of his own violent impulses after he falls in love with Neela Mahendra.

There is also a suggestion in *Fury* that Solanka's anger is partly triggered by a common theme associated with modernity: the experience of urban life. Earlier in the novel it appears that the acoustic signs and visual codes of contemporary New York compound Solanka's 'demons of the past'. In one passage, for example, the narrator conveys Solanka's psychological struggle between reason and passion:

> Sitting on the steps of the great museum, caught in a sudden burst of slanting, golden afternoon sunlight, scanning the *Times* while he waited for Neela, Professor Malik Solanka felt more than ever like a refugee in a small boat, caught between surging tides: reason and unreason, war and peace, the future and the past. ... And after the terror and the thirst and the sunburn there was the noise, the incessant adversarial buzz of voices on a taxi driver's radio, drowning his own inner voice, making thought impossible, or choice, or peace. How to defeat the demons of the past when the demons of the future were all around him in full cry? (145)

The narrator's comparison of Solanka to 'a refugee' in this passage is significant in that Solanka seems to have no clear sense of national belonging as an Indian migrant, who recently left England for the United States. Yet the analogy is of course limited by the fact that Solanka, unlike a refugee, is a member of an educated and cosmopolitan elite, who is able to scan *The Times* and write scripts for television.

If Rushdie's narrator in *Fury* seems to announce the futility of anti-American sentiments on the grounds that it only reinforces America's imperial hegemony in the early twenty-first century, Solanka's involvement in the liberation struggle of the fictional Southern-Pacific nation of Lilliput–Blefuscu raises questions about the Third World writer's political commitment in the era of contemporary US imperialism. Indeed, such a questioning is borne out by the narrator's comparison between Solanka's 'unpredictable temper', which is described as 'a thing of pathetic insignificance' and the 'group fury' of Neela Mahendra and the oppressed people of Lilliput–Blefuscu, which is 'born of long injustice' and is described as a 'higher, antipodean rage' (193).

Solanka's subsequent involvement in the counter-coup in Lilliput–Blefuscu is motivated by his desire for Neela Mahendra rather than a political commitment to the cause of the Filbistani Resistance Movement. As a former academic philosopher and doll maker, who created a popular history of philosophy for television in the 1970s entitled *The Adventures of Little Brain*, Malik Solanka becomes a significant player in the global culture industry of the late 1990s. His science fiction fairy tale of the Puppet Kings is launched as a spin-off merchandising initiative as well as a children's book by an Internet marketing company called webspyders with 'Major production, distribution and marketing agreements' with multi-national corporations such as 'Mattel, Amazon, Sony, Columbia [and] Banana Republic' (214). In this respect, Malik Solanka's literary empire seems to parallel Rushdie's own status as celebrity in the global literary marketplace.

The reproduction of the Puppet Kings as toys and characters in computer games might suggest that the value of Solanka's story – like the 'spin-off merchandising' associated with 'the *Star Wars* phenomenon' (224) – is defined by its market success as a cultural commodity. Such a reading is however complicated by the appropriation of the Puppet Kings' costumes by the Filbistani Resistance Movement as part of a counter-coup in Lilliput–Blefuscu: 'Filbistanis, FRM, Fremen … had taken on the identities of [Solanka's] fictions' (234). In 'a strange piece of mask theatre' (235), the meaning of Solanka's fictional puppets is altered by the Fiblistani resistance movement who identify with the plight of the Puppet Kings in Solanka's story, and adopt the costumes of his characters as part of their own political identity. In this

> Theatre of Masks, the original, the man with no mask, was perceived as the mask's imitator: the creation was real while the creator was the counterfeit! It was as though he were present at the death of God and the god who had died was himself. (239)

Many of *Fury's* reviewers attacked the novel on the grounds that it seems to be a thinly veiled and rather solipsistic autobiography concerned with Rushdie's own success as a celebrated author in the global literary marketplace (Kumar 2001). Yet such a reading overlooks the significance of the fictional 'Third World' coup and counter-coup that takes place in the latter part of the novel. For the critic Sarah Brouillette, the 'fictional account of a national liberation struggle' in *Fury* is 'largely based on the real political turmoil in Fiji in 1999 and 2000', and also refers *The Jaguar Smile* (1986), Rushdie's non-fictional travel narrative about Nicaragua after the Sandinista revolution (Brouillette 2005: 139).

The reference to the political turmoil in Fiji corresponds most explicitly with the story of Neela Mahendra, whose name bears an uncanny resemblance to that of the former Indo-Fijian Prime

Minister Mahendra Pal Chaudhry. As an Indo-Lilliputian, whose ancestors were disenfranchised indentured Indian labourers in Lilliput–Blefescu (238), Neela Mahendra also resembles the Indo-Fijians who fought for their social and political equality as part of a counter-coup against ethnic Fijians (Brouillette 2005: 141, 147). The reason for this ethnic coup in Fiji in 2000 was that ethnic Fijians perceived the left-wing coalition government, led by the first Indo-Fijian political leader Mahendra Pal Chaudhry, as a threat to the power and hegemony of ethnic Fijians (Brouillette: 137). This political antagonism between the Indo-Fijians and the ethnic Fijians is paralleled in the novel by the dominance of the Elbees, whose constitution denied the Indians the 'right to own real estate on either island' (158). Yet this ethnic struggle over land is complicated by the fact that whereas the indigenous Elbee culture is based on a principle of collective ownership, the 'Big-Endia Wallahs' are advocates of 'free-market mercantilism and profit mentality' (158). By characterising the Filbistani Resistance Movement as supporters of a free market ideology led by a nefarious dictator called Babur rather than a left wing struggle for the minority rights of Indo-Lilliputians, Rushdie could be seen to comment on the ways in which contemporary liberation struggles are increasingly shaped and influenced by America's global economic and military hegemony.

Yet, at the same time, the Filbistani Resistance Movement's identification with Solanka's story of the Puppet Kings and their appropriation of the Puppet Kings' costumes suggests that cultural texts are open to a more radical re-signification. Such a process of re-signification is implied but not explicitly stated in Rushdie's 1986 travel narrative *The Jaguar Smile*. At one point in his travel narrative, for example, Rushdie describes a visit with Daniel Ortega, the leader of the Sandinista movement, and observes how many of his children 'were wearing "Masters of the Universe" T-shirts', which featured 'the eternal battle of He-Man and Skeletor' (51). For Rushdie, the fact that Ortega's children are wearing T-shirts that depict characters from a popular American television cartoon series is 'another indication of the omnipresence of US culture' in Nicaragua.

Rushdie's anecdotal account of the Ortega children wearing ' "Masters of the Universe" T-shirts' may seem to parallel the Filbistani Resistance Movement's appropriation of the Puppet

Kings' costumes in *Fury*, in that both the ' "Masters of the Universe" T-shirts' and the Puppet Kings' costumes are cultural commodities produced in the United States, and are *ipso facto* signifiers of American cultural dominance. Yet Rushdie's suggestion that ' "Masters of the Universe" T-shirts' are a transparent sign of US cultural influence in Nicaragua seems to rule out the possibility that such signifiers of American popular culture can be given different meanings in different cultural and political contexts. As the anthropologist Arjun Appadurai has argued, 'the United States is no longer the puppeteer of a world system of images but is only one node of a complex transnational construction of imaginary landscapes' (Appadurai 1996: 31). Crucially for Appadurai, theories that equate globalisation with the global dominance of American commodity culture tend to ignore the ways in which American culture is indigenised in different cultural contexts (Appadurai 1996: 32). Following Appadurai, I would suggest that the Ortega children's wearing of the Masters of the Universe T-Shirts and the Filbistani Resistance Movement's appropriation of the Puppet Kings' masks can be read as instances of indigenisation, in which the symbolic codes of the Puppet Kings or the Masters of the Universe are linked to an indigenous struggle against American cultural and political dominance.

Such a reading is further borne out by the ultimate failure of the Indo-Lilliputian counter-coup at the end of the novel which attempts to promote the neoliberal ideology of the global market. This failure of the Indo-Lilliputians to successfully replace the existing collectivist government with a government that supports the free market is partly facilitated by Neela Mahendra. For not only is Neela Mahendra sympathetic to the political cause of the Elbee culture because 'they're collectivists' (158), but she also betrays the cause of the Filbistani Resistance Movement by organising 'the Fremen who were sick of Babur' (253). Significantly, this final twist in the political plot of *Fury* seems to anticipate Rushdie's controversial contribution to the public debate about the case for the war in Iraq that began in March 2003. In an article published in the *Washington Post* in November 2002, Rushdie makes what he calls 'the extremely strong anti-Saddam Hussein argument' by distinguishing between a 'war of liberation' from the brutal dictatorship of Saddam Hussein and the Bush administration's argument for regime change based on a 'comprehensively unproven' connection between

Saddam Hussein and al Quaeda. Rushdie is clearly mindful of the various challenges facing the American military campaign in Iraq, since he mentions the parallels with America's military campaign in Vietnam, the 'internal divisions and separatist tendencies' within Iraq, and the risk of establishing an 'American puppet' government in Iraq. Furthermore, in his argument for a 'war of liberation' that is linked to 'Iraqi opposition groups in exile', Rushdie invokes a spirit of resistance that may seem to recall what Neil Lazarus calls the 'energy, dynamism and optimism of the decolonising and immediate post-independence era' (Lazarus: 13). Yet, in making what Rushdie describes as a liberal argument for the war in Iraq, it is difficult to see how Rushdie can ultimately avoid supporting the Bush administration's decision to go to war in Iraq. Indeed, it is precisely this liberal dilemma facing the contemporary Third World writer who seeks to condemn political repression in the Third World while remaining resolutely non-aligned with the First World in an age of post-communist American imperialism that the narrator articulates in *Fury*.

DIASPORAS OF TERROR IN SALMAN RUSHDIE'S *SHALIMAR THE CLOWN*

If *Fury* highlights the global expansion of American economic and political power from the cosmopolitan standpoint of a South Asian New Yorker, Salman Rushdie's ninth novel *Shalimar the Clown* (2005) embeds a story about the militarisation of Kashmir in a broader narrative of neoliberal globalisation and US foreign policy in South Asia from the Bretton Woods Agreement to the US-led war in Afghanistan following the attacks on America of September 11 2001. In so doing, Rushdie attempts to find a literary form appropriate to describe the transnational social and political relations that underpin globalisation. As the narrator puts it, 'Everywhere was a part of everywhere else. Russia, America, London, Kashmir. Our lives, our stories, flowed into one another's, were no longer our own, individual, discrete. This unsettled people' (Rushdie 2005: 37).

It is significant also that *Shalimar the Clown* appeared three weeks after Rushdie, in an article published in *The Washington Post* on August 7 2005, called for a reformation of Islam in the aftermath of the London bombings of July 7 2005. Rushdie opens this article (entitled 'The Right Time for An Islamic Reformation') with a discussion of the significance of Sir Iqbal Sacranie's public acknowledgement that members of the British Muslim community were responsible for the London bombings, and questions the Blair government's treatment of Sacranie as the 'acceptable face of "moderate", "traditional" Islam' (Rushdie 2005: B07). One of the reasons why Rushdie questions Blair's support for Sacranie and the Muslim Council of Britain is that Sacranie was among some of the British Muslims who called for the proscription of Rushdie novel *The Satanic Verses* in 1989. For Sacranie, as Rushdie goes on to explain, had said in 1989 that ' "Death is perhaps too easy" ' for the author of *The Satanic Verses*. Against the Blair government's attempt to eradicate Islamic extremism by working closely with the Muslim Council of Britain, Rushdie calls for a reformation of Islam, which would allow Muslims to 'study the revelation of their religion as an event inside history, not supernaturally above it' (Rushdie 2005: B07). Such an argument clearly reiterates Rushdie's repeated defence of *The Satanic Verses* as a fictional representation of Islamic history, which aimed to encourage critical discussion and debate about the meaning of revelation in the Islamic faith.

Like his 'liberal argument' in favour of the war in Iraq, Rushdie's call for the reformation of Islam may appear – however unwittingly – to correspond with those contemporary discourses of counter-terrorism, which have clearly articulated the war against terrorism and the struggle for global security to the control of immigration, as well as the criminalisation of Islam. As A. Sivanandan has argued in 'Race, terror and civil society', 'the war on asylum and the war on terror … have converged to produce a racism which cannot tell a settler from an immigrant, an immigrant from an asylum speaker, an asylum speaker from a Muslim, a Muslim from a terrorist' (Sivanandan 2005: 2). In the context of this conflation of counter-terrorism and the state regulation of migrant populations, what is at stake in Salman Rushdie's call for a reformation of Islam in response to the July 7 bombings? As a middle-class migrant writer, who is often associated with a Western liberal ideology, and a secular Muslim, who was also the victim of the death sentence issued by Ayatollah Khomeini in 1989, Rushdie occupies an ambivalent position in relation to the convergence of the war on asylum and the war on terror described by Sivanandan. But how is this ambivalence registered in Rushdie's *Shalimar the Clown*, a novel that was published at the same time as Rushdie's call for a reformation of Islam? This section seeks to address this question by examining how Rushdie explodes the conventions of national allegory that he established in *Midnight's Children* and *Shame* to represent the conflict in Kashmir, and its place in contemporary geopolitics.

'How does newness come into the world?' asks the narrator in *The Satanic Verses* as Saladin Chamcha and Gibreel Farishta fall from the wreckage of Air India flight 420 above the English Channel. For postcolonial theorists such as Homi K. Bhabha, this question is concerned with the experience of postcolonial migration from South Asia to Britain during the 1980s, and with the acts of cultural translation that such an experience engenders. The demonisation and brutalisation of Saladin Chamcha by British immigration officers as an illegal South Asian immigrant shortly after his fantastic survival of a terrorist attack might suggest that this episode in *The Satanic Verses* prefigured the relationship between terrorism and migration described by Sivanandan. Yet *The Satanic Verses* tends to be read as an exemplary narrative of cultural hybridity, in which Saladin Chamcha's negotiation of English and South Asian cultural practices are contrasted with the cultural purity of Gibreel Farishta, who is plagued by visions of the life of the Prophet, and of being a messenger of Allah. Such readings tend also to romanticise and mythologise transnational migration in such a way that elides the precarious lives of many immigrants. As Amitava Kumar has suggested, Chamcha and Farishta's miraculous survival of a terrorist attack belies the grim fate of migrants who, in their desperation to earn a living, are willing to risk their lives by travelling as stowaways in the undercarriage of an aeroplane (Kumar 2002: 232–234).

Yet if the experience of migration in *The Satanic Verses* is synonymous with the valorisation of difference, hybridity, cultural translation and border crossing (as Homi K. Bhabha has suggested), *Shalimar the Clown* (2005) shifts the focus away from the transformative potential of migration in the West to a focus on the way in which political events in Kashmir during the latter half of the twentieth century have impacted on the lives and transnational mobility of people. By doing so, Rushdie situates the experience of South Asian migration and diaspora in relation to the partition of

Kashmir, the rise of so-called Islamic fundamentalism in neighbouring Pakistan and Afghanistan, and US foreign policy in South Asia from the Johnson administration to the Bush administration. Moreover, by foregrounding the history of Kashmir from India's partition to the war on terror from the standpoint of the Kashmiri people, Rushdie encourages readers to consider what Judith Butler calls the 'precarious life of the Other' (Butler 2004: xviii). Writing in the context of the US-led war on terror, Butler invokes Emmanuel Levinas' idea of the face of the other in order to present an ethical argument against the various aspects of the war on terror, including the wars in Afghanistan and Iraq, the indefinite detention of enemy combatants in Guantánamo Bay, and the US support for the militarised expansion of Israeli settlements into the Palestinian territories. By applying Butler's concept of precarious life to Rushdie's representation of Kashmir in *Shalimar the Clown*, this part of the chapter assesses the extent to which *Shalimar the Clown* offers an ethical challenge to US foreign policy in South Asia from the Cold War to the war on terror.

Rushdie's concern with the partition of Kashmir was clearly evident in the first section of *Midnight's Children*. As Patrick Colm Hogan argues, the character of Aadam Aziz in *Midnight's Children* represents the 'beginning of modernity in Kashmir' (Colm Hogan 2001: 531). For Hogan, Aadam Aziz's exile from Kashmir in 1915 is significant because it marks the year when a second major road was built linking Srinagar with Jammu, as well as the period during which telephone lines were introduced to the region. In a similar vein, Ananya Kabir observes how Rushdie's pre-lapsarian representation of Kashmir in book one of *Midnight's Children* is marked by 'the politics-ridden present' of a divided and militarised Kashmir (Kabir 2002: 252). More recently, Rushdie's concern with Kashmir was reflected in an article he wrote for the *Washington Post* on August 28 2002. In this article, Rushdie criticises the Bush administration's foreign policy in South Asia for ignoring the Kashmir crisis. As Rushdie puts it, 'In the heat of the dispute over Iraq strategy, South Asia has become a side show' and 'Pakistani-backed terrorism in Kashmir will be winked at because of Pakistan's support for the "war against terror" on its frontier'. It is against this political context of the sidelining of the crisis in Kashmir by the Bush administration that Rushdie makes the 'politics-ridden present' of Kashmir the central focus of his novel *Shalimar the Clown*.

The conflict over Kashmir can be traced back to the partition of India in 1947. After the British left India in August 1947, Kashmir initially remained a Princely State under the autocratic rule of the Maharaja, a Hindu prince. However, during Lord Mountbatten's involvement in the negotiation of India's independence as the viceroy of India, he urged many of the leaders of the Princely States to 'opt either for Pakistan or India' (Bennett-Jones 2002: 58). Furthermore, Mountbatten's interference in the recommendations of the Boundary Commission, the committee appointed to divide India after independence, made both India and Pakistan suspicious of Britain's neutrality in the partition of South Asia, especially where Kashmir was concerned. Following the invasion of Kashmir by tribesman from Pakistan in October 1947, the Maharaja acceded Kashmir to India in exchange for military support from India against the Pakistani tribesmen.

The partition of India and the escalation of violence from the deployment of Indian troops in the Kashmir valley in October 1947 to Pakistan's cooperation with the Bush administration during the 2001 war in Afghanistan form part of the historical backdrop to *Shalimar the Clown*. This historical and geopolitical backdrop is significant because it marks a failure in US foreign policy to either comprehend or influence the ongoing conflict in Kashmir. This 'failure of the United States to translate its power into influence in the subcontinent' was partly a consequence of a tendency within successive US administrations to approach the 'interests, priorities and needs' of Third World nations 'with a Cold War yardstick that distorted far more than it illuminated' (McMahon 1994: 345). Such a tendency was particularly evident in the Truman administration's embracing of Pakistan as a strategic ally against the Soviet Union in the Middle East rather than South Asia during the early 1950s (McMahon 153). In response to this US alliance with Pakistan, the Indian Prime Minister Nehru expressed a genuine fear 'that an influx of American armaments might embolden Pakistani leaders to seek a military solution in Kashmir' (McMahon: 150). By setting his novel in twentieth-century Kashmir, Rushdie thus draws attention to the competing narratives of Cold War geopolitics, Western imperialism and religious fundamentalism that circumscribe the region.

Shalimar the Clown also complicates the postcolonial metaphors of migrancy Rushdie established in *The Satanic Verses* by drawing a parallel between the migrant narratives of Max Ophuls, a holocaust survivor who becomes a US ambassador to India, and that of his Kashmiri assassin, Shalimar. The novel itself is structured into three sections, which correspond with the names of the three protagonists: Max, Shalimar the Clown and Kashmira. Max Ophuls, a fictional US ambassador to India, has an affair with the Kashmiri dancer Boonyi Noman, and subsequently deserts her after she conceives a child with him. Ophuls is a Strasbourg-born Jewish graduate in law and international relations, who worked for the French resistance during the Second World War, after the Nazis captured his parents in Strasbourg. Ophuls' escape from the Nazis is figured as a heroic act of resistance to genocide and anti-Semitism in the novel. Yet this experience of the holocaust and resistance to Nazi oppression is subsequently contrasted with Ophuls' employment as a leading figure in the formulation of post-war United States economic and foreign policy. Ophuls is also instrumental in the development of the Bretton Woods' Agreement; an agreement, which the narrator says will 'shape the postwar recovery of Europe and address the problems of unstable exchange rates and protectionist trade policies' (173). Further, Ophuls is employed by US President Lyndon Johnson to visit Kashmir as the US ambassador to India.

In some respects, Ophuls would appear to resemble his real life successor, the former American ambassador to India, Chester Bowles. Bowles was inspired by Woodrow Wilson's liberal capitalist vision of an international order inscribed in Wilson's 14 points, and 'believed that the United States had a global responsibility to protect all nations' quests for freedom from domination, political and economic' (Dauer 2005: 7). During his first period in office as American ambassador to India from 1951–1953 (under President Truman's administration), Bowles campaigned for a US economic aid programme to India in the broader context of Truman's Cold War foreign policy, and argued that if India did not 'make reasonable economic progress in alleviating its poverty' this would 'encourage communist propaganda and the growth of the Communist Party of India' (Dauer 50).

Bowles was also conscious of the historical conditions which had led to the conflict between India and Pakistan over Kashmir, and had insistently argued for 'the partition of Kashmir as a means of bringing about a settlement' (Schaffer 1993: 102). In his

1954 *Ambassador's Report*, Bowles describes a visit to Kashmir in 1952 during the ceasefire between India and Pakistan, in which 'the UN effort to achieve a Kashmir settlement inevitably took on the character of an American operation' (Bowles 1954: 254). He proceeded to describe how Cold War American foreign policy had failed to 'recognize fully the explosive nature ... of the India-Pakistan dissension' and cautioned against the US becoming 'partisans' of either India or Pakistan (Bowles 254–255). Bowles continued to argue for a 'final settlement' in 'the form of an autonomous or semi-autonomous Vale of Kashmir, with the rest of the state partitioned between the two rivals' during his second appointment as US ambassador to India (Schaffer: 257), and added that the US should play a less central role as a mediator in the conflict and should 'do what it could to persuade India and Pakistan to develop a moderate dialogue' (Schaffer: 256).

Like Chester Bowles, Max Ophuls is a liberal intellectual who had 'published a theoretical model of how Third World economies might flourish by learning to bypass the U.S. dollar' (178). As a liberal internationalist, Ophuls believes in the 'utopian fallacy' that

> the global structures he had helped to build, the pathways of influence, money and power, the multinational associations, the treaty organizations, the frameworks of cooperation and law whose purpose had been to deal with a hot world turned cold, would still function in the future that lay beyond what he could foresee. (20)

In Ophuls' utopian vision, 'the emerging economies of India, Brazil, and a newly-opened up China' would provide 'counterweights to the American hegemony of which he had always as an internationalist disapproved' (20).

Against Lyndon Johnson's reluctance to 'favour India' over Pakistan, Max is advised by his Washington contacts, who include the national security adviser, McGeorge Bundy, and Chester Bowles to 'discuss urgently, "on the front burner", what India wanted most: to purchase American supersonic fighter jets in significant numbers and on advantageous terms' (180). This fictionalised presentation of US foreign policy seems to correspond with the recommendations to offer India sustained military assistance that two former US ambassadors to India – John Kenneth Galbraith and Chester Bowles – made to President Kennedy. Yet, rather than campaigning for military aid, Rushdie's fictional ambassador Ophuls devises a plan for India and Pakistan to work on multilateral projects, including a fuel exchange programme, as well as hydroelectric and irrigation projects (188) to counter the escalation of military conflict over Kashmir.

By 'using the language of the unpronounceable acronyms which was the true lingua franca of the subcontinent's political class' (188) to describe these projects, Rushdie's narrator exposes the emptiness of Ophuls' plan, and by extension the failure of US foreign policy in South Asia since the end of the Second World War (188). Ophuls' use of the word 'oppressors' (198) to describe the militarisation of the Kashmiri valley by the Indian army and the Pakistani militia clearly departs from the non-partisan position on the Kashmir conflict, which Chester Bowles argued the US should adopt in his 1954 *Ambassador's Report*. Indeed, it is Ophuls' public comment, combined with the news of his extra-marital affair with Boonyi Noman, that leads to the end of Ophuls' career as US ambassador in the novel. In this respect, the narrator suggests that Ophuls' foreign policy recommendations are shaped and influenced by his sexual desire for Boonyi. Such a connection between Ophuls' desire for Boonyi and his decision-making over US foreign policy in South Asia certainly encourages a reading of Ophuls relationship with Boonyi as an allegory of American foreign policy in South Asia. Yet, as this chapter will suggest, Rushdie ultimately subordinates this allegory of American imperialism to an elegy for Kashmir.

Max Ophuls' subsequent appointment as 'an ambassador for counterterrorism' might suggest that his political influence in South Asia and Kashmir comes to an end at this point in the narrative (272). Moreover, this change in Ophuls' job description would seem to parallel Rushdie's recent criticism of the Bush administration's foreign policy in South Asia for focusing on Afghanistan and Iraq to the exclusion of Kashmir. For Ophuls' new position as ambassador for counterterrorism involves him supporting terrorist groups such as the Taliban, who worked for America's geopolitical interests during the Russian war with Afghanistan. As the narrator puts it, 'The person who held the job could not be named, his movements were not mentioned in the newspapers; he slipped across the globe like a shadow, his presence detectable only by its influence on the actions of others' (335).

In Kashmira's words, Max is now the 'occult servant of American geopolitical interest' (335). In this sense, Ophuls' escape from the threat of death in the Nazi concentration camps, and his rise to political power in the United States mirrors the distinction that the political theorist Giorgio Agamben makes between the figure of bare life (the person who can be tortured and killed outside the jurisdiction of the law), and the figure of sovereign power (the figure who decides on the exception to the law which allows bare life to be tortured and killed) (Agamben 1998).

By juxtaposing the conflict in Kashmir and the contemporary US-led war on terrorism, Rushdie also seems to question the assumption that the rise of so-called jihadist violence in Kashmir was causally connected to the rise of the Taliban in Afghanistan during the war with the Soviet Union, and is separate from the Indo-Pakistan conflict over Kashmir. Such a challenge seems to anticipate the argument of historian Praveen Swami that the 'jihad in Jammu and Kashmir had in fact raged on ever since Jammu and Kashmir acceded to the Union of India in 1947, and Indian troops landed in Srinagar to defend the state against Pakistani irregulars' (Swami 2007: 3).

Rushdie's portrayal of Bulbul Fakh also reinforces the idea that so-called Islamic jihad in Kashmir was part of the conflict in Kashmir. Although the 'firebrand Islam' of Bulbul Fakh, the iron mullah, is declared to be 'positively un-Kashmiri and un-Indian as well' (122), he is, nonetheless, regarded as the reincarnation of Bulbul Shah, 'a fabled saint who had come to Kashmir in the fourteenth century' (116). What is more, Bulbul Fakh's influence in the valley of Kashmir during the intervention of the Indian military is framed in the fantastical terms of a non-secular, oral narrative, which links the mullah's rise to power to the disused Indian military hardware in the valley (115).

By suggesting that the mullah's political power is the result of a miraculous anthropomorphic transformation of the Indian military's scrap metal, Rushdie offers a non-partisan response to the political, military and technological forces of postcolonial modernity in the valley of Kashmir. Further, Rushdie's metaphor of the iron mullah suggests that the 'firebrand Islam' (115) Bulbul Fakh preaches is a historical product of an increasingly militarised and divided postcolonial Kashmir rather than an essential theological principle of Islam.

Like Bulbul Fakh's political theology, Rushdie's fictional construction of Shalimar the Clown seems on a first reading to reinforce the Western media's conflation of migrants, Muslims and terrorists. Shalimar's training in an Islamic military camp in Kashmir with the iron mullah, his subsequent training with the Taliban, and his clandestine infiltration of the United States to assassinate Max Ophuls mirrors the media fiction of an international terrorist network such as Al Quaeda. Indeed, Shalimar's transnational movements from Kashmir to Pakistan, Afghanistan, the Philippines and to Seattle via Vancouver resemble the transnational movements of an international terrorist. At one point in the novel, the character Zainab Azam compares Shalimar's assassination of Max Ophuls to Shaheed Udham Singh's assassination of Sir Michael O'Dwyer in London in 1940. As the former colonial governor of Punjab, O'Dwyer was widely believed to be responsible for the 1919 Jallianwala Bagh massacre. Such a comparison between the assassination of O'Dwyer and Ophuls is significant not only because it implies a link between the transnational movements of India's freedom fighters in the early twentieth century and the global terrorist networks of the early twenty-first century but also because it suggests a parallel between British colonialism in India and American foreign policy in South Asia.

Shalimar's decision to assassinate Ophuls 'around the time' (243) of the end of the Bangladesh war and the agreement signed by Indira Gandhi and Zulfikar Ali Bhutto at Simla in 1971 is significant in that this agreement not only transformed the ceasefire line between India and Pakistan into a line of control, which was effectively an international border between India and Pakistan but also omitted any reference to a referendum for the people of Kashmir (Schofield 2003: 117–119). If Shalimar's decision to murder Ophuls is read as a response to the omission of a referendum for the people of Kashmir, his decision could be understood as part of a struggle to assert Kashmiri sovereignty against India, Pakistan and the United States. The fact that Shalimar's assassination of Ophuls is primarily motivated by a desire to avenge Max Ophuls' affair with his wife Boonyi rather than any specific ideological opposition to Ophuls' position as an agent of US imperial power might appear to undermine the reading of *Shalimar the Clown* as an allegory of US foreign policy in South Asia.

Yet to focus exclusively on the revenge plot in *Shalimar the Clown* (as many reviews of the novel have done) would be to overlook the significance of Boonyi and Ophuls' daughter Kashmira in the novel. Clearly, the name Kashmira suggests a connection between Ophuls' daughter and Kashmir. Yet Kashmira is not only a sign of Max Ophuls' sexual relationship with Boonyi; she is also a symbol of American imperialism in South Asia. As the narrator explains:

> A Kashmiri girl ruined and destroyed by a powerful American gave the Indian government an opportunity to look like it would stand up and defend Kashmiris against marauders of all types – to defend the honour of Kashmir as stoutly as it would defend that of any other integral part of India ... the new president Zakir Hussain, was making angry statements in private about the godless American's exploitation of an innocent Hindu girl ... And Indira Gandhi was out for blood. (206)

By placing the scandal of Ophuls' relationship with Kashmira in the context of the Indo-Pakistani war in Kashmir and the American war in Vietnam, the narrator highlights the way in which American foreign policy in South Asia was viewed with suspicion by both India and Pakistan. Rather than offering a straightforward allegory of US foreign policy in South Asia, however, Rushdie calls into question the very idea that allegory is an appropriate literary form for a divided and militarised Kashmir.

Moreover, by representing Kashmir from the perspective of the people of Pachigam, a fictional Kashmiri village, Rushdie tries to avoid taking sides with either Indian or Pakistani versions of Kashmir's history and the origins of the conflict. In the section of the novel entitled 'Boonyi', for instance, the narrator focuses on the cosmopolitanism of the villagers, and the way that a dispute between the villagers of Pachigam and Shirmal is settled at the insistence of the maharaja:

> After the pot war, contact between the two village headmen came to an acrimonious end, until messengers from the maharaja himself arrived in both Pachigam and Shirmal, demanding that to augment the staff of the palace kitchen they set aside their quarrels and pool their resources to provide food (and theatrical entertainment) at a grand Dassehra festival banquet in the Shalimar garden. (71)

This festival and banquet involved a celebration of Kashmir's hybrid cultural heritage. As Pandit Pyarelal Kaul declares:

> Today our Muslim village, in the service of our Hindu maharaja, will cook and act in a Mughal — that is to say Muslim — garden, to celebrate the anniversary of the day on which Ram marched against Ravan to rescue Sita. ... Who tonight are the Hindus? Who tonight are the Muslims? Here in Kashmir, our stories sit happily side by side on the same double bill, we eat from the same dishes, we laugh at the same jokes ... .(71)

This performance of hybridity and the confusion of communal identities might seem to construct an idealised image of Kashmir as more cosmopolitan under the semi-autonomous rule of the Hindu maharaja than after India's independence and partition. Yet this ignores the influence of the British colonial administration in dividing the Kashmiri population along ethnic lines by identifying Kashmiri people either as Hindu, Muslim or Buddhist. Through bureaucratic techniques of power such as the census, the British colonial administration 'fundamentally changed the conceptualization of an identity in that it inculcated a strong sense of *self* versus *other* among individuals as well as communities' (Behera 2000: 40). It is perhaps for this reason that Firdaus Noman reads the maharaja's demand that the people of Pachigam perform their hybrid cultural heritage as a sign that 'bad trouble is on the way' (71).

The prophetic and proleptic powers that the narrator attributes to Firdaus serve to place the history of India's partition and the subsequent conflict in Kashmir within the non-secular, oral historical world-view of the villagers. Such a world-view is further registered in the narrator's account of the rumours, which 'seemed like a new species of living thing' and asserted that ' "an army of *kabailis* from Pakistan has crossed the border, looting, raping, killing ... and it is nearing the outskirts of the city" ' (85). By representing the historical experience of communal violence in the form of a rumour, the narrator powerfully evokes the villagers' understanding of political events and their rising panic in the face of what she describes as 'the most persistent' and 'most puissant rumours' (85).

In a related discussion of rumour in the context of peasant insurgency in colonial South Asia, the postcolonial theorist Gayatri Chakravorty Spivak has suggested that the rumour of subaltern insurgency operated as a system of writing with no identifiable source, and 'the mistake of the colonial authorities was to take rumor for speech, to impose the requirements of speech in the narrow sense upon something that draws its strength from writing in the general sense' (Spivak 1987: 292). For Spivak, rumours are a radical medium of communication for political insurgents because they operate as a form of writing that can be passed on without leaving a trace of the insurgent who started the rumour. Like Spivak, Rushdie's narrator certainly identifies the way in which rumours are both anonymous and transitive (Rushdie: 86–87). Yet, whereas subaltern rumours circulate the message of anti-colonial insurgency, Rushdie's rumours portend the terror of political violence in Kashmir. By placing the rumours of India and Pakistan's territorial claims on the valley of Kashmir in apposition, Rushdie evokes the perspective of the Kashmiri people, who are caught in the middle of these contending rumours. Moreover, by representing the violent repression of the Kashmiri people by both the Indian military and the Pakistani militias, the narrator conveys the way in which the conflict in Kashmir is overdetermined by multiple historical narratives. Yet, in so doing, the narrator also appears to support the secular nationalism of the Kashmiri separatist movement against both the influence of the Indian military and the iron mullahs from Pakistan.

Such support is implied in Rushdie's characterisation of the Indian General Kachhwaha as a Hindu fundamentalist, who regards the idea of 'Kashmir for the Kashmiris' as 'moronic' (101); who believes that 'Every Muslim in Kashmir should be considered a militant' (291); and who orders the Indian military to ethnically cleanse the village of Pachigam. While General Kachhwaha 'despised the fundamentalists, the jihadis [and] the Hizb' he 'despised the secular nationalists more' (299) on the grounds that they have no God. As Kachhwaha expostulates, 'What sort of God was secular nationalism?' (299). By invoking the idea of 'secular nationalism' in the context of the conflict over Kashmir, the narrator suggests that the secular struggle for Kashmiri liberation from both India and Pakistan corresponds with the Nehruvian rhetoric of secular nationalism that promoted the co-existence of Muslims and Hindus in India and Pakistan.

Yet if General Kachhwaha's military campaign of terror against Kashmiri Muslims in the Valley of Kashmir gives the lie to Nehru's legacy of secularism and tolerance by exposing the hegemonic and military power of India's Hindu majority, Rushdie's account of the secular nationalism of the Jammu Kashmir liberation front in *Shalimar the Clown* seems to embody what the postcolonial theorist Homi K. Bhabha calls subaltern secularism (Bhabha 1996). For the secular nationalism of the Jammu and Kashmir liberation front (JKLF) is precisely subaltern in the sense that it reflects the view of the Kashmiri people rather than the elite, a people 'of no more than five million souls, landlocked, preindustrial, resource rich but cash poor, perched thousands of feet up in the mountains' (253). As Rushdie's narrator explains, 'the liberation front was reasonably popular and *azadi* was the universal cry!' (253). Furthermore, the JKLF's call for *azadi* (the Urdu word for freedom) refers to the

> Freedom to be meat-eating Brahmins to saint-worshipping Muslims, to make pilgrimages to the ice-lingam high in lakeside mosque, to listen to the santoor and drink salty tea … to make honey and carve walnut into animal and boat shapes and to watch the mountains push their way, inch by inch, century by century, further up into the sky. (253)

Such a spirit of freedom is reinforced by the way in which the people of Kashmir treat the 'de facto line of partition [between India and Pakistan] with contempt' by walking 'across the mountains whenever they so chose' (97).

All of which is not to say that Rushdie is simply an uncritical defender of the JKLF. At one point in the novel, for instance, the narrator states that the word 'Azadi … sounded like a fantasy, a children's fable' (256). Further, Rushdie's account of the rise of jihadi groups in the ' "free"—Azad—sector of Kashmir' (270) traces the way in which the secular nationalism of the JKLF is increasingly co-opted by the Islamic political theology of the iron mullah, Bulbul Fakh. While Fakh promises Shalimar that he will liberate Kashmir (264), he does so in a training camp 'for worldwide Islamist-jihadist activities set up by Pak Inter-Services Intelligence' (264). The daily routine of the warriors enlisted in this camp involves training exercises on 'firing ranges with moving targets', the formal ritual of 'five daily prayers', and attending lectures delivered by the iron mullah on the doctrine of Holy War (264). Shalimar's ability to perform these rituals, and to convince the iron mullah of his devotion to the ideological cause of holy war against the infidel is made possible by his training as an actor in the village of Pachigam. By passing as an Islamic fundamentalist, Shalimar not only infiltrates a transnational terrorist network in order to assassinate Max Ophuls, but he also suggests that belief is nothing more than the performance of rituals of religious devotion.

Shalimar's feeling that the iron mullah's 'business of finding young boys and even young girls who were ready to blow themselves up' is 'demeaning', and his subsequent decision to 'break with the iron mullah' in such a way 'that wouldn't lead to his execution for desertion' (318) might suggest that the secular and private motive for Shalimar's killing of Max Ophuls is morally superior to the iron mullah's use of political theology to train young suicide bombers in the name of Islam. In a related discussion, the anthropologist Talal Asad has called into question the correlation of religion and violence. For Asad, what is often described in the Western media as 'the Islamic roots of violence' is rather misleading because it assumes a necessary correlation between religion and violence, where there is in fact no such correlation. As Asad explains:

> [V]iolence does not *need* to be justified by the Qur'ān – or any other scripture for that matter. When General Ali Haidar of Syria, under the orders of his secular president Hafez al-Assad, massacred 30,000 to 40,000 civilians in the rebellious town of Hama in 1982 he did not invoke the Qur'ān – nor did the secularist Saddam Hussein when he gassed thousands of Kurds and butchered the Shi'a population in Southern Iraq. Ariel Sharon in his indiscriminate killing and terrorizing of Palestinian civilians did not – so far as is publicly known – invoke passages of the Torah, such as Joshua's destruction of every living thing in Jericho. Nor has any government (and rebel group), whether Western or non-Western, *needed* to justify its use of indiscriminate cruelty against civilians by appealing to the authority of sacred scripture. They might in some cases do so, because that seems to them just – or else expedient. But that's very different from saying that they are *constrained* to do so. (Asad 2003: 10)

If Asad questions the assumption that there is something inherently violent about Islam by highlighting acts of 'indiscriminate cruelty' carried out in the name of secularism, Rushdie's narrator seems to almost condone Shalimar's military training on the grounds that it is carried out in the name of a secular nationalist cause rather than a religious ideology. Even though Shalimar does not adhere to the religious beliefs or methods of Bulbul Fakh, his motivation for training in the terrorist methods of a *jihadi* group funded by the Pak Inter-Services Intelligence is no less violent or rational because of its secular character.

Moreover, in the aftermath of the attacks on America of September 11 2001, the identification of Shalimar as 'a known associate of more than one terrorist group' (371) collapses the distinction between an act of political violence and private revenge, and constructs Shalimar as a terrorist because of his Muslim identity: 'After the bombing of the World Trade Centre in New York … it was a dangerous time in prison for a Muslim man accused of being a professional terrorist' (377). Such a representation not only foregrounds the way in which the discourse of terrorism post-September 11 2001 collapses the obvious differences between Muslims, migrants and terrorists (as Sivanandan suggests) but also ignores the historical singularity of the conflict in Kashmir.

It is precisely this historical singularity that the narrator foregrounds in Kashmira's observation that this was not 'an American story. It was a Kashmiri story' (372). Against Shalimar's 'disappearance beneath the alien cadences of American speech' (372) – a phrase which itself evokes the power and authority of America's legal and political discourses – Rushdie centres Kashmir in the imaginative global political geography of *Shalimar the Clown*. This centring is achieved through the narrator's self-conscious reflection on an appropriate literary mode to mourn the loss of human life associated with the conflict in Kashmir. Such literary self-consciousness is exemplified in Kashmira's reference to A. E. Housman's pastoral poem about rural Shropshire, *A Shropshire Lad* (1896): 'There were collisions and explosions. The world was no longer calm. She thought of Housman in Shropshire. *That is the land of lost content.* For the poet, happiness was the past. It was that other country where they did things differently' (37). Writing in the global historical context of the second Boer war, Housman framed idyllic life in the local context of rural Shropshire as a 'land of lost content'. By invoking this poem in the global political context of a discussion of the ongoing conflict between India and Pakistan over the local territory of Kashmir, Rushdie suggests that the myth of Kashmir as a land of paradise is a belated fantasy.

Moreover, by framing Kashmira's grief over the death of her father, and the loss of the homeland she never lived in with the biological mother she never knew in terms of a pastoral elegy, Rushdie draws attention to the political dimension of mourning that the social theorist Judith Butler has recently described in *Precarious Life* (2004). Against President George W. Bush's assertion on September 21 2001 that 'we have finished grieving and that *now* it is time for resolute action to take the place of grief' (cited in Butler 2004: 29), Butler argues that grief can be a 'resource of politics' if it leads to 'a consideration of the vulnerability of others' (Butler 2004: 30) and a questioning of the political norms that determine why the lives of Americans are grievable and the lives of Iraqis, Palestinians and Afghanis are not (Butler 2004: 34). Further, by arguing that 'the world itself as a sovereign entitlement of the United States must be given up, lost and mourned' (Butler 2004: 40), Butler offers a radical democratic vision of global political relations in the twenty-first century.

Against the history of American foreign policy in South Asia, Rushdie offers a similar vision of the global political future in *Shalimar the Clown*. By framing Shalimar's murder of Max Ophuls as a 'Kashmir story' rather than an 'American story', Kashmira grieves for Kashmir against the political norms and 'alien cadences of American speech' (372) which define Shalimar's murder of Ophuls as a terrorist action against America's global political sovereignty. In so doing, Rushdie offers a political elegy for Kashmir that highlights the limitations of American foreign policy in postcolonial South Asia from the Truman administration to the Bush administration, and mourns the lives of many Kashmiris, whose deaths have been overshadowed by the Cold War and the US-led war on terrorism.

8

CONCLUSION

If Rushdie's newspaper articles on anti-Americanism and the wars in Afghanistan and Iraq post-September 11 2001 suggest a shift in the broadly anti-imperialist position reflected in his book *The Jaguar Smile* and his essay 'The Empire Writes Back with a Vengeance', the geopolitical imagination of Rushdie's fiction seems to complicate this picture. For, as this book has suggested, Rushdie's fiction has from the outset been concerned with re-framing and re-imagining the long history of Western imperialism – from British territorial colonialism to US military and economic expansion – from the standpoint of South Asia's political modernity, its independence and subsequent partition. By placing the situation in Kashmir, the partition of India, India's state of emergency, the legitimation crisis in India's discourse of state secularism and the rise of the Hindu right in an international frame, Rushdie's fiction has raised questions about the political legacies of British colonialism, and the viability of a Third World alternative to Western capitalism and Soviet communism during the Cold War period and its aftermath. The Satanic Verses affair and the collapse of the Soviet Union may have seemed to mark a crisis in Rushdie's position as a tricontinental intellectual, as the end of the Cold War was replaced with what Rushdie himself describes as 'narrower, ever more fanatical definitions of ourselves', which are at once 'religious, regional, [and] ethnic' (Rushdie 2003: 301).

Yet, Rushdie's re-writing of religious texts, South Asian history and modern forms of political sovereignty has produced fictional worlds that do not merely satirise the competing rhetorics of secular democracy, global capitalism and political theology but also imagine alternative political futures. Rushdie's marginal reference to the Zapatistas in *The Ground Beneath Her Feet*, his coded reference

to the coup and counter-coup in Fiji in *Fury* and his representation
of the Kashmiri separatist movement in *Shalimar the Clown* may be
read as a sign that Rushdie's fiction increasingly dissolves the aesthetic into media representations of world politics. Indeed, it is
such allusions to contemporary international events that have
prompted critics such as Timothy Brennan to conclude that
Rushdie's fiction is 'current events collage' (Brennan 2006: 74). But
as Deepika Bahri cautions,

> If criticism is prone to attach too much meaning to artistic and intel-
> lectual expression as political work, as the many critics of postcolo-
> nialism rightly charge, it is also true that a criticism uninterested in
> exploring its aesthetic dimension will fail to glean its possible contri-
> bution to the emancipatory project. (Bahri 2003: 17)

Rushdie certainly highlights the limitations of Nehru's secular
democratic vision of postcolonial India in *Midnight's Children* and
The Moor's Last Sigh, and the rhetoric of Islamic revivalism in *Shame*
and *The Satanic Verses*. Moreover, his juxtaposition of fictional worlds
and histories, such as Jahilia and Ellowen Deeowen in *The Satanic
Verses*, or New York and Lilliput Blufescu in *Fury* creates an aesthetic
form inspired by the narrative conventions of Bombay cinema,
Latin American magical realism and Anglo-American postmodern
literature that is not only appropriate to register the complexities
and contradictions of South Asia's postcolonial modernity, but
which also encourages readers to imagine an alternative to the systematic inequalities of global capitalism and the false and reductive
dichotomy between the Islamic world and the West.

In his insightful essay, 'Salman Rushdie: Paradox and Truth'
Robert Eaglestone has argued that Rushdie's work 'is simply too
lacking in unity, too paradoxical and continually shifting for any
firm view which relies on a single position properly to embody
it' (Eaglestone 2006: 100). Using an analogy from philosophy,
Eaglestone characterises this 'paradoxical' and 'continually-shifting'
quality of Rushdie's writing as a form of 'dream reasoning' or 'paralogical thinking' which does not follow 'the strict rules of logic'
or aim to establish a consensus (Eaglestone 101). Such a form of
thinking is a suggestive way of describing the conceptual process
through which Rushdie's writing refuses to resolve the critical
conflict between readers 'who favour existential questions and

those who turn to historical particulars' (Eaglestone 100). Yet, if Rushdie's writing is analogous to paralogical thinking, it is a paralogical thinking that also challenges the teleological narrative of Western modernity, and its universalising aspirations. Deepika Bahri has argued in a related discussion that the 'postcolonial writer attempting to catalog "the dissonant character of modern life" is forced to confront the idea of emancipation as non-teleological and of temporality itself as ambivalent' (Bahri 2003: 99). As I suggested in Chapter 3, such an approach to the temporal dissonance of postcolonial modernity is exemplified in Rushdie's representation of India's chronological transition from British colonial rule to political independence in *Midnight's Children*, which is framed as an anticlimax that ultimately results in Saleem Sinai's loss of hope in the nation state as a structure that can deliver social and political liberation. In a similar vein, Rushdie's treatment of secularism in *Midnight's Children* and *The Moor's Last Sigh* raises questions about the limitations of secularism as a concept that was first formulated in post-Enlightenment liberal culture as an attempt to recognise the minority status of the Jews in Europe, and was subsequently adopted in India by Jawaharlal Nehru as an attempt to recognise the minority status of Muslims in India in the aftermath of partition (Mufti 2007). Indeed, as Chapter 5 suggested, Moraes Zogoiby's assertion of his Jewish ancestry in *The Moor's Last Sigh* is precisely a response to the limitations of the liberal ideology of secularism, as it has been adopted in postcolonial India. Moreover, by juxtaposing the worldly and otherworldly dimensions of modern South Asia in novels such as *The Satanic Verses*, Rushdie contests the belief that modernity involves a smooth temporal transition from an age of religion, superstition and feudalism to an age of enlightenment, secularism and social democracy. By blurring the boundaries between Islamic history and representations of Islamic history in the fictional Bombay cinema genre of the theological, *The Satanic Verses* suggests that the coexistence of religion, technology and popular culture characterises the temporal dissonance of modernity in postcolonial India and its diasporas.

As well as challenging the evolutionary logic of modernity, Rushdie's fiction raises important questions about modernity's geographical provenance in Western Europe. If, as some commentators have argued, the seeds of contemporary global modernity were sown in the age of European colonial expansion, Rushdie's fiction redraws the map of global modernity in a way that is analogous to the social and political process of provincialising Europe described by the South Asian historian Dipesh Chakrabarty. Rushdie's surreal juxtaposition of the fictional worlds of seventh-century Jahilia and late twentieth-century London, for instance, is precisely an attempt to re-imagine one of Europe's imperial cities from the non-secular perspective of a postcolonial migrant. The global dominance of American popular culture is also challenged in Rushdie's novel *The Ground Beneath Her Feet* in the narrator's (albeit fictional) suggestion that rock 'n' roll music was first invented in Bombay/Mumbai. Moreover, as I suggested in Chapter 7, the narrator's assertion in *Shalimar the Clown* that the assassination of Max Ophuls was 'a Kashmiri story' rather than an 'American story' (372) re-centres Kashmir in the imaginative political geography of the novel and the post-9/11 world to which it refers.

Rushdie's fictional writing post-*The Satanic Verses* has been criticised by some commentators for being increasingly solipsistic, and for foreclosing the aporias and paradoxes that Robert Eaglestone identifies in his fictional corpus. Amitava Kumar, for instance, has said of *Fury* that 'what is likely to drive the reader to fury is the narrator's relentless discourse on success and wealth and chic consumer products even while appearing to denounce them' (Kumar 2001); whereas Roger Y. Clark has suggested that Rushdie's later fiction abandons the fictional space left for belief despite his scepticism that we see in earlier novels (183). Timothy Brennan, in contrast, detects a conservative streak in Rushdie's fictional writing from *Midnight's Children* onwards; in Brennan's reading, Rushdie's 'satire' of the communist characters in *Midnight's Children* is proleptic of the post-communist new world order (2006: 91); his representation of West Indians in *The Satanic Verses* are so 'embarrassing and offensive' (1989: 164) that one 'wonders why the first protests [against the novel] did not come from the Afro-British communities' (2006: 89); and his 'parody of "dub" poetry' in the same novel is 'hollow and out of touch' (1989: 164). For Brennan, such examples of Rushdie's elitism prefigure his more recent public expressions of support for the Bush administration's wars in Afghanistan and Iraq in the first decade of the twenty-first century; expressions which have certainly damaged his reputation as a politically engaged writer amongst many critics on the left. More recently, Rushdie's acceptance of a knighthood from the British monarchy in 2007 seems to confirm his rejection of a more radical, anti-establishment position, in which he was as critical of racism, anti-immigration legislation and Raj nostalgia in Britain, as he was of religious fundamentalisms. As Priya Gopal argued in a response to Rushdie's acceptance of a knighthood, the post-fatwa, post-911 Rushdie

> recalls his own creation Baal [in *The Satanic Verses*], the talented poet who becomes a giggling hack corralled into attacking his ruler's enemies. Denuded of texture and complexity, it is no accident that this fiction since the early 90s has disappeared into a critical wasteland. The mutation of this relevant and stentorian writer into a pallid chorister is a tragic allegory of our benighted times, of the kind he once narrated so vividly. (Gopal 2007)

The crucial problem for Timothy Brennan in his 1989 study *Salman Rushdie and the Third World* is that the aesthetic form of Rushdie's fiction stops short of fictionalising the Third world national struggle (1989: 166) that is evident in the work of many other postcolonial writers before and after Rushdie, from G. V. Desani and Jose Carlos Mariategui to A. Sivanandan and Farrukh Dhondy. Brennan is of course quite right to question the reasons why Salman Rushdie, in particular, has been celebrated as an exemplary South Asian writer in the global literary marketplace, and not other, more politically engaged writers. For Rushdie's status in the global literary marketplace may say as much about the literary marketplace's desire to package the Third World for Western consumption as it does about the formal nuances of Rushdie's fiction.

Moreover, it may be tempting to dismiss Rushdie's more recent fictional writing in light of his controversial statements about the Bush administration's foreign policy in the Middle East, and his recent acceptance of a knighthood from the British monarchy. But rather than simply equating Rushdie's writing with his political views in the front pages of the British and American broadsheets, I would like to conclude this study with a different observation. If Rushdie's fiction is preoccupied with the historical experience of postcolonial modernity, it is concerned with both the progressive and the retrograde dimensions of postcolonial modernity in South Asia at the same time. By holding progressive ideas such as secularism, decolonisation and social democracy, and retrograde phenomena such as communal violence, state repression or neo-colonialism in a state of perpetual tension, Rushdie's fiction refuses to represent a vision of emancipation in a disenchanted global economic system or to simply write off the social and political achievements of decolonisation in South Asia as a failure. And it is this refusal of straightforward political closure that makes Rushdie's fiction engaging to readers of different critical persuasions and ideological perspectives. To invoke Saleem Sinai's oxymoron in *Midnight's Children*, if the optimism associated with national independence is a disease, Rushdie fiction suggests that it is a disease that is worth enduring.

PART III
Criticism and Contexts

9

OTHER WRITINGS

Rushdie is a prolific essay writer, as well as a novelist, and has participated in various public discussions and debates ranging from racism in Thatcher's Britain, the political establishment in India and Pakistan, the legacies of Britain's imperial culture and the representation of India in British films of the 1980s to the controversy surrounding the publication of *The Satanic Verses* and Rushdie's period in hiding, the rise of the Hindu right, the death of Princess Diana, the political crisis in Kashmir and the terrorist attacks on America of September 11 2001. Moreover, this book has suggested that Rushdie's non-fictional writings provide a useful resource for tracking Rushdie's shifting critical and political positions, and for situating his writing in a precise historical, cultural and political context. It is also worth noting that Rushdie has been an important critical voice in the literary world, and has written reviews of many contemporary novelists, including for example, Julian Barnes, Saul Bellow, John Berger, John le Carré, J. M. Coetzee, Nuruddin Farah, Nadine Gordimer, Günter Grass, Gabriel Garcia Marquez, V. S. Naipaul, Philip Roth and Kurt Vonnegut. This section of the appendix assesses Rushdie's reflections on the politics of Third World literature in his non-fictional writings in order to map the trajectory of Rushdie's geopolitical imagination from the 1980s to the first decade of the twenty-first century.

Many of the essays collected in his 1991 collection *Imaginary Homelands* help to situate Rushdie's own fictional writing in relation to British cultural representations of South Asia, and the emergence of postcolonial literatures in English. His essay 'Commonwealth Literature Does Not Exist', for example, rejects the term 'Commonwealth Literature' on the grounds that it 'places Eng. Lit. at the centre and the rest of the world at the periphery' (66), and reduces particular literary texts to authentic expressions of a national culture. Against the attempt to homogenise Anglophone writing from former British colonies under the general umbrella of 'Commonwealth Literature', Rushdie tries to define a 'Third World' literature, which identifies a 'commonality' between 'writers from ... poor countries, or deprived minorities in powerful countries' (69).

Rushdie's earlier essay 'The Empire Writes Back with a Vengeance' (published in 1982) further articulates the political imperative of what he calls 'Third World' literature by suggesting that his fiction, along with that of writers as diverse as James Joyce, Samuel Beckett, Anita Desai and Ngugi wa Thiong'o challenge and complicate the often negative and stereotypical representations of Ireland, South Asia and Africa in English literature and culture. Invoking the Indian writer G. V. Desani's novel *About H. Hatterr* (first published, 1948), Rushdie argues that 'Desani's triumph was to take babu-English, *chamcha*-English, and turn it against itself: the instrument of subservience became a weapon of liberation, it was a weapon of great liberation. It was the first great stroke of the decolonizing pen' (1982: 8). By aligning Desani's writing with a struggle for national liberation, Rushdie suggests that 'Third World' literature participates in the cultural and political process of decolonisation in India. Despite Rushdie's reference to Desani as an important precursor, however, Rushdie fails to acknowledge the 'presence of a growing and heterogeneous body of Black and Asian writing in Britain' in the twentieth century, an omission that not only reflects 'a general myopia in the cultural politics of the mainstream publishing and literary world' (Nasta 145), but which also distinguishes the bourgeois liberal sensibility of Rushdie's migrant writing from the social realism of writers such as Samuel Selvon and Farrukh Dondy (Nasta 148–149).

To the extent that the fiction of Desani, Lovelace, Naipaul, Ngugi and Rushdie challenge the stereotypes and negative representations of India and Africa in the literature of empire, one can see how what Rushdie calls 'Third World' literature might participate in the process of what Ngugi wa Thiong'o has elsewhere called decolonising the mind. Indeed, Rushdie's critical essays on Rudyard Kipling, David Lean's adaptation of E. M. Forster's novel *A Passage to India*, Paul Scott's *A Raj Quartet* and Richard Attenborough's film *Gandhi* further reinforce this argument. In his reading of Kipling, for instance, Rushdie argues that 'There will always be plenty in Kipling that I will find difficult to forgive, but there is also enough truth in these stories to make them impossible to ignore' (80). Despite Kipling's obvious 'racial bigotry' (74), Rushdie argues that 'No other Western writer has ever known India as Kipling knew it, and it is this knowledge of place, and procedure, and detail that gives his stories their undeniable authority' (75). And in his essay, 'Outside the Whale', Rushdie criticises what he calls the Raj Revival in British cinema, popular culture and fiction during the early 1980s on the grounds that 'the rise of Raj revisionism, exemplified by the huge success of these fictions, is the artistic counterpart of the rise of conservative ideologies in modern Britain' (92). In the face of these conservative ideologies, Rushdie argues that there is a 'genuine need for political fiction, for books that draw new and better maps of reality, and make new languages with which we can understand the world' (100).

Rushdie's challenge to the conservative ideology underpinning Raj revivalism in 1980s Britain is laudable. But if his plea for 'books that draw new and better maps of reality' (100) refers to the 'Third World fiction' that he invokes in 'Commonwealth Literature Does Not Exist', it is not clear how this 'political fiction' will challenge the capitalist dynamics of imperialism and globalisation that circumscribe the contemporary world. 'Like world music, the world novel is a category to be distrusted', argues Michael Denning in a related discussion of Gabriel Garcia Marquez' *One Hundred Years of Solitude*,

> if it genuinely points to the transformed geography of the novel, it is also a marketing device that flattens distinct regional and linguistic traditions into a single cosmopolitan world beat, with magical realism serving as the aesthetic of globalisation, often as empty and contrived

a signifier as the modernism and socialist realism it supplanted. (Denning 2004: 51)

If magical realism is an 'empty signifier', the aesthetic ideology of Rushdie's 'Third World' fiction is bound in part by the class structures of postcolonial India, of which Rushdie himself is a product. In 'The Empire writes back with a vengeance', Rushdie implies without explicitly stating that the social class that collaborated with the British Empire in India, whom he calls *chamchas* or *babus*, form the privileged subject of Indian fiction in English. It is for this reason that the Indian literary critic Tabish Khair has argued that 'what passes for Indian English fiction (especially in its most successful versions) is written by the most privileged sections of the Babus. Indian English fiction is Babu fiction' (Khair 2001: x). Rushdie's controversial claim in his preface to *The Vintage Book of Indian Writing 1947–1997* that 'prose writing – both fiction and non-fiction – created in this period by Indian writers working in English is proving to be a more interesting body of work than most of what has been produced in the sixteen "official languages" of India, the so-called "vernacular languages" ' (Rushdie 2002:160) reinforces the social and cultural elitism that Khair attributes to Indian fiction in English. In so doing, Rushdie also seems to consolidate rather than decolonise the social, cultural and linguistic power of the *chamcha* class that he criticises in 'The Empire Writes Back with a Vengeance'.

If Rushdie's valorisation of Indian fiction in English in the late 1990s suggests both a conservative and an anti-imperialist position in questions of literary and cultural value, his essays during the 1980s on political repression and corruption in India and Pakistan, the social marginalisation of Black Britons under the Thatcher administration and his support for the Sandinistas in Nicaragua, reveal a more left-wing position in matters of politics. In his essay on the assassination of Indira Gandhi, for example, Rushdie criticises her administration's removal of political power from the states that constitute India to the centre, and the 'peculiarly monarchic style of government which Mrs Gandhi developed' (43). In a similar vein, Rushdie's essay on Pakistan's military leader Zia ul-Haq compares Zia to a goblin in the *Arabian Nights*, and argues that Zia's 'Islamization programme was the ugliest possible face of the faith', which erased the 'strong strain of pluralistic

Sufi philosophy' which had 'developed historically along moderate lines' (54) in the Indo-Pakistani subcontinent. Such criticisms are not, however, meant to highlight the failures of decolonisation; but rather emphasise the need for persistent social and democratic transformation in India and Pakistan. As Edward Said has written in a related discussion of Rushdie's fiction, 'Rushdie's novels are scathingly critical, not to say insurrectionary, about the present rulers of India and Pakistan, but one never gets the impression from *Midnight's Children* or *Shame* that the critique is disengaged, or haughty, or disapproving of the entire postcolonial enterprise' (Said 1987: 10).

Rushdie was also vocal in his opposition to the British Parliament's passing of the Nationality Act of 1981, which abolished the *ius soli* (law of the soil, which automatically granted citizenship rights to anyone born on English soil) in an attempt 'to deprive black and Asian Britons of their citizenship rights' (136); and to the language of integration, racial harmony and multiculturalism that circulated in the dominant British media and political sphere on the grounds that such language is a 'sham' (133), which masks the social control of the black British population by the police force. Rushdie concedes that 'Britain isn't South Africa' or 'Nazi Germany', but he also argues that 'British thought, British society, has never been cleansed of the filth of imperialism' (131). In saying this, Rushdie implies that the liberal ideology upon which British imperialism was based aids and abets the persistence of imperial attitudes in contemporary British society and culture. Rushdie's criticism of race politics in 1980s Britain is developed further in his essay 'An Unimportant Fire', which invokes the deaths of Mrs Abdul Karim, a Bangladeshi woman, and her two children in slum housing in the London Borough of Camden, to reflect on the racism of social housing in 1980s British society.

Rushdie's travelogue *The Jaguar Smile* documents his travels around Nicaragua in 1986. This short book reveals a writer who is broadly sympathetic to the political struggle of the left-wing Sandinistas against the CIA-backed Contras on the grounds that he regards the struggle of the Sandinistas against the US imperialist war by proxy as analogous to the national liberation struggle of India from the British Empire. If Rushdie's political support for the Sandinistas reveals a tricontinental socialism that parallels his vision of a 'Third World' literature, in which he identified common literary strategies between and among writers from decolonising countries, he is also critical of the ways in which religion increasingly came to dominate politics at the end of the Cold War period, as socialism failed to provide a real political alternative to capitalism's global expansion in the 'Third World'.

In an essay titled 'In God We Trust' (published in *Imaginary Homelands*), Rushdie clearly articulates his position as a 'wholly secular person' who has been 'drawn towards the great traditions of secular radicalism – in politics, socialism; in the arts, modernism and its offspring' (377). Such a position is further reflected in his account of Islamic revivalism in Pakistan and Iran, and Hindu fundamentalism in India. For Rushdie, a religious revival is not 'a religious event', but rather 'a political event that is almost always nationalist in character' (380). While Rushdie emphasises that 'Khomeini's revolution was intensely nationalistic in character', he also considers the significance of Ali Shariati's phrase 'a revolt against history' (383). Invoking Benedict Anderson's argument that the nation state emerges in 'homogeneous empty time' – an idea, which Rushdie also satirises in Mountbatten's ticktock in *Midnight's Children* – Rushdie argues that when 'religion enters the political arena today … it does so as an event in linear time; that is, as a part of the world of the nation-state, and not a rejection of it' (382). Such an argument is instructive for reading *The Satanic Verses*, for it clarifies that the novel's satirical representation of the anti-historical Imam and Gibreel Farishta's dream of seventh-century Mecca was specifically opposed to the anti-historical premise of Khomeini's political ideology of Islamic revivalism in late twentieth-century Iran, and the assumption that the birth of Islam took place outside of history, rather than simply seeking to denigrate Islam (as many of the novel's critics suggested).

As well as interrogating Khomeini's political ideology of Islamic revivalism in 'In God We Trust', Rushdie addresses the rise of communal violence in India and the popularity of the Christian right in the United States. Against the criticism that Nehru's idea of state secularism in India is no more than a slogan, Rushdie examines the historical context in which secularism was formed. In Rushdie's analysis, it was the fear 'that a Hindu *imperium* might take the place of the British Raj' as well as the 'terrible killings of the Partition riots', which underpinned Nehru's 'idea of a godless State' (385). Rushdie concludes his essay by arguing that the 'religious fundamentalism of the United States is as alarming as anything in the much feared world of Islam' (389). In view of Rushdie's recent pronouncements about Islam and his support for the US-led wars in Afghanistan and Iraq, however, this criticism of the Christian right, as well as his criticism of American foreign policy in Latin America during the 1980s would seem to represent a broadly left-wing, anti-imperialist position that Rushdie has since abandoned.

Rushdie's British Film Institute study of *The Wizard of Oz* offers some interesting insights into the ways in which both Hollywood and Bombay cinema has influenced the aesthetic form of his fiction. As well as recounting how his first experiment with fiction as a child was inspired in part by viewing the *Wizard of Oz* alongside Hindi movies at Bombay's Metro Cinema, Rushdie criticises the conservative message at the end of the film – 'there's no place like home' – on the grounds that 'there is no longer any such place *as* home: except of course, for the home we make, or the homes that are made for us, in Oz: which is anywhere and everywhere, except the place from which we began' (Rushdie 57). Such an argument echoes Rushdie's claim in *Imaginary Homelands* that when the migrant writer or the writer in exile looks back, they do so in the knowledge 'that [they] will not be capable of reclaiming precisely the thing that was lost' and that as a consequence the 'homelands' that they create will be 'imaginary' (Rushdie 1991: 10).

The production of a stage version of *Midnight's Children* first performed at London's Barbican Theatre in January 2003 may appear to reinforce the status of Rushdie's second novel as a contemporary classic. The play utilised the visual media alluded to in *Midnight's Children* by placing a film screen depicting 'the infinite crowd that is India today' on the stage (Rushdie 2003a: 1), and by re-playing Nehru's political speeches as an auditory contextual backdrop to the dialogue. In the stage version of the novel, however, Saleem's digressive, hyperbolic and fast-paced narrative is transformed into a truncated dialogue with a smaller cast of characters than the multitude which populates the novel. As one reviewer observed in *The New York Times*:

> The stage version – shaped by Mr. Rushdie in collaboration with Tim Supple, the show's director, and Simon Reade, its dramaturge – never finds a theatrical means of conveying this galloping momentum. In striving for clarity, it consistently muffles its own climaxes and flattens its Dickensian twists of plots. (Brantley 2003: 5)

Rushdie's second volume of essays and non-fiction, *Step Across this Line*, contain a range of essays on popular culture and popular music, literature and politics. The volume is perhaps most valuable to readers of Rushdie's fiction as a critical resource, which provides some insights into the trajectory of Rushdie's thinking and writing in the aftermath of *The Satanic Verses* affair, and the time Rushdie spent living in safe houses. Rushdie's characterisation of the period following the death sentence publicly announced by the Ayatollah Khomeini on February 14 1989 as the 'plague years' and his claim that the so-called *fatwa* is a 'straightforward terrorist threat' because it 'exceeds its author's jurisdiction', 'contravenes fundamental principles of Islamic law' and was 'issued without the faintest pretence of any legal process' (250) is consistent with the secularist ethos of Rushdie's fiction and criticism. Such writings may offer an index to what the literary critic Madelena Gonzalez has called Rushdie's 'traumatic biography' (Gonzalez 2005: 6) during his life in hiding under the shadow of Khomeini's death sentence, but they also prefigure a shift in Rushdie's political position after the attacks of September 11 2001. Rushdie's experience of living in fear of death for several years may certainly account for what he calls his liberal support for the US-led wars in Afghanistan and Iraq (discussed in Chapter 6), even though they do not justify such a position.

Step Across this Line also includes reflections by Rushdie on globalisation, the American elections of 2000, Rock Music, celebrity photography, Kashmir, anti-Americanism, Reality-TV, the coup led by George Speight against the Indian migrant population of Fiji in June 2000 and the communal riots in Gujarat in March 2002. If, as Timothy Brennan has suggested, there is a 'seamless edge between [Rushdie's] journalism and his novels' (Brennan 2006: 74), the following extract from Rushdie's essay on the anti-establishment ethos of rock 'n' roll music seems to capture Rushdie's complex and contradictory position as a diasporic, Third Worldist, Indian secular Muslim dwelling in New York:

> The collapse of communism, the destruction of the Iron Curtain and the Wall, was supposed to usher in a new era of liberty. Instead, the post-Cold War world, suddenly formless and full of possibility, scared many of us stiff. We retreated behind smaller curtains, built smaller stockades, imprisoned ourselves in narrower, ever more fanatical

definitions of ourselves – religious, regional, ethnic – and readied ourselves for war. Today, as the thunder of one such war drowns out the sweet singing of our better selves, I find myself nostalgic for the old spirit of independence and idealism, which once, set infectiously to music, helped bring another war (in Vietnam) to an end'. (Rushdie 301)

Such a nostalgic impulse not only helps to situate Rushdie's engagement with rock 'n' roll in novels such as *The Ground Beneath her Feet* but also helps to map the trajectory of Rushdie's geopolitical imagination between the end of the Cold War in the 1980s and the US-led wars in Afghanistan and Iraq in the first decade of the twenty-first century.

10

CRITICAL RECEPTION

Throughout this study I have referred to critical essays and studies of Rushdie's fiction in journals and books to support the case for reading Rushdie's literary and non-literary texts as fictions of postcolonial modernity. This section of the book aims to supplement the account of Rushdie's criticism presented in Chapters 1–7 by providing a short and selected history of Rushdie's critical reception. In this chapter, I concentrate mainly on reviews of Rushdie's writing, partly to avoid repetition, and partly to assess the ways in which Rushdie's writing has been read and evaluated in the global literary marketplace, as well as in the pages of academic journals and monographs. While some critics have suggested that Rushdie's fiction post-*The Satanic Verses* lacks the formal and philosophical complexity of the earlier novels (Clark 2001), others have noted a shift in the narrative structure and style of Rushdie's fiction that corresponds with Rushdie's traumatic biography (Gonzalez 2005). However, such a critical framing of Rushdie's fictional work before and after the so-called Rushdie affair can overlook the development of what Timothy Brennan has called a uniquely situated cosmopolitan perspective in Rushdie's fictional work from the start of his literary career (Brennan 2006). This cosmopolitan or worldly outlook may, as Brennan suggests, also assume a privileged transnational class position in relation to the working-class subjects that are represented in the novels. But as this book has suggested, Rushdie's literary fiction from *Midnight's Children* to *Shalimar the Clown* presents a complex and often contradictory vision of the modern postcolonial world, which allows for readings that brush against the grain of this elite, cosmopolitan perspective.

A SHORT HISTORY OF RUSHDIE'S
CRITICAL RECEPTION

Critical interest in Rushdie's first novel *Grimus* (1975) was relatively scant at first, with reviewers such as David Wilson not only praising its ambition and confidence but also describing the novel as 'a strikingly convoluted fable about the human condition' and an 'elaborate statement of the obvious decked out in the mannerisms of Oxford philosophy' (Wilson 1982: 364). A reviewer for *Publishers Weekly* also praises Rushdie's 'artful first novel' for its 'notably witty prose' (364), and argues that 'Rushdie is a talent to watch' (*Publishers Weekly* 1982: 364). *Grimus* has been re-assessed following the publication of *Midnight's Children, Shame* and *The Satanic Verses*, however, with Catherine Cundy noting parallels between the divided protagonists of *The Satanic Verses* and *Grimus*, as well as Rushdie's allusions to Dante's *Comedy* and Attar's *The Conference of the Birds*, and D. C. R. A. Goonetilleke examining the novel's subversion of conventional gender roles. Ib Johansen contends that '*Grimus* is worth studying for its own sake as a formal experiment: a strange blend of mythical or allegorical narrative, fantasy, science fiction and Menippean satire' (Johansen 24–25) and proceeds to claim that 'the clash between different systems of values and between the people of the *third world* and their *European* colonizers is largely carried out in *metaphorical* terms, as part of a literary experiment with time, space and language' (33). Some critics have also posited a theological reading of the novel. Uma Parmeswaran (1994), for instance, links the narrative structure of *Grimus* to the cyclical structure of Hindu mythology, while Roger Y. Clark suggests that *Grimus* opens the 'doors of cosmological and narratological speculation' (55) in order to demonstrate that there are 'more philosophies and cosmologies than any one mind can dream of' (57).

In contrast to *Grimus*, contemporary reviews of *Midnight's Children* were generally positive, and have no doubt helped to establish Rushdie's public reputation as one of the world's leading writers of contemporary fiction. In one review the Indian novelist Anita Desai praises the book's 'exuberance and fantasy', its 'full and copious language' and concludes that '*Midnight's Children* will surely be recognized as a great tour de force, a dazzling exhibition of the gifts of a new writer of courage, impressive strength, the power of both imagination and control and sheer stylistic brilliance' (Desai 1982: 365). For the novelist Clark Blaise, *Midnight's Children* 'sounds like a continent finding its voice' (365), but he qualifies this rather sweeping generalisation with the observation that *Midnight's Children* is 'a Bombay book', which is 'coarse, knowing, comfortable with Indian pop culture, and, above all, aggressive' (365). Like Blaise, K. B. Rao argues that Rushdie is 'authentic when he writes about Bombay' but adds that 'when Rushdie writes about the rest of India, he is neither so forceful nor so authentic' (Rao 1982: 367). For the critic Valentine Cunningham, however, the novel's achievement is not only its representation of India's 'crowded' character but also its capacity to 'cope with the daunting vastnesses, the multiplicities of things and persons' (Cunningham 1982: 366). Maria Couto identifies one of the limitations of Rushdie's Anglo-Indian perspective in her review of *Midnight's Children*. She observes that Saleem 'cannot think in the language of the masses of India' and questions whether Rushdie's 'inherited Indo-British sensibility, uprooted from Indian reality, can encompass the paradoxes of India's strength and future' (Couto 1982: 369). In doing so, Couto anticipates the criticisms of Aijaz Ahmad and Timothy Brennan, which question the elite, bourgeois sensibility underpinning much of Rushdie's fiction.

Critical studies of *Midnight's Children* have focused on the novel's representation of history, its narrative structure, figurative language and use of generic conventions. Both Timothy Brennan and Neil ten Kortenaar have interpreted the novel as an allegory of India's independence, which self-consciously foregrounds the novel's failure to adequately represent the Indian nation state coming into being (Brennan 1990; ten Kortenaar 2004). For John Clement Ball, the novel's 'pessoptimism' with the Indian nation's postcolonial future is an effect of Rushdie's use of Menippean satire – which is exemplified in Saleem's ambitious attempt to narrate the multitudinous histories of the Indian nation state (Ball 1998: 65). Anuradha Dingwaney Needham reads the novel as a deconstructive re-playing of British colonial and elite nationalist representations of the Indian subcontinent and its history (Needham 2000: 53), while Nalini Natarajan suggests that Rushdie's representation of women in *Midnight's Children* borrows and subverts the myth of the gendered body as a metaphor for the nation in Bombay cinema (Natarajan 165–181). For Mac Fenwick the novel dramatises the connection between metaphorical and metonymical modes of interpretation through the relationship between the narrator Saleem and Padma, who is both a metaphorical reader and a reader who stands in for the masses (Fenwick 2004: 53–54). What many of these critics gesture towards is an important tension in *Midnight's Children* between the progressive forces of India's postcolonial modernity, exemplified by the optimism disease associated with Nehru's secular vision of India's modernity, and the more coercive aspects of India's postcolonial modernity, such as partition, communal violence, the India-Pakistan war and the emergency.

The question of Rushdie's standpoint as migrant writer, which some critics of *Midnight's Children* have raised, also marks Rushdie's imaginative representation of Pakistan in *Shame*, which as the narrator explains is 'learned' in 'fragments of broken mirrors' (70–71). Many contemporary reviewers of the novel draw comparisons between *Midnight's Children* and *Shame*, and note how Rushdie's magical realist style conceals a thinly veiled political criticism of Pakistan's political leadership. The novelist Blake Morrison, for instance, argues that the ' "masculine saga" of "power, patronage, betrayal, death, revenge" ' in *Shame* is 'factually based if scarcely documentary realism', and proceeds to suggest that this saga is 'balanced by a more obviously fantastic "feminine" plot' (Morrison 1985: 353). For Timothy Hyman, '*Shame* stands to *Midnight's Children* very much as Pakistan to India: a smaller book for meaner world' (Hyman 1985: 354). In Hyman's reading of *Shame*, Pakistan is presented as a mistake from the start, in striking contrast to the India of *Midnight's Children*, which 'remained throughout the book a magnificent possibility' (Hyman 354). Una Chaudhuri echoes this reading of the novel's representation of the Pakistani state in her observation that 'Sufiya Zenobia is the utterly convincing and terrifying product of a culture lost in falsehood and corruption' (Chaudhuri 1985: 357). Many of these reviews identify some of the principle critical questions that animate *Shame*, such as the extent to which Pakistan is fictionalised in the novel, and the question of whether the fantastic story of Sufiya Zinobia provides an effective counterpoint to the narrator's thinly veiled political satire. Yet they stop short of explaining how the fantastic account of Sufiya Zinobia in the novel embodies the public secret of state repression in *Shame*.

In an article published on US foreign policy in the Middle East and Latin America during the so-called Irangate Affair in the

London Review of Books in 1987, the postcolonial critic Edward Said praises Rushdie's travelogue about Nicaragua *The Jaguar Smile* on the grounds that it contests the mainstream American media portrayals of Nicaragua and the Sandinistas. As Said puts it, 'To the extent that Rushdie has given Sandinismo a human face, he has perhaps staved off some indifference and some jingoism in America, which has declared war on a movement whose avowed aim is to shake off Yankee tutelage' (Said 1987: 10). Yet Said also suggests that Rushdie's criticism of Reagan's foreign policy in Nicaragua and his caution against the censorship of the press in Nicaragua does not go far enough, and that *The Jaguar Smile* – as an example of what Said calls 'the emerging alternative movement' – needs to do more to 'formulate solutions, ideas, and even utopian hopes' (10). Said's review is significant because it identifies a left-wing position in Rushdie's non-fictional writings of the 1980s, especially with regard to American foreign policy; a position that many critics feel Rushdie abandoned in his journalistic reflections on the Bush administration's wars in Afghanistan and Iraq in the first decade of the twenty-first century.

The publication of the paperback edition of the *Satanic Verses* in 1989 has generated a surfeit of responses in the world press, radio and television, as well as academic books and journals. As Joel Kuortti has argued in his *Salman Rushdie Bibliography*, the *Satanic Verses* affair received such wide coverage in the press that it would be impossible to document all of this material (Kuortti 1997a: 7). Many of the critical responses to *The Satanic Verses* adopted a position of either defending Rushdie's novel in accordance with the enlightenment principle of free speech, or attacking the novel on the grounds that it denigrated Islam by rehearsing Orientalist stereotypes of the Prophet and the *Qur'ān*. Rather than simply rehearsing these arguments, the following section presents a selective critical assessment of reviews and essays that engage with the novel itself.

Madhu Jain in a review of the novel published in *India Today* praises the 'kaleidoscopic' quality of the novel, and links its radical shifts in time and space to the aesthetics of Bombay cinema; yet he also adds that the novel is 'an uncompromising, unequivocal attack on religious fanaticism and fundamentalism, which is largely Islamic' (Jain 1988: 215) and which is 'bound to trigger an avalanche of protests from the ramparts' (Jain 216). In a similar vein, the literary critic Hermione Lee, in a review that was originally published in the London *Observer* on September 25 1988, notes the cinematic quality of the novel and describes Rushdie's fictional reinvention of Islamic history as 'the Koran rewritten as science fiction by Burroughs or Ballard' (Lee 1988: 217). Yet, at the same time, Lee argues that there is 'about this massive, wilful undertaking a *folie de grandeur* which sends its brilliant comic energy, its fierce satiric powers, and its unmatchable, demonic inventiveness plunging down, on melting wings, towards unreadability' (Lee 1988: 217). Patrick Parrinder's review of *The Satanic Verses*, originally published in *The London Review of Books*, situates the novel in relation to historical accounts of the apocryphal Satanic Verses episode, and Western translations of the Islamic scriptures which 'argue that the Koran as a whole is a forgery' (Parrinder 1988: 218). Rather then elaborating on the broader significance of this history, and speculating on the possible repercussions of Rushdie's allusions to this history in his novel, however, Parrinder concludes that the novel is 'damnably entertaining, and fiendishly ingenious' (Parrinder: 218–219). In an astute review of the novel's embedded narratives for the *Times Literary Supplement*, Robert Irwin notes that the connections between Rushdie's 'story of the Imam, a grim religious bigot in exile in London (who is and is not the Ayatollah Khomeini in exile in Paris)', as well as the distorted echo of the historical origins of Islam in Rushdie's story of Jahilia (Irwin 1998: 220). Ian Sinclair is less enthusiastic about *The Satanic Verses*, and in a barely veiled criticism of Rushdie's representation of Margaret Thatcher's Britain, argues that the 'authorial voice is ... uniformly decent in its attitude towards the mean-spirited culture with which it seems forced to deal' (Sinclair 1988: 219). Such a reading seems to anticipate Timothy Brennan's critique of Rushdie's representation of Black-British culture and the working-class characters of Jahilia in *The Satanic Verses*.

In response to the novel's proscription in India, the riots it prompted in Pakistan, and the burning of *The Satanic Verses* in Bradford, England, Rushdie expressed his sadness about 'Labour councillors in Bradford, and Labour MPs in Westminster joining forces with the mullahs' (Rushdie 1988: 223); and argued that *The Satanic Verses* is not 'an anti-religious novel' but 'an attempt to write about migration, its stresses and transformations, from the point of view of migrants from the Indian subcontinent to Britain' (Rushdie: 223). In a similar vein, Michiko Kakutani argued that the novel 'deals only incidentally with Islam', and is more concerned with 'the broader questions of good and evil, identity and meta-morphosis, race and culture' (Kakutani 1988: 223). Jonathon Yardley echoes this view in his claim that *The Satanic Verses* is a 'relatively non-political book' in comparison to *Shame* and *Midnight's Children*, and is more of a 'philosophical novel about the tangled relationship between good and evil, the angelic and the satanic' (Yardley 1988: 224).

What many of the literary reviews of *The Satanic Verses* in the British and American press assume, however, is a global readership that is both familiar with the codes and conventions of contemporary fiction and which shares its secular values. Some of the critical responses to the novel certainly reject the secular values upon which the novel's representation of Islamic history is based. As one commentator puts it:

> Rushdie not only reviles the Prophet in the most vulgar ways, but also portrays the Prophet's wives in the most shameful and indecent manner. The Prophet's wives, according to Qur'ānic parlance, are the 'mothers of the Faithful' and are respected by Muslims in the same way that the Prophet is revered. By calling the brothel a 'curtain' and locating it in the Ka'ba, Rushdie on the one hand, ridicules the Islamic tradition of *Hijab* (Muslim women's dress) and on the other, defiles the sanctity of the Ka'ba, the House of God, the symbol of Muslim unity, towards which Muslims the world over face in their five daily prayers. (Ahsan and Kidwai 1993: 33)

In this quoted passage, the use of verbs such as 'reviles', 'defiles' and 'ridicules' clearly suggest that *The Satanic Verses* was regarded as an obscene representation of the life of the Prophet rather than raising epistemological questions about the structure of belief and revelation (as Rushdie argued in his defence of the novel). Such a response is echoed in Shabbir Akhtar's observation that 'There is nothing in *The Satanic Verses* which helps to bring Islam into a fruitful confrontation with modernity, nothing that brings it into thoughtful contact with contemporary secularity and ideological pluralism' (Akhtar in Bowen 1994: 29).

As Chapter 4 suggested, *The Satanic Verses* affair became part of a global political debate in what Aamir Mufti calls the Islamic public sphere, especially after Ayatollah Khomeini declared that it was the responsibility of Muslims around the world to kill Rushdie (see

Mufti in Booker). Yet, to attribute all expressions of Muslim out-
rage to the novel to 'fundamentalists and the mullahs' is, as Tariq
Modood has suggested, a form of racism, which treats all Muslims
as the same, and forecloses rational critical debate (Modood 1990:
155). The so-called Muslim response to *The Satanic Verses* is complicated by an edited collection of essays entitled *For Rushdie*, which
offers a series of responses from leading Muslim intellectuals and
writers to *The Satanic Verses* in defence of Rushdie. Many of these
responses criticise Khomeini's political tyranny, and suggest that
Rushdie's 'condemnation to death ... is contrary to the spirit of
Islam' (Adnan in *For Rushdie* 16). Others question the legitimacy of
Ayatollah Khomeini's *fatwa* (Al-Azmeh in *For Rushdie* 22), his charge
that Rushdie is an 'apostate' (Gandjeih in *For Rushdie* 153), and argue
that 'the critical position taken by Rushdie is actually essential to
the modern historical development of the Arab and Muslim
worlds' (Al-Azmeh in *For Rushdie* 26).

It is also worth noting that many commentaries on *The Satanic
Verses* affair do not actually engage with the novel itself. This may
be a consequence of the way in which Rushdie and his novel was
transformed into a symbol of the cultural values of the secular
British nation state, as Jean Kane argues, 'Whether depicted as a
person, a book, or as the nation-state itself, the metonymic structure of the individual in these binaries is structured as a fetish'
(Kane 2006: 432). Such a reading is, however, based on the premise
that Rushdie is a British writer rather than a secular diasporic
Indian Muslim writer, whose satirical reflections on migration and
Islamic history in *The Satanic Verses* are partly informed by the cultural practices of both Bombay cinema and Urdu poetry.

Catherine Cundy's reading of Rushdie's *Haroun and the Sea of
Stories* in her 1996 study of Salman Rushdie situates the novel in relation to Rushdie's own plight as a writer following the death sentence
pronounced by the Ayatollah Khomeini, the break up of his marriage, his imposed exile and the impact that all of this might have on
his son, Zafar. But she also traces the text's allusions to the *Arabian
Nights*, Attar's *Conference of the Birds*, Bombay cinema, such as Satyajit
Ray's 1969 film *Goopy Gyne Bagha Byne*, and the Hollywood classic
The Wizard of Oz. For Roger Y. Clark, however, one 'of the more interesting aspects of *Haroun* is the way Attar's twelfth-Century Persian
paradigm slides into Somadeva's eleventh-Century Sanskrit one'
(Clark 2001: 186). In Clark's reading, Rushdie's synthesis of these

two religious paradigms 'strengthens the pro-unity moral Rushdie is aiming at' (Clark 188).

Many of the critical readings of Rushdie's short story collection *East, West* note how Rushdie's stories were first published in a number of different journals, and how the collection lacks the richness and complexity of some of his novels. Damian Grant, for instance, suggests that the form of the short story is 'perhaps not the most congenial form of expression for Rushdie' (Grant 1999: 106), and D. C. R. A. Goonetilleke argues that the 'achievement of *East, West* is modest but significant' (Goonetilleke 132). In spite of such criticism, both Grant and Goonetilleke suggest that the geographical structure of the collection provides it with a formal coherence, and consider how themes familiar to readers of Rushdie's other works such as home and migration, India's state of emergency, the secular and the non-secular are developed in *East, West*.

The reviews of Rushdie's sixth novel *The Moor's Last Sigh* (1995) tended to concentrate either on the parallels between Rushdie's fate after the death sentence pronounced by Ayatollah Khomeini and that of his fictional protagonist Moraes Zogoiby, or on Rushdie's satirical representation of the Hindu fundamentalist Shiv Sena party, and its leader Bal Thackeray. In an insightful review of the novel published in *New Statesman and Society*, for example, the writer Aamer Hussein argues that Raman Fielding is 'a twin soul of the real-life demagogue Bal Thackeray, whose pseudo-ideologies, proclaimed by his Shiv Sena party, Fielding shares' (Hussein 1997: 285). Yet he also praises Rushdie's ability 'to integrate fantastic narrative with historical insight' (286), a skill which is exemplified by the 'guiding metaphor of Aurora's paintings' in *The Moor's Last Sigh* (Hussein 286). Michael Wood's review of *The Moor's Last Sigh* not only picks up on the garrulousness, hyperbole and melodrama of the novel but also praises the success of Rushdie's use of Aurora's paintings as a structural device in the novel (Wood 1997: 286–289). The novelist Orhan Pamuk in a review published in *The Times Literary Supplement* reads the novel as 'a grand family chronicle' (Pamuk 1997: 289), which 'most resembles *Midnight's Children*' in 'its scope, its ambition and its magic' (290). Pamuk also notes how *The Moor's Last Sigh* juxtaposes two sides of Bombay: 'the many headed cosmopolis of diverse cultures' and the 'new Bombay of religious and nationalistic fanaticism' (291). In a review for *The New York Times*, Michiko Kakutani also compares the novel to *Midnight's Children*, and argues that 'The *Moor's Last Sigh* traces the downward spiral of expectations experienced by India as post-independence hopes for democracy crumbled during the emergency rule declared by Prime Minister Indira Gandhi in 1975, and early dreams of pluralism gave way to sectarian violence and political corruption' (Kakutani 1997: 295). Kakutani also draws parallels between Rushdie's own fate and that of Moraes Zogoiby at the end of *The Moor's Last Sigh*.

Like Kakutani, one reviewer in *Publisher's Weekly* suggests that 'Rushdie's own plight' informs the pages of *The Moor's Last Sigh*, but adds that this is 'always integrated into plot and character' (Publisher's Weekly 1997: 292); while another reviewer for the Canadian magazine *Maclean's* argues that the novel 'reads like the vision of a harried mind that has lost touch with the pace and amplitude of everyday life' (Bemrose 1997: 293). In a more detailed treatment of the novel first published in *The New York Review of Books*, the South African writer J. M. Coetzee examines Rushdie's use of the palimpsest as 'a novelistic, historiographical and autobiographical device' (Coetzee 1997: 321), and argues that 'the darkly prophetic imagination of Aurora Zogoiby' dominates Rushdie's use of ekphrasis in the novel (322). Coetzee also asks what it means for Moraes to declare that he is a Jew, and to 'assert, however symbolically, solidarity with persecuted minorities worldwide' (323). As I argued in Chapter 5, such a question is significant because it raises questions about the limitations of liberal secularism in postcolonial India.

Critical essays on *The Moor's Last Sigh* have tended to concentrate on Rushdie's representation of the rise of Hindu fundamentalism and the limitations of secularism in postcolonial India, as well as the significance of Aurora Zogoiby's palimpsest paintings. Jonathan Greenberg examines what is at stake in Rushdie's half-buried intertextual allusion to Shakespeare's *Othello*, while Stephen Heninghan builds on Timothy Brennan's reading of the Indian-Latin American connection in Rushdie's fiction by tracing the parallels between *The Moor's Last Sigh* and Juan Ruolfo's novel *Pedro Páramo* (Henighan 1998). Rachel Trousdale (2004) examines the rise of Hindu fundamentalism and globalisation in Bombay, and Jill Didur (2004) argues that *The Moor's Last Sigh* offers an ethical counterpoint to the liberal discourse of secularism upon which Nehru's rhetoric of secular socialism was based.

If the critical assessment of *The Moor's Last Sigh* was generally positive in its praise of Rushdie's cosmopolitan vision of India, the reception of Rushdie's seventh novel *The Ground Beneath Her Feet* was rather mixed. Pankaj Mishra, in a review published in *New Statesman and Society*, criticised the 'cartoon-like simplicity of the novel' with 'its banal obsessions', 'empty bombast', 'pseudo-characters' and 'non-events', and argued that the novel 'does little more than echo the white noise of the modern world' (Mishra 2004: 248). David Caute suggests that the problem with *The Ground Beneath Her Feet* is its attempt to represent England or America, which results in 'a strained satirical stridency', and 'a constant cartoon quality' which 'induces periodic weariness and boredom' (Caute 2004: 249). In a similar vein, Bruce King suggests that the narrative voice of *The Ground Beneath Her Feet* sounds more like Kurt Vonnegut than Salman Rushdie, and concludes from his reading of the novel that Rushdie, like V. S. Naipaul, faces the problem of 'what to write about after using up memories of "home" ' (King 2004: 285).

The absence of Rushdie's eighth novel *Fury* from the long list of the 2001 Booker Prize could be interpreted as an indication of Rushdie's declining success as an international writer in the early twenty-first century. Such a view would appear to be supported by Robert Edric's criticism of Rushdie's 'excessively explicatory and self-regarding prose', which renders his characters 'cold and uninteresting' (Edric 2004: 307) and by Lee Siegel's claim that 'Rushdie's intelligence [in *Fury*] gets in the way of his fantastically gifted viscera' (Siegel 2004: 309). In a biographical reading of the novel, James Wood argues that *Fury* is a 'flailing apologia' (Wood 2004: 311) that dramatises 'how America has seduced and even, on occasion, compromised [Rushdie's] soul' (313). This view of Rushdie's ambivalent relationship to the United States and its foreign policy is echoed by Simon and Sabina Sawhney in their article on Rushdie's post-911 journalism. As they put it, 'If Rushdie indeed wishes his voice to be heard in the countries of South and West Asia, he will not be helped by his endorsement of the "war on terror" ' (Sawhney and Sawhney 2001: 437).

The reception of Rushdie's novel *Shalimar the Clown* has been more upbeat. Jason Cowley in a review published in the London *Observer* claims that in contrast to *Fury* '*Shalimar* is an altogether different book: calmer, more compassionate wiser'. He proceeds to argue that '*Shalimar the Clown* is Rushdie's most engaging book since

Midnight's Children', not only because it combines elements of a lament, a love story and a revenge story but also because it 'grapples imaginatively with the shock of September 11 2001 and the wars that have followed' (Cowley 2005). For Natasha Walter in a *Guardian* review, however, the novel reads as 'an impassioned lecture on the roots of violence and the awful fate of Kashmir' with 'an increasingly absurd plot', in which the characters are 'almost crushed by the freight of nations that they carry around on their shoulders', and a 'style that is more and more mannered' (Walter 2005). In a more sophisticated critical reading of *Shalimar*, Robert Eaglestone argues that the final aporia of the novel in which the arrow that Kashmira fires at Shalimar is frozen in time and space exemplifies Rushdie's 'dream reasoning': 'the generation of ideas without the aim of consensus, without following the strict rules of logic'. 'Unless we attend to his work as this sort of thinking', Eaglestone concludes 'Rushdie's work will continue to elude us' (Eaglestone in Tew and Mengham 2006: 101).

BIBLIOGRAPHY

WORKS BY RUSHDIE

—— *Grimus*. London: Vintage, 1996, 1975.

—— *Midnight's Children*. London: Picador, 1982, 1981.

—— 'The Empire writes back with a vengeance' *The Times*, Saturday July 8, 1982.

—— *Shame*. London: Picador, 1984, 1983.

—— *The Jaguar Smile*. London: Picador, 1987.

—— *The Satanic Verses*. London: Vintage, 1998, 1988.

—— 'Choice between Light and Dark'. *Contemporary Literary Criticism* 55, Detroit, MI: Gale Research Inc., 1988, p. 223.

—— *Two Stories by Salman Rushdie*. Privately printed by Sebastian Carter in Great Britain, Number 13 of 72 held in the British Library Cup. 510. cc. 109, 1989.

—— *Haroun and the Sea of Stories*. London: Viking, 1999, 1990.

—— *Imaginary Homelands*. London: Granta, 1992, 1991.

—— *East, West*. London: Vintage, 1994.

—— *The Moor's Last Sigh*. London: Vintage, 1996, 1995.

—— *The Ground Beneath Her Feet*. London: Vintage, 2000, 1999.

—— *Fury*. London: Vintage, 2002, 2001.

—— *Step Across This Line*. London: Jonathon Cape, 2003.

—— *Shalimar the Clown*. London: Jonathon Cape, 2005.

—— The Right Time for an Islamic Reformation' *Washington Post*. Sunday, August 7, 2005; p. B07.

INTERVIEWS

Chahan, Pradyumna S., ed., *Salman Rushdie Interviews: A Sourcebook of His Ideas*. Westport: Greenwood Press, 2001.

SECONDARY CRITICISM

Adnan, Etel. 'On the Subject of Rushdie'. *For Rushdie: A Collection of Essays by 100 Arabic and Muslim Writers*. New York: George Braziller, 1994, pp. 16–17.

Agamben, Giorgio. *Homo Sacer: Sovereign Power and Bare Life*. Trans. Daniel Heller-Roazen. Stanford: Stanford University Press, 1998.

Ahmad, Aijaz. *In Theory: Classes, Nations, Literatures*. London: Verso, 1992.

Ahsan, M. M. 'The "Satanic" Verses and the Orientalists', eds M. M. Ahsan and A. R. Kidwai *Sacrilege Versus Civility: Muslims Perspectives on 'The Satanic Verses' Affair*, Leicester: the Islamic Foundation, 1991, pp. 131–141.

Ahsan, M. M. and Kidwai, A. R. (eds). *Sacrilege Versus Civility: Muslim Perspectives on the Satanic Verses Affair*. Markfield: Islamic Foundation, 1993.

Aji, Aron R. ' "All Names Mean Something": Salman Rushdie's *Haroun* and the Legacy of Islam', *Contemporary Literature*, Vol. 36, No. 1, Spring 1995, pp. 103–129.

Akhtar, Shabbir. 'Be Careful with Muhammad', ed., David Bowen *The Satanic Verses: Bradford Responds*. Bradford: Bradford and Ilkley Community College, 1994, pp. 28–32.

Al-Azm, Shadik J. 'Is the Fatwa a Fatwa?', *For Rushdie: A collection of essays by 100 Arabic and Muslim Writers*. New York: George Braziller, 1994, pp. 21–23.

Al-Azmeh, Aziz. 'Rushdie the Traitor', *For Rushdie: A collection of essays by 100 Arabic and Muslim Writers*. New York: George Braziller, 1994, pp. 24–27.

—— *Islams and Modernities*. London: Verso, 1993.

Al-Hakim Al-Tirmidhi. *The Concept of Sainthood in Early Islamic Mysticism*. Trans. Bernd Radtke and John O'Kane. Richmond, Surrey: Curzon, 1996.

Appadurai, Arjun, *Fear of Small Numbers: An Essay on The Geography of Anger*. Durham, NC.: Duke University Press, 2006.

—— *Modernity at Large: Cultural Dimensions of Globalization*. Minneapolis: University of Minnesota Press, 1996.

Aravamudan, Srinivas. ' "Being God's Postman is No Fun, Yaar": Salman Rushdie's *The Satanic Verses*', ed., M. D. Fletcher. *Reading Rushdie: Perspectives on the Fiction of Salman Rushdie*. Amsterdam: Rodopi, 1994, pp. 187–208.

Asad, Talal. *Formations of the Secular: Christianity, Islam, Modernity*. Stanford, California: Stanford University Press, 2003.

—— *Genealogies of Religion: Discipline and Reasons of Power in Christianity and Islam*. Baltimore: Johns Hopkins University Press, 1993.

Bader, Rudolf. 'Indian Tin Drum', *International Fiction Review*, 11, 1984, 75–83.

Bahri, Deepika. *Native Intelligence: Aesthetics, Politics, and Postcolonial Literature*. Minneapolis: University of Minnesota Press, 2003.

Bakhash, Shaul. 'What's Khomeini Up To?' *Contemporary Literary Criticism* 55, Detroit, MI: Gale Research Inc., 1988, pp. 236–7.

Ball, J. Clement. 'Pessoptimism: Satire and the Menippean Grotesque in Rushdie's *Midnight's Children*' *English Studies in Canada*. Vol. 24, No. 1, 1998, pp. 61–82.

Barthes, Roland. *The Eiffel Tower and other mythologies*. Trans. Richard Howard. Berkeley: University of California Press, 1997.

Baucom, Ian. *Out of Place: Englishness, Empire, and the Locations of Identity*. Princeton, N. J.: Princeton University Press, 1999.

Behera, Navnita Chadha. *State, Identity and Violence: Jammu, Kashmir and Ladakh.* New Delhi: Manohar, 2000.

Bemrose, John. 'Tower of Babble', *Contemporary Literary Criticism* 100, Detroit, MI: Gale Research Inc., 1997, pp. 292–293.

Bennett, Robert. 'National Allegory or Carnivalesque Heteroglossia? *Midnight's Children's* Narration of Indian National Identity', *Bucknell Review: A Scholarly Journal of Letters, Arts and Sciences.* Vol. 43, No. 2, 2000, pp. 177–194.

Bennett-Jones, Owen. *Pakistan: Eye of the Storm.* New Haven: Yale University Press, 2002.

Bhabha, Homi K. 'Unpacking My Library … Again', eds Iain Chambers and Lidia Curtis, *The Post-Colonial Question: Common Skies, Divided Horizons.* London and New York: Routledge, 1996, pp. 199–211.

—— *The Location of Culture.* London: Routledge, 1994.

Bhargava, Rajeev, ed., *Secularism and Its Critics.* Delhi: Oxford University Press, 1998.

Bharucha, Rustom. *In the Name of the Secular: Contemporary Cultural Activism in India.* Delhi: Oxford University Press, 1998.

Blaise, Clark. 'A Novel of India's Coming of Age', *Contemporary Literary Criticism* 23, Detroit, MI: Gale Research Inc., 1982, pp. 365–366.

Bob, Clifford. *The Marketing of Rebellion: Insurgents, Media and International Activism.* New York: Cambridge University Press, 2005.

Booker, M. Keith, ed., *Critical Essays on Salman Rushdie.* New York: GK. Hall, 1999.

—— Booker, M. Keith. 'Midnight's Children, History, and Complexity: Reading Rushdie after the Cold War', *Critical Essays on Salman Rushdie,* pp. 283–314.

Bowers, Maggie Ann. *Magic(al) Realism.* Abingdon: Routledge, 2004.

Bowles, Chester. *Ambassador's Report* (An account of the author's impressions and activities as US. Ambassador to India and Nepal, 1951–1952). Victor Gollancz: London, 1954.

Ben Brantley. 'Theater Review – An Abundance of Plot, Flashes and Videos', *The New York Times* March 25, 2003, p. 5.

Brennan, Timothy. *Salman Rushdie and the Third World: Myths of the Nation.* Basingstoke: Macmillan, 1989.

—— *Wars of Position: The Cultural Politics of Left and Right.* New York: Columbia University Press, 2006.

Bronfen, Elisabeth. 'Celebrating Catastrophe', *Angelaki,* Vol. 7, No. 2, August 2002, pp. 175–186.

Brouillette, Sarah. 'Authorship as crisis in Salman Rushdie's *Fury*', *Journal of Commonwealth Literature,* Vol. 40, No. 1, 2005, pp. 137–156.

Brown, Wendy. *Regulating Aversion: Tolerance in the Age of Identity and Empire.* Princeton, NJ.: Princeton University Press, 2006.

Butler, Judith. *Precarious Life: The Powers of Mourning and Violence*. London: Verso, 2004.

—— Laclau, Ernesto and Zizek, Slavoj. *Contingency, Hegemony, Universality: Contemporary Dialogues on the Left*. London: Verso, 2000.

Cadava, Eduardo. *Words of Light: Theses on the Photography of History*. Princeton, NJ.: Princeton University Press, 1997.

Caute, David. *Contemporary Literary Criticism* 191, Detroit, MI: Gale Research Inc., 2004, pp. 248–251.

Chakrabarty, Dipesh. *Provincializing Europe: Postcolonial Thought and Historical Difference*. Princeton, NJ.: Princeton University Press, 2000.

Chatterjee, Partha 'Secularism and Toleration', *A Possible India: Essays in Political Criticism*. Delhi: Oxford University Press, 1997, pp. 228–262.

—— 'Talking about Our Modernity in Two Languages', *A Possible India: Essays in Political Criticism*. Delhi: Oxford University Press, 1997, pp. 263–285.

—— *Nationalist Thought and the Colonial World: a Derivative Discourse?* London: Zed, 1986.

Chaudhuri, Una. 'Review of *Shame*', *Contemporary Literary Criticism* 31, Detroit, MI: Gale Research Inc., 1985, p. 357.

Clark, Roger Y. *Stranger Gods: Salman Rushdie's Other Worlds*. Montreal: McGill-Queen's University Press, 2001.

Cleary, Joe. *Literature, Partition and The Nation State: Culture and Conflict in Ireland, Israel and Palestine*. Cambridge: Cambridge University Press, 2002.

Coetzee, J. M. 'Palimpsest Regained', *Contemporary Literary Criticism* 100, Detroit, MI: Gale Research Inc., 1997, pp. 319–324.

Communist Party of India. *CPI's fight Against the Caucus, Sterilisation and Demolition*. New Delhi: Communist Party of India, 1977.

Cossman, Brenda and Ratna, Kapur. *Secularism's Last Sigh? Hindutva and the (mis)Rule of Law*. New Delhi: Oxford University Press, 1999.

Couto, Maria. '*Midnight's Children* and Parents', *Contemporary Literary Criticism* 23, Detroit, MI: Gale Research Inc., 1982, pp. 367–369.

Cowley, Jason. 'From Here to Kashmir', *The Observer*, Sunday September 11, 2005.

Cundy, Catherine. *Salman Rushdie*. Manchester: Manchester University Press, 1996.

—— 'Through Childhood's Window: Haroun and the Sea of Stories', ed. M. D. Fletcher, *Reading Rushdie: Perspectives on the Fiction of Salman Rushdie*. Amsterdam: Rodopi, 1994, pp. 335–341.

Cunningham, Valentine. 'Nosing out the Indian Reality', *Contemporary Literary Criticism* 23, Detroit, MI: Gale Research Inc., 1982, p. 366.

Dauer, Richard P. *A North-South Mind in an East-West World: Chester Bowles and the Making of United States Cold War Foreign Policy, 1951–1969*. Westport, Conn.: Praeger, 2005.

Deleuze, Gilles and Guattari, Felix. *A Thousand Plateaus: Capitalism and Schizophrenia*. Trans. Brian Massumi. Minneapolis: University of Minnesota Press, 1987.

Denning, Michael. *Culture in the Age of Three Worlds*. London: Verso, 2004.

Desai, Anita 'Where Cultures Clash by Night', *Contemporary Literary Criticism* 23, Detroit, MI: Gale Research Inc., 1982, p. 365.

Desani, G. V. *About H. Haterr*. London: Francis Aldor, 1948.

Didur, Jill. 'Secularism beyond the East/West divide: Literary Reading, Ethics, and *The Moor's Last Sigh*', *Textual Practice*, Vol. 18, No. 4, December 2004, pp. 541–562.

Eaglestone, Robert. 'Salman Rushdie: Paradox and Truth', eds Phillip Tew and Rod Mengham, *British Fiction Today*. London: Continuum, 2006, pp. 91–101.

Edric, Robert. *Contemporary Literary Criticism* 191, Detroit, MI: Gale Research Inc., 2004, pp. 248–251.

Erickson, John D. *Islam and Postcolonial Narrative*. Cambridge: Cambridge University Press, 1998.

Fenwick, Mac. 'Crossing the Figurative Gap: Metaphor and Metonymy in *Midnight's Children*', *Journal of Commonwealth Literature*, Vol. 39, No. 3, 2004, pp. 45–68.

Fletcher, M. D. 'Rushdie's *Shame* as Apologue', ed. M. D. Fletcher, *Reading Rushdie: Perspectives on the Fiction of Salman Rushdie*. Amsterdam: Rodopi, 1994, pp. 97–108.

Foucault, Michel. *Society Must be Defended: Lectures at the Collège de France, 1975–1976*. Trans. David Macey, London: Allen Lane, 2003.

Gandjeih, Ayatollah Djalal. 'For Rushdie', *For Rushdie: A Collection of Essays by 100 Arabic and Muslim Writers*. New York: George Braziller, 1994, pp. 149–156.

Gonzalez, Madelena. *Fiction after the fatwa: Salman Rushdie and the Charm of Catastrophe*. Amsterdam: Rodopi, 2005.

Grant, Damian. *Salman Rushdie*. Plymouth: Northcote House in Association with the British Council, 1999.

Grass, Günter. *The Tin Drum*. Trans. by Ralph Manheim. London: Secker & Warburg, 1962. First published 1959.

Greenberg, Jonathan. "'The Base Indian" or "The Base Judean"?: *Othello* and the Metaphor of the Palimpsest in Salman Rushdie's *The Moor's Last Sigh*'. *Modern Language Studies*, Vol. 29, No. 2, Autumn 1999, pp. 93–107.

Goonetilleke, D. C. R. A. *Salman Rushdie*. Basingstoke: Macmillan Press, 1998.

Gregory, Derek. *The Colonial Present: Afghanistan, Palestine, and Iraq*. Oxford: Blackwell, 2004.

Grewal, Inderpal. 'Salman Rushdie: Marginality, Women, and *Shame*', ed. M. D. Fletcher, *Reading Rushdie: Perspectives on the Fiction of Salman Rushdie*. Amsterdam, Netherlands: Rodopi, 1994, pp. 123–144.

Hamilton, Ian. 'The First Life of Salman Rushdie', *The New Yorker*. December 25, 1995/ January 1, 1996, pp. 90, 92–97, 99–102, 104–108, 110, 112–113.

Harvey, David. *The New Imperialism*. Oxford: Oxford University Press, 2003.

Hassumani, Sabrina. *Salman Rushdie: A Postmodern Reading of His Major Works*. Madison, NJ: Fairleigh Dickinson University Press, 2002.

Heehs, Peter. *The Bomb in Bengal*. Delhi: Oxford University Press, 2004.

Henighan, Stephen. 'Coming to Benengeli: The Genesis of Salman Rushdie's Rewriting of Juan Rulfo in *The Moor's Last Sigh*', *Journal of Commonwealth Literature*, Vol. 33, No. 2, 1998, pp. 55–74.

Hirschkop, Ken. *Mikhail Bakhtin: an Aesthetic for Democracy*. Oxford: Oxford University Press, 1999.

Hogan, Patrick Colm. ' "*Midnight's Children*": Kashmir and the Politics of Identity',*Twentieth Century Literature*, Vol. 47, No. 4, Winter 2001, pp. 510–544.

Houen, Alex. *Terrorism and Modern Literature from Joseph Conrad to Ciaran Carson*. Oxford: Oxford University Press, 2002.

Huggan, Graham. *The Postcolonial Exotic: Marketing the Margins*. London: Routledge, 2001.

Huntington, Samuel P. *The Clash of Civilizations and the Remaking of World Order*. New York: Simon and Schuster, 1996.

Hussein, Aamer. 'City of Mongrel Joy', *Contemporary Literary Criticism* 100, Detroit, MI: Gale Research Inc., 1997, pp. 285–286.

Hutcheon, Linda. *A Poetics of Postmodernism: History, Theory, Fiction*. New York: Routledge, 1988.

Hyder, Rehan. *Brimful of Asia: Negotiating Ethnicity on the UK Music Scene*. Aldershot: Ashgate, 2004.

Hyman, Timothy. 'Fairy-Tale Agitprop', *Contemporary Literary Criticism* 31, Detroit, MI: Gale Research Inc., 1985, p. 354.

Ibn Hisham, Abd al-Malik. *The Life of Muhammad: A Translation of Ishaq's Sirat Rasul Allah*. Trans. A. Guillaume. Karachi: Oxford University Press, 1967.

Idris, Farhad B. 'Salman Rushdie', *Dictionary of Literary Bibliography, Volume 323: South Asian Writers in English*, ed. Fakrul Alam. Detroit and London: Thomson Gale, 2006, pp. 314–330.

India Today. 'Salman Rushdie: Satanic Storm', *Contemporary Literary Criticism* 55, Detroit, MI: Gale Research Inc., 1988, pp. 260–263.

Indian Sociologist. June 1908, p. 23.

Irwin, Robert. 'Original Parables', *Contemporary Literary Criticism* 55. Detroit, MI: Gale Research Inc., 1988, p. 220.

Jain, Madhu. 'An Irreverent Journey', *Contemporary Literary Criticism* 55, Detroit, MI: Gale Research Inc., 1988, pp. 215–216.

Johansen, Ib. 'The Flight from the Enchanter: Reflections on Salman Rushdie's *Grimus*', ed. M. D. Fletcher. *Reading Rushdie: Perspectives on the Fiction of Salman Rushdie*. Amsterdam: Rodopi, 1994, pp. 23–34.

PHY

Veekly. 'Science Fiction: *Grimus*', *Contemporary Literary Criticism*
it, MI: Gale Research Inc., 1982, pp. 364–5.

ariq. *Western Muslims and the Future of Islam*. Oxford: Oxford
y Press, 2004.

Ruvani. 'The *fatwa* and its Aftermath', ed. Abdulrazak
The Cambridge Companion to Salman Rushdie. Cambridge
ge University Press, 2007, pp. 45–60.

sia and the Pacific: *Midnight's Children*, *Contemporary Literary*
23, Detroit, MI: Gale Research Inc., 1982, p. 367.

Terror and the Sublime in Art and Critical Theory: from Auschwitz t
a to September 11. Basingstoke: Palgrave Macmillan, 2005.

. 'Unravelling Sharam: Narrativisation as a Political Act i
Rushdie's Shame, *Wasafiri: The Transnational Journal of Internationa*
Vol. 39, Summer 2003, pp. 55–61.

iona. 'The Desecrated Shrine: Movable Icons and Literar
nce In Salman Rushdie's "The Prophet's Hair"', *SOAS Literar*
., Summer 2000. http://www.soas.ac.uk/soaslit/

w and Kristin Ross, eds. *Anti–Americanism*. New York: New Yor
ity Press, 2004.

y and Judith Colp Rubin. *Hating America: A History*. New Yor
University Press, 2004.

alman and Elizabeth West, eds. *The Vintage Book of Indi*
1947–1997. London: Vintage, 1997.

an Rushdie's Midnight's Children, adapted for the theatre b
Rushdie, Simon Reade and Tim Supple. London: Vintag

lph. 'Getting to Know Ghalib', *The Oxford India Ghalib*, ed.Ralp
Delhi: Oxford University Press, 2003, pp. 283–324.

Malise. *A Satanic Affair: Salman Rushdie and the Rage of Isla*
: Chatto & Windus, 1990.

hamad. *A History of Urdu Literature*. London: Oxford Universi
964.

rd. 'Irangate', *London Review of Books*. 7 May 1987, pp. 7–10.

Vorld, the Text, and the Critic. London: Vintage, 1991. First pu
981.

a C. *Salman Rushdie's Postcolonial Metaphors: Migration, Translati*
y, Blasphemy, and Globalization. Westport, Connecticut: Greenwo
001.

Sabina and Simona Sawhney. 'Introduction: Reading Rush
eptember 11, 2001', *Twentieth Century Literature*, Vol. 47, No.
, 2001, pp. 431–443.

loward B. *Chester Bowles: New Dealer in the Cold War*. Cambrid
Harvard University Press, 1993.

Jussawalla, Feroza F. 'Rushdie's Dastan-E-Dilruba: *The Satanic Verses* as
Rushdie's Love Letter to Islam',ed. M. Keith Booker, *Critical Essays on
Salman Rushdie*. New York: G.K. Hall, 1999, pp. 78–106.

Kabir, Ananya Jahanara. 'Subjectivities, Memories, Loss: Of Pigskin Bags,
Silver Spittoons and the Partition of India', *Interventions*, Vol. 4, 2002,
pp. 245–264.

Kakutani, Michiko. 'Serious, Crammed Yet Light', *Contemporary Literary
Criticism*. 100, Detroit, MI: Gale Research Inc., 1997, pp. 295–296.

—— 'Review of *The Satanic Verses*'. *Contemporary Literary Criticism* 55,
Detroit, MI: Gale Research Inc., 1988, pp. 223–224.

Kane, Jean M. 'Embodied Panic: Revisiting Modernist "Religion" in the
Controversies over *Ulysses* and *The Satanic Verses' Textual Practice*, Vol. 20,
No. 3, 2006, pp. 419–440.

—— 'The Migrant Intellectual and the Body of History: Salman Rushdie's
Midnight's Children', *Contemporary Literature*, Vol. 37, No. 1, Spring,
1996, pp. 94–118.

Katz, Nathan. *Who Are the Jews of India?* Berkeley: University of California
Press, 2000.

Kaushik, Surendra Nath. *Politics of Islamization in Pakistan: A Study of the Zia
Regime*. New Delhi: South Asian Publishers, 1993.

Khair, Tabish. *Babu Fictions: Alienation in Contemporary Indian English Novels*.
Delhi: Oxford University Press, 2001.

Khan, Yasmin. *The Great Partition: The Making of India and Pakistan*. New
Haven, Conn.: Yale University Press, 2007).

Khosrokhavar, Farhad. *Suicide Bombers: Allah's New Martyrs*. Trans. David
Macey London: Pluto, 2005.

King, Bruce. 'Review of *The Ground Beneath Her Feet* by Salman Rushdie',
Contemporary Literary Criticism 191, Detroit, MI: Gale Research Inc., 1999,
pp. 245–248.

The Koran. Trans. by N. J. Dawood. London: Allen Lane, 1978.

Kortenaar, Neil ten. *Self, Nation, Text in Salman Rushdie's 'Midnight Children'*.
Montreal and London: McGill-Queen's University Press, 2004.

—— 'Midnight's Children and the Allegory of History', *Ariel* 26.2, 1995, 41–62.

Kumar, Amitava. *Bombay, London, New York*. London: Routledge, 2002.

—— 'Review of *Fury* by Salman Rushdie and *Half a Life* by V. S. Naipaul',
The Nation. November 26, 2001.

Kuortti, Joel. *The Salman Rushdie bibliography: A Bibliography of Salman
Rushdie's Work and Rushdie Criticism*. Frankfurt am Main: Peter Lang,
1997a.

—— *Place of the Sacred: The Rhetoric of The Satanic Verses Affair*. Frankfurt am
Main: Peter Lang, 1997.

—— 'The Satanic Verses: 'To be Born Again, First You Have to Die' in *The
Cambridge Companion to Salman Rushdie*, edited by Abdulrazak Gurnah
Cambridge: Cambridge University Press, 2007, pp. 125–38.

Lazarus, Neil. 'Postcolonial Studies after the Invasion of Iraq', *New Formations*. No. 39, Autumn 2006, pp. 10–22.

Lee, Hermione. 'Falling towards England', *Contemporary Literary Criticism* 55, Detroit, MI: Gale Research Inc., 1988, p. 217.

Lele, Jayant. 'Saffronization of the Shiv Sena: The Political Economy of City State and Nation', eds Sujata Patel and Alice Thorner, *Bombay: Metaphor for Modern India*, Oxford: Oxford University Press, 1995, 185–212.

McMahon, Robert J. *The Cold War on the Periphery: the United States, India, and Pakistan*. New York: Columbia University Press, 1994.

Macaulay, Thomas Babington. *Speeches by Lord Macaulay, with His Minute on Indian Education*. Selected, with an introduction and notes, by G. M. Young (London: World's Classics, 1935).

Mamdani, Mahmood. 'The Politics of Culture Talk in the Contemporary War on Terror', *Hobhouse Memorial Public Lecture*. LSE, 8 March 2007. Transcript available at http://www.lse.ac.uk/collections/LSEPublic LecturesAndEvents/events/2007/20061219t1346z001.htm

Man, Paul de. *Blindness and Insight: Essays in the Rhetoric of Contemporary Criticism*. London: Methuen, 1983.

Massignon, Louis. *The Passion of al-Hallaj Mystic and Martyr of Islam Volume 2: The Survival of al-Hallaj*. Princeton: Princeton University Press, 1982.

Mayer, Arno J. *The Furies: Violence and Terror in the French and Russian Revolutions*. Princeton: Princeton University Press, 2000.

Meisami, Julie Scott and Paul Starkeys, eds. *Encyclopaedia of Arabic Literature*. Volume 1, London: Routledge, 1998.

Menon, Ritu and Kamla, Bhasin. *Borders and Boundaries: Women in India's Partition* (New Delhi: Kali for Women, 1998.)

Merivale, Patricia. 'Saleem Fathered by Oscar: Intertextual Strategies in *Midnight's Children* and *The Tin Drum*', *Reading Rushdie: Perspectives on the Fiction of Salman Rushdie* ed. M. D. Fletcher. Amsterdam: Rodopi, 1994, pp. 83–96.

Mijares, Loretta. '"You Are an Anglo-Indian?": Eurasians and Hybridity and Cosmopolitanism in Salman Rushdie's *Midnight's Children*' *Journal of Commonwealth Literature*, Vol. 38, No. 2, Spring 2003 pp. 125–145.

Mishra, Pankaj. 'The Emperor's New Clothes', *Contemporary Literary Criticism* 191. Detroit, MI: Gale Research Inc., 2004, pp. 245–248.

Modood, Tariq. 'British Asian Muslims and the Rushdie Affair', *Political Quarterly* 61. No. 2, April 1990, pp. 143–160.

Morrison, Blake. 'On a Magic Carpet', *Contemporary Literary Criticism* 31, Detroit, MI: Gale Research Inc., 1985, pp. 353–354.

Mufti, Aamir. *Enlightenment in the Postcolony: The Jewish Question and the Crisis of Postcolonial Culture*. Princeton: Princeton University Press, 2007.
—— 'Towards a Lyric History of India', *Boundary* 2, Vol. 31, No. 2, Summer 2004, pp. 245–274.

—— 'Reading the Rushdie Affair: "Islam M. Keith Booker, *Critical Essays on Salma* 1999, pp. 51–77.
—— 'Auerbach in Istanbul: Edward Sa Question of Minority Culture' *Critical* 1998, pp. 95–125.

Muir, Sir William. *The Life of Mohammad:* John Grant, 1912.

Mujeebuddin, Syed. 'Centres and Margir Rajeshwar Mitapalli and Joel Kuort *Insights*, Vol.1. New Delhi: Atlantic Pu pp. 131–149.

Mukherjee, Meenakshi, ed. *Rushdie's Midn* Delhi: Pencraft International, 1999.

Nandy, Ashis. 'The Politics of Secularism Toleration', ed. Rajeev Bhargava, *Secula* University Press, 1998, pp. 321–344.

Nasr, Seyyed Vali Reza. *Mawdudi and t* Karachi: Oxford University Press, 199

Nasta, Susheila. *Home Truths: Fictions A Britain*. Basingstoke: Palgrave, 2001.

Natarajan, Nalini. 'Women, Nation and ed. Mukherjee, Meenakshi, *Rushdie's Readings*. Delhi: Pencraft International

Needham, Anuradha Dingwaney. *Using tl Literature of the African and South-Asian D* 2000.

Ngai, Sianne. *Ugly Feelings*. Cambridge, N 2005.

Nehru, Jawaharlal. *The Discovery of India*. De

Pamuk, Orhan. 'Salaam Bombay', *Cor* Detroit, MI: Gale Research Inc., 1997,

Pandey, Gyanendra. *Routine Violence: Nati* Stanford University Press, 2006.

Parmeswaran, Uma. 'New Dimensions C Word Play in *Grimus*', ed. M. D. Fletch the Fiction of Salman Rushdie. Amsterda

Parrinder, Patrick. 'Let's Get the Hell O *Criticism* 55, Detroit, MI: Gale Researc

Pathak, Zakia and Rajan, Rajeswari Sund the Political, Judith Butler and Joan London: Routledge, 1992, pp. 257–279

Publisher's Weekly. 'A review of *The l Literary Criticism* 100. Detroit, MI: Gale

Publish
23,
Ramad
Uni
Ranasi
Gur
Can
Rao, K
Criti
Ray, Ge
Hiro
Raza, H
Salm
Writ
Richard
Irrev
Revie
Ross, An
Univ
Rubin, E
Oxfo
Rushdie
Writi
—— Sa
Salm
2003
Russell,
Russe
Ruthven
Lond
Sadiq, M
Press,
Said, Edv
—— The
lished
Sanga, Ja
Hybrid
Press,
Sawhney
after
Winte
Schaffer,
Mass.:

Schimmel, Annemarie. *A History of Indian Literature Volume III: Classical Urdu Literature from the Beginning to Iqbal*. Wiesbaden: Otto Harrassowitz, 1975.

Schmitt, Carl. *Political Theology: Four Chapters on the Concept of Sovereignty*. Trans. George Schwab. Cambridge, Mass.: MIT Press, 1985.

Schofield, Victoria. *Kashmir in Conflict: India, Pakistan and the Unending War*. London: Tauris, 2003.

Sharma, Ashwani 'Sounds Oriental: The (Im)possibility of Theorising Asian Musical Cultures', eds. Sanjay Sharma, John Hutnyk and Ashwani Sharma, *Dis-Orienting Rhythms: The Politics of the New Asian Dance Music*. London and New Jersey: Zed Books, 1996, pp. 15–31.

Siegel, Lee. 'Wild in the Streets', *Contemporary Literary Criticism* 191. Detroit, MI: Gale Research Inc., 2004, pp. 307–310.

Silva, Neluka. 'The Politics of Repression and Resistance in Salman Rushdie's *Shame*', eds. Rajeshwar Mitapalli and Joel Kuortti *Salman Rushdie: New Critical Insights*. Vol.1, New Delhi: Atlantic Publishers and Distributors, 2003, pp. 150–170.

Sinclair, Ian. 'Imaginary Football Teams', *Contemporary Literary Criticism* 55, Detroit, MI: Gale Research Inc., 1988, p. 219.

Sinha, Braj Mohan. *Operation Emergency*. Delhi: Hind Pocket Books, 1977.

Sivanandan, A. 'Race, terror and civil society', *Race and Class* 47, 2006, pp. 1–8.

Smith, Neil. *The Endgame of Globalization*, New York: Routledge, 2005.

—— 'After the American *Lebensraum*', *Interventions*, Vol. 5, No. 2, 2003, pp. 249–270.

Spivak, Gayatri Chakravorty. *In Other Worlds: Essays in Cultural Politics*. New York: Methuen, 1987.

Stauffer, Andrew M. *Anger, revolution, and romanticism*. Cambridge: Cambridge University Press, 2005.

Suleri, Sara. *The Rhetoric of English India*. London: University of Chicago Press, 1992.

Swami, Praveen. *India, Pakistan and the Secret Jihad: the Covert War in Kashmir, 1947–2004*. London: Routledge, 2007.

Tarlo, Emma. *Unsettling Memories: Narratives of the Emergency in Delhi*. London: C. Hurst, 2003.

Taussig, Michael. *Defacement: Public Secrecy and the Labour of the Negative*. Stanford: Stanford University Press, 1999.

—— *The Nervous System*. London: Routledge, 1992.

Tomlinson, John. *Globalization and Culture*. Chichester: Polity Press, 1999.

Trousdale, Rachel. '"City of Mongrel Joy": Bombay and the Shiv Sena in *Midnight's Children* and *The Moor's Last Sigh*', *Journal of Commonwealth Literature*, Vol. 39, No. 2, June 2004, pp. 95–110.

Van der Veer, Peter. 'Satanic or Angelic? The Politics of Religious and Literary Inspiration', *Public Culture*, Vol. 2, No. 1, Fall 1989, pp. 100–106.

Virno, Paolo. *A Grammar of the Multitude: For an Analysis of Contemporary Forms of Life.* Los Angeles: Semiotext(e), 2004.

Walter, Natasha. 'The Children of Paradise', *The Guardian*, September 3, 2005.

Wilson, David. 'Fiction: *Grimus*', *Contemporary Literary Criticism* 23, Detroit, MI: Gale Research Inc., 1982, pp. 364–5.

Wood, James. 'Escape to New York', *Contemporary Literary Criticism* 191. Detroit, MI: Gale Research Inc., 2004, pp. 311–313.

Wood, Michael. 'Shenanigans', *Contemporary Literary Criticism* 100. Detroit, MI: Gale Research Inc., 1997, pp. 286–289.

Yardley, Jonathon. 'Wrestling with the Angel', *Contemporary Literary Criticism* 55. Detroit, MI: Gale Research Inc., 1988, pp. 224–225.

Young, Robert J. C. *Postcolonialism: An Historical Introduction.* Oxford: Blackwell, 2001.

—— *Colonial Desire: Hybridity in Theory, Culture and Race.* London: Routledge, 1995.

INDEX